A Global Political Economy of Intellectual Property Rights

It has become a commonplace that there has been an information revolution, transforming both society and the economy. Increasingly, knowledge and information are seen as important resources; ownership of which confers competitive advantage. In 1995 the Trade Related Aspects of Intellectual Property Rights (TRIPs) agreement aimed to harmonise protection for property in knowledge throughout the global system. This book questions whether the current arrangements are either just or sustainable.

This volume considers the political construction of intellectual property, and how it is linked to the economics of knowledge and information in the contemporary global political economy. *A Global Political Economy of Intellectual Property Rights* examines contemporary disputes about the ownership of knowledge resources – as in the cases of genetically modified foods, the music industry or the internet – and the problematic nature of the TRIPs agreement.

This book argues that there are solutions in the form of political moves to establish the social availability of information, and in reattaching property to the innovating individual. In this highly topical book, Christopher May reveals that, because of problems with the TRIPs agreement, at present the balance in international property rights between public good and private reward is, more often than not, weighted towards the latter.

Christopher May is Senior Lecturer in International Political Economy at the University of the West of England.

Routledge/RIPE studies in global political economy

Series Editors: Otto Holman, Marianne Marchand (*Research Centre for International Political Economy, University of Amsterdam*) and Henk Overbeek (*Free University, Amsterdam*)

This series, published in association with the *Review of International Political Economy*, provides a forum for current debates in international political economy. The series aims to cover all the central topics in IPE and to present innovative analyses of emerging topics. The titles in the series seek to transcend a state-centred discourse and focus on three broad themes:

- the nature of the forces driving globalisation forward
- resistance to globalisation
- the transformation of the world order.

The series comprises two strands:

Routledge/RIPE Studies in Global Political Economy is a forum for innovative new research intended for a high-level specialist readership, and the titles will be available in hardback only. Titles include:

Globalization and Governance
Edited by Aseem Prakash and Jeffrey A. Hart

Nation-States and Money
The past, present and future of national currencies
Edited by Emily Gilbert and Eric Helleiner

A Global Political Economy of Intellectual Property Rights
The new enclosures?
Christopher May

The *RIPE Series in Global Political Economy* aims to address the needs of students and teachers, and the titles will be published in hardback and paperback. Titles include

Transnational Classes and International Relations
Kees van der Pijl

Gender and Global Restructuring:
Sightings, sites and resistances
Edited by Marianne H. Marchand and Anne Sisson Runyan

A Global Political Economy of Intellectual Property Rights

The new enclosures?

Christopher May

London and New York

First published 2000 by Routledge
11 New Fetter Lane, London EC4P 4EE

Simultaneously published in the USA and Canada
by Routledge
29 West 35th Street, New York, NY 10001

Routledge is an imprint of the Taylor & Francis Group

© 2000 Christopher May

Typeset in Baskerville by Keystroke, Jacaranda Lodge, Wolverhampton
Printed and bound in Great Britain by TJ International Ltd., Padstow, Cornwall

British Library Cataloguing in Publication Data
A catalogue record for this book is available from the British Library

Library of Congress Cataloging in Publication Data
May, Christopher, 1960–
    A global political economy of intellectual property rights : the new enclosures?/
Christopher May.
        p. cm. — (The RIPE series in global political economy)
    Includes bibliographical references and index.
    ISBN 0–415–22904–9 (HB) ✓
    1. Intellectual property. 2. Intellectual property—Economic aspects. 3. Critical theory.
I. Title. II. Series.
K1401.M39 2000
346.04′8—dc21   99–057173

For Hilary

Contents

Series editors' preface   ix
Acknowledgements   xi

Introduction   1
The emerging information society   2
Property in knowledge   6
Property, intellectual property, political economy   11
The argument in outline   14

1   On institutions and property   16

Property as an institution   18
Justificatory schemata of property   22
Institutions as structures of knowledge   29
A model of change in the global political economy   39
A critique of intellectual property rights   42

2   Developing intellectual property   45

Characterising property   45
From property to intellectual property   47
Of authors and markets   50
Leasehold as a model for intellectual property?   54
Trade secrets, contracts and tacit knowledge   57
A set agenda   59
Disposing of intellectual property?   61
The thin line between public and private   65

3   TRIPs as a watershed   67

An outline of the TRIPs agreement   68
The importance of the agreement   72

Likely implications of the TRIPs agreement 76
The emergence of TRIPs 80
The triumph of the knowledge structure 85

4   Sites of resistance: patenting nature, technology and skills?   91

General and immanent critiques of IPRs 92
Some problems with intellectual property 98
Intellectual property – but not for me? 125

5   Sites of consolidation: legitimate authorship?   127

Key knowledge industries 128
Piracy, piracy everywhere 150
And real individuals? 157

6   Between commons and individuals   162

The global information society 164
Re-enlarging social utility 167
Re-balancing individuals' rights 172
A change is going to come 178

Notes   182
References   185
Index   196

Series editors' preface

By now it is common sense to speak of an 'information society' in which control over knowledge has replaced control over matter as the ultimate source of power. The commodification of information and knowledge, although not entirely new, has only recently accelerated so strongly as to reach a qualitative threshold. This crucial aspect of the process of global restructuring has put the need to unravel the essence of 'intellectual property' and to expose the power relations in the knowledge structure on the top of the agenda of critical theory.

In *A Global Political Economy of Intellectual Property Rights: The New Enclosures?* Christopher May responds to this challenge. taking the analytical framework of Susan Strange's *States and Markets* as the point of departure he develops a major critique of the construction and institutionalisation of knowledge as 'property'. May meticulously traces the legal construction of 'intellectual property', culminating in the General Agreement on Tariffs and Trade (GATT) Agreement on Trade Related Aspects of Intellectual Property Rights (TRIPs) coming out of the Uruguay Round.

The Uruguay Round saw the emergence of intellectual property and its protection as a major international trade issue. During the negotiations resulting in the TRIPs agreement, developed and developing states defended different positions, indicating that two different perspectives were at stake: developed states were primarily concerned with protecting the rights belonging to owners ('sanctity of property') whereas the developing countries wanted to link IPRs to their developmental strategies and priorities. This site of contestation reflects the fact that in the global economy of today economic prosperity stems not so much from natural resources or the production of industrial goods, but rather from the production of new ideas and new products. Indeed, the differences between rich and poor countries in terms of science, technology and knowledge are perhaps more important today than differences in income. According to Jeffrey Sachs, developed states own approximately 99 per cent of the stock of patents registered in the USA and Europe. In the end, May argues, the TRIPs agreement privileged the position of developed countries and will, at least in the short to medium term, further increase the wealth gap between those who own IPRs and those who wish to use them.

The GATT thus played a crucial role in the codification of a very specific conception of private property of information and knowledge. The TRIPs Agreement, as May convincingly argues, has in fact launched a new 'enclosures' movement in which previously 'social' (public, communal) property or non-property (such as individual genetic codes) is privately appropriated and exploited for profit. And as in history, the new enclosures movement produces its own forms and sites of resistance (intellectual and physical), ranging from Western universities where lecturers' course materials are turned into 'software' to be marketed by the university to the Indian countryside where villagers confront Western multinationals who have patented properties of the Neem tree which have been applied in traditional medicine and other social uses for many generations.

May ends with a passionate and (in his own words) 'reformist' plea for a two dimensional political project aimed at re-balancing *individual* (private) rights and simultaneously re-enlarging and strengthening global *social* utility in knowledge.

Future struggles in the knowledge structure of power must determine whether there is scope for such a project in the forcefield between Rousseau (*la propriété c'est le vol*) and Smith (the invisible hand of market forces). May's study provides ample material and food for thought for those wishing to contribute to these struggles and debates.

Acknowledgements

This book could not have been written without the long-term support of my wife, Hilary Jagger-May or my parents John and Laurie May. My father died in December 1998, but though he never saw the final text, this book would not have been the same without him. My parents were my earliest and greatest intellectual influences, for which I have always remained in their debt. Hilary has managed to keep me sane while this project developed and for that alone deserves fulsome praise. She also helped me develop an earlier piece of research regarding the clothing industry where many of these ideas were originally formed. Without her help then, this project would not have developed in the way it has.

Many people have heard me talk about these ideas and I thank them for asking me awkward questions, as well as suggesting new avenues, at the conferences and seminars where these arguments have been presented over the last few years. I would like to especially thank Robin Brown, Phil Cerny, Stephen Chan, Claire Cutler, Chris Farrands, Andrew Gamble, Randy Germain, Stephen Gill, Hannes Lacher, Norman Lewis, Stella Maile, Duncan Matthews, Ronen Palan, Tony Payne, Lloyd Pettiford, Susan Sell, Tim Sinclair, Roy Smith, Roger Tooze and Frank Webster who provided useful and crucial criticisms during the time I was working on this book. I am also indebted to Andrew Chadwick and Dimitrios Christophoulos at UWE and Susan Sell at George Washington University, as well as my late father, all of whom read draft chapters. However, the shortcomings remain my own.

The late Susan Strange was very supportive, even when she disagreed with me, and I was grateful to her for taking the time to correspond with me even though I was never one of her students, or attended an institution at which she taught. She will be greatly missed by those like me whom she always took time to help despite her busy schedule. Many years have passed since I first returned to higher education through the Open University, but I still benefit from the excellent training they provide. A special thanks is owed to Mike Pugh who was my tutor on the first International Relations course I took many years ago, and who set me on this path, which is very different from his own. Hazel Smith and Stephen Chan (during my time at the London Centre of International Relations) helped me develop my overall perspective on International Political Economy (IPE) and remain good friends. I also want to thank Chris Farands at Nottingham Trent

University who provided guidance and intellectual sustenance during the groundwork for this project while I completed my doctorate.

Lloyd Pettiford and Hazel May have both been invaluable friends who saw me through the dark hours when I thought I would never finish this book. They both knew exactly what I needed in times of stress and despair, and I hope I have been able to do the same for them. Lloyd also read the entire text during the later stages and gave me invaluable advice, though of course I absolve him from all blame for overall direction and argument of this book. Finally, I want to thank the editors of the RIPE series who believed in and supported my work on this book while it developed.

Earlier versions of parts of Chapters 1 and 2 originally appeared as 'Thinking, Buying, Selling: Intellectual Property Rights in Political Economy', *New Political Economy*, vol. 3 no. 1, March 1998, pp. 59–78.

Introduction

I was in a Vietnamese restaurant with a few friends and at the end of the meal we were all offered a fortune cookie. The message enclosed in mine was: 'Good ideas come free of charge'. Unfortunately this is not always the case. In this book I explore the reason why many good ideas are in fact rather expensive and look at some of the problems which beset a market in knowledge.

It is frequently asserted that an information society is emerging to replace modern industrial society. Though all societies may be communication systems centred on the exchange of information, the informational content of goods and services is increasingly the basis of economic value rather than social value. Information and knowledge are becoming important market commodities, priced accordingly. And though many Internet sites carry strident assertions that 'information wants to be free', there are institutional barriers which inhibit the free flow of information. The transfer and use of all sorts of information and knowledge are constricted through its designation as intellectual property which institutionalises payment for use. Thus, the benefits of information society flow to those who own the information and knowledge resources which have been rendered as intellectual property rather than those whose need for such information and/or knowledge might be greatest.

My critique of intellectual property is intended to contribute to its reformation, to try and shift the developmental path of the emerging global information society away from its current direction. Thus, I explicitly adopt a perspective which has the purpose Robert Cox suggests for critical theory. Such theory

> stands apart from the prevailing order of the world and asks how that order came about. [It] does not take institutions and social power relations for granted but calls them into question by concerning itself with their origins and how and whether they might be in the process of change . . . [It] is theory of history in the sense of being concerned not just with the past but with a continuing process of historical change . . . Critical Theory allows for a normative choice in favour of a social and political order different from the prevailing order, but it limits the range of choice to alternative orders which are feasible transformations of the existing world. A principal objective of critical theory, therefore is to clarify this range of possible alternatives.
>
> (Cox 1996: 88–90)

The history of global capitalism has (re)produced vast inequalities between the rich and poor. It is possible that the global information society will produce a 'computer generated caste system' between the information rich and information poor, continuing this history (Curtis 1988). Before embarking on this study of intellectual property therefore I will outline some of the elements of the notion of an information society as this has a direct relevance to much that follows.

The emerging information society

Ideas about the emergence of an information society are not a particularly recent phenomena (Webster 1995; Kumar 1995). One 'bibliometric inquiry' (Duff 1995) suggests the concept was quite widely utilised in various types of publication (from academic reports to policy documents) between 1986 and 1993. At the end of this period its use seemed to be in decline. But, at the turn of the millennium, once again variations of the information society thesis are widespread, perhaps as a response to Manuel Castells' widely read and cited three-volume work *The Information Age* (1996; 1997a; 1998). Certainly, the arrival of e-commerce and the explosion of web-sites have suggested to many commentators that the Internet is ushering in a profound change in social and economic relations.

On the one hand, this may be a continuance of processes that stem from the Industrial Revolution. Beniger (1986) suggests the emergence of information society is predicated on the 'control revolution', a response to the forces unleashed by mechanisation and automation. The use and valuing of information developed out of largely successful attempts to utilise information to control and direct mechanised production in the last century. Conversely, for many observers the information society is a revolution in socio-economic organisation. The movement of material goods is now much less important than flows of information and knowledge. Suggesting the arrival of a 'weightless economy' Quah concludes that 'the term "industrialised countries" no longer carries any resonance: now, no advanced and growing country is dependent on production industries' (Quah 1997: 55). But as Anthony Smith has suggested, some of these writings have

> a Hegelian ring about them. Information technology [is] penetrated by the historic spirit . . . [and] the very act of formulating this idea of an information and communication society has exercised much of the transforming power, or at least has provided the political acceleration.
>
> (Smith 1996: 72)

Arguments for the emergence of the information society have reinforced the observed dynamic, and may have contributed to the actualisation of socio-economic relations they purported only to 'recognise'. This information technology-based revolution is also a key element of globalisation discourse with great importance put on the 'shrinking world' of instantaneous knowledge dissemination. The global system is becoming more interconnected through our knowledge of distant places, events and communities. As communities have always been built on systems of information exchange (through communication), the ability to communicate at a distance in real time engenders a global (information) society.

In his influential analysis Castells suggests the emergence of the information society is the result of three developments: the information technology revolution; the restructuring of capitalism in the 1980s; and the long-term effects of political and social movements in the 1960s and 1970s (Castells 1997b: 7). The information technology revolution has produced a technological paradigm which is instrumental in shaping the way the information society is conceived: certain directions of further development are 'possible', others are not. Because information is integral to all human activity, information technology is much more pervasive than previous technologies, and thus this technological paradigm is far more flexible than its predecessors. Information technology is able to integrate and connect diverse aspects of social and economic relations through its impact on the flows of information that make up these relations (Castells 1996: 61ff.). There is therefore a clear technological element to the emergence of the information society. However, despite the technological determinist nature of much literature proclaiming the information society (e.g. Negroponte 1995; Toffler 1980), Castells stresses the actual deployment of information technology 'in the realm of conscious social action, and the complex matrix of interaction between technological forces unleashed by our species and the species itself, are matters of enquiry rather than fate' (Castells 1996: 65). In the first instance this leads Castells to identify two other elements behind the emergence of information society: the economic restructuring of the 1980s and the development of identity politics.

As Castells sums up, the reformation of capitalism in the 1980s revolved around four main elements:

> deepening the capitalist logic of profit seeking in capital-labour relationships; enhancing the productivity of labour and capital; globalising production, circulation and markets, seizing the most advantageous conditions for profit making everywhere; and marshalling the state's support for productivity gains and competitiveness of national economics, often to the detriment of social protection and public interest regulations.
>
> (Castells 1996: 19)

The information society remains a capitalist society, though economic restructuring benefits greatly from the information technology revolution it was not caused by it. And, despite claims this reformation has marginalised the state, as the OECD point out:

> Government action is important since the developments taking place in the information economy can be harnessed to better meet some of the key challenges they face, such as the need to stimulate sustainable economic growth, the need for greater social cohesion and issues arising from ageing populations.
>
> (OECD 1997: 104)

Though the reformation of capitalism has arguably led to a decline in social provision, states still retain responsibility for legislating to support further economic development where necessary while still ameliorating some of its effects. Establishing robust intellectual property law is one such key activity of the state in an information society.

Third, the de-massification of politics is linked to the information revolution and the reformation of capitalism as precursors to the information society. Castells devotes an entire volume of his trilogy to the 'power of identity' (Castells 1997a). He argues that social movements, clustered around issues rather than classes, are questioning the social outcomes the contemporary social system is producing. These movements have a long history but developed swiftly during the 1960s and more recently have constructed global networks through cheap communications technology and the possibilities of the Internet. The information revolution did not produce identity politics but has enabled it to develop more widely and speedily than before. These movements are based on the formation of new identities (a recognition of new communities of interest) for their participants. Their strength lies in 'their autonomy *vis-à-vis* the institutions of the state, the logic of capital, and the seduction of technology' (Castells 1998: 352). These developmental trends have worked to construct an increasingly global information society.

Recognition of this new set of social relations is often centred on the identification of two key social and economic shifts emblematic of the information society: the development of information/knowledge as a new economic resource, value added is increasingly reliant on non-material inputs into products or services; and the changing character of the knowledge being mobilised in social relations, global flows of specialised (analytical) knowledge are now vital to wealth creation and greatly influence political affairs.

Though capitalism still revolves around markets and profit, economic organisation is presented as fundamentally changed. In Drucker's analysis 'there is less and less return on the traditional resources: labour, land and (money) capital. The main producers of wealth have become information and knowledge' (Drucker 1993: 183). There has been a move away from material inputs providing the critical elements in the production of material outputs, with ideas or knowledge inputs now contributing significant value to products. While often taking a material form these products owe their value to the information used in their realisation (Lash and Urry 1994; Masuda 1980; Morris-Suzuki 1988). Furthermore, knowledge-related inputs (such as design, marketing, 'quality' and technological novelty) are becoming the key aspects of competition as understood by market actors (Hamel and Prahalad 1994; Micklethwait and Wooldridge 1996: 134ff.; Nonaka and Takeuchi 1995). Knowledge-based capitalism in an information society breaks with previous patterns of economic organisation by virtue of its key resources, the use it makes of them and the sorts of products or service it produces. But the use of knowledge is changing the nature of enterprise as well as its products, which is changing ways of working.

Reich has famously suggested that the information society represents the rise of the 'symbolic analyst'. These new information adept workers whose ability to mobilise knowledge resources allows them to produce innovative goods and services, are the vanguard of the new economy (Reich 1991). Furthermore, given the technological aspects of the information society, primarily the massively expanded capabilities of cheap and reliable computing, low-level information work will (and is already being) deskilled. Much information work (possibly up to 80 per cent of 'white-collar' tasks) is 'relatively routine transformation of information from one form into another – from an invoice into a payment, and so on' (Ducatel and Millard 1996: 124). Mechanisation through computerisation has allowed lower level entrants to the information workforce, but has also limited the benefits of this employment. And though Reich recognises that the beneficiaries of the new information rich economy are likely to be a limited elite of information professionals, less careful analyses sometimes seem to assume that all information work is highly rewarding, high satisfaction labour.

Previously the information or knowledge elements of a commodity were embedded in its realisation. Now, as information and knowledge have been accorded separate values they have become dis-articulated from their carriers. Thus, the ascendant knowledge industries are those in which value added stems primarily from the utilisation of information in one form or another. This ranges from the use of branding, and the provision of information-services (such as design and marketing) to companies which mine data to provide information on consumers or their credit ratings. In these industries the most important input is non-material, though not necessarily to the total exclusion of material inputs or components. The ability to control, direct and profit from flows of vast amounts of information and knowledge-based resources sets this form of economic organisation aside from that which preceded it.

It is not data and information that are most highly valued in information society, however, though this is in no way to argue they are worthless. Rather, theoretical knowledge is the subject of heightened and furious competition. Twenty-five years ago Bell argued that the services which indicate the emergence of an information society are those which prompt the 'expansion of a new intelligentsia – in the universities, research organisations, professions and government' (Bell 1974: 15). What was distinctive about the information society was

> the change in the character of knowledge itself. What has become decisive for the organisation of decisions and the direction of change is the centrality of *theoretical* knowledge – the primacy of theory over empiricism and the codification of knowledge into abstract systems of symbols that . . . can be used to illuminate many different and varied areas of experience.
>
> (ibid.: 21)

Though Reich accords more weight to private institutions, he too sees the knowledge and information-rich sectors of the workforce as holding a pivotal role in contemporary (and future) society (Reich 1991: 177ff.). While concern with information and knowledge has been a recurring refrain for twenty-five years, the supposition of collective provision of knowledge development has been replaced by an individualised responsibility (Stehr 1994). This move away from expectations of large-scale state involvement in knowledge development is linked to the reformation of capitalism instituting market provision more widely.

The emergence of an information society therefore has involved a greater emphasis on knowledge over information. This might be seen as a false distinction; the terms information and knowledge are often used interchangeably and certainly the borderline is diffuse and difficult to clarify. But if information refers to data, characterised as a passive resource which can be packaged and transferred in discrete units, then knowledge refers to the theoretical or intellectual tools that are needed to produce further (knowledge-related) resources from this raw information. In this sense information has become (or perhaps always was) a commodity, whereas knowledge is more akin to skill and expertise, the higher order intellectual ability needed to produce new knowledge from knowledge itself. The social and economic importance put upon the mobilisation and control of knowledge is the crucial second element to the posited emergence of an information society.

The information society self-avowedly develops its knowledge resources through research and development, through education, and through the manipulation of extensive knowledge of the known to reveal the unknown. Social development no longer starts from the material but is rather predicated on the manipulation of theoretical knowledge (codified by scientific and technical principles). Webster argues that 'a major difficulty with this notion is defining with any precision what is meant by theoretical knowledge' (Webster 1996: 104). Nevertheless, responding to this element of the posited information society, much attention has been paid to how such knowledge might be codified and controlled. Whereas information can easily be collected and stored (the database being the defining example), theoretical knowledge is altogether a more complex issue. Much scientific theory is codified for use (and is generally in the public realm), however theoretical knowledge about economic processes (from macro to micro levels) is altogether different. Not only is it hard to fix (as economic model-makers know to their cost), it is difficult to decide what actually represents valuable knowledge in any case.

This has led to a growing recognition that the tacit knowledge of workers and managers is often one of a company's most valuable (yet difficult to quantify) assets and inputs. As knowledge has grown as an element in the value added for any particular product or service relative to the material properties of commodities, so capitalists wish to capture such knowledge for their exclusive control. Though knowledge has always fed into productive processes and services, it is now increasingly subject to attempts to render it as property. The needs and interests of the expanding knowledge industries have included the firm requirement for a clear legal institutionalisation of property in knowledge.

Property in knowledge

The emergence of an information society, where knowledge industries are accorded increasing importance, forms the background to the contemporary debates regarding intellectual property rights (IPRs). Some broad definitions of the various elements of intellectual property will help establish the terrain over which we will range.

When knowledge or information becomes subject to ownership, IPRs express ownership's legal benefits including the right to charge rent for use, to receive compensation for loss and collect payment for transfer or sale. Like material property, these rights are usually justified on the basis of some combination of three arguments. There are two separate ethical approaches to justifying property as well as an economic defence, and arguing from metaphor, intellectual property is regarded as being similarly justified. First, utilising John Locke's well-known discussion of property as labour's 'just desert', intellectual property is seen as a suitable reward for intellectual labour. The effort expended to produce any particular knowledge or information should be rewarded by the award of property in whatever is produced. This encourages further intellectual activity by establishing a clear benefit: intellectual endeavour is rewarded by intellectual property (which can be converted into a monetary reward through the market). Conversely, drawing on the ideas of Georg Hegel, (intellectual) property is seen as the expression of self. Hegel argued that individuals define themselves through their control of possessions, their property. In the case of knowledge, our ideas are an expression of our identity. Intellectual property is a recognition of the individual's sovereignty over their thoughts. The expression of self through the creative act therefore should be protected as this represents the product of selfhood and is the property of the self.

While these first two arguments are based on ethical concerns, a third way of justifying intellectual property is merely concerned with economic outcomes. It is frequently argued that only by allocating value to a particular resource (in this case knowledge or information) will it be used to its best advantage and further beneficial developments encouraged. By allocating a price through a market for property, users are constantly required to assess the return that use generates and to think about how this might be maximised. This promotes a more efficient use of resources as well as innovations in the methods of use. By fostering progress in economic organisation and increased efficiency, society as a whole benefits. All three ways of justifying (intellectual) property (or 'justificatory schemata') are mobilised in the debates about IPRs, though in varying combinations. For instance, they repeatedly resurface in popular debates regarding patents for genes, unauthorised copying of CDs or the illegal use of trademarks. These three justificatory schemata are discussed at some length in the next chapter.

Intellectual property rights are divided into a number of groups, of which two generate most discussion: industrial intellectual property (patents) and literary or artistic intellectual property (copyrights). Conventionally the difference is presented as between patent's protection of an idea, and copyright's protection of its expression. Additionally, given the different character of knowledge *vis-à-vis* other forms of property (which I shall return to), a key element to any legal settlement has been the balance between private rewards from limited distribution and a public interest in free availability of knowledge. This tension has historically been settled through time limits on IPRs, though these vary by type of intellectual property.

Patents

For patents the knowledge which is to be registered and thus made property should be applicable in industry or other economic activities. If it fits the following three criteria an idea is generally regarded as patentable. The idea should be:

- *new,* and thus not already in the public domain or the subject of a previous patent;
- *not obvious,* which is to say it is not common sense to any accomplished practitioner in the field when asked to solve a particular practical problem, it should not be a self-evident solution using available skills or technologies;
- *useful,* or *applicable in industry*, the idea must have a stated function, which has a practical use and could immediately be manufactured to fulfil this function.

If these conditions are met, then the idea can be patented, becoming intellectual property. The interpretation of these criteria is at the root of many disputes regarding the widening of patents, such as those around the patenting of genetic information (which is possibly neither new nor non-obvious) as will be explored in Chapter 4.

The patent is lodged at the patent office (usually a department of state) which for an agreed fee will allow others access to the ideas as expressed in the patent document. Perhaps more importantly for the patent holder the office will police and punish unauthorised usage. However, some patent documents are written with unnecessary detail and technical jargon resulting in formal availability being obscured beneath a veneer of description. Also, by embedding an idea in a complex of separate patents such high fees may be required to license all the relevant patents that effective technological transfer is again obstructed. Nevertheless the creator, or holder of the patent, cannot keep patented knowledge completely to themselves, but does receive a due reward each time the idea is utilised by a third party.

Copyright

Copyright is concerned with 'literary and artistic works'. Copyright therefore covers:

- literary works (fiction and non-fiction);
- musical works (of all sorts) including audio recordings;
- artistic works (of two- and three-dimensional form and importantly irrespective of content – from 'pure art' and advertising to amateur drawings and children's doodles);
- maps;

- technical drawings;
- photography; *etc*
- audio-visual works (including cinematic works, video and new forms of multi-media such as CD-ROMs).

Combinations of these different forms will also be covered, and these categories are neither exclusive nor exhaustive. In some jurisdictions for instance copyright also covers broadcast transmissions and typographical arrangements of publications (WIPO 1993: 43/44). There have also been moves to copyright as literary expressions the lines of code which make up computer programmes. However, in general the underlying ideas, the plot, the conjunction of colours, the process governed by instructions do not receive protection. Only specific expressions attract copyright.

Copyright forbids reproduction without the express permission of the creator (or the owner of the copyright, which may have been legally transferred to another party). In many jurisdictions this is limited to an economic right: the creator (or copyright owner) is legally entitled to a share of any return that is earned by the utilisation or reproduction of the copyrighted knowledge, but may be unable to finally control the form or context of use. Copyright holders wishing to halt further reproduction or use of their copyright can refuse to come to terms leading their rights to be formally protected and unauthorised use deterred. Failure to agree terms prior to an act of reproduction or duplication may result in all income being awarded to the original copyright holder by the court if an infringement is deemed to have taken place. In some jurisdictions there is an additional moral right which can be asserted allowing the original creator some control over the use and amendment of their expressions. Under this sort of legal regime copyrighted knowledge can only be used in ways the original creator is willing to accept.

Unlike patents, however, copyright resides in the work from the moment of creation. To prove infringement, unauthorised use or reproduction of the original work, it needs to be shown that the item has been copied after the fact of original creation. However, co-creation, two or more people expressing an idea in a similar way at similar times does not impinge any copyright, sanction must be based on proof of *actual* copying.

Trademarks and industrial designs

Though copyright and patent are the most generally recognised forms of intellectual property and are certainly at the centre of both popular and academic accounts, trademarks and industrial designs are a further area of considerable debate and conflict. Trademarks serve to distinguish the products of one company from another. Their legal development parallels the emergence of large companies seeking to differentiate themselves in commodity goods markets (Wilkins 1992). Trademarks can be made up of one or more distinctive words, letters, numbers, drawings or pictures, emblems or other graphic representations. They need to be registered, and during the act of registration a check is carried out to ensure that no other companies currently have registered the same trademark. The pre-registration use of a trademark may establish its viability and support its subsequent legal recognition. But a particular trademark is unlikely to succeed in being registered if it is too similar to, or liable to cause confusion with, a trademark already registered by another company (a criminal activity usually referred to as 'passing off'). Neither will it attract protection if the form of the mark is already in common public usage (similar to the 'new' criteria for patents), which explains the odd spelling utilised by companies seeking to trademark their name, such as Kall-kwick, Prontaprint or Spud-U-Like.

In some jurisdictions the outward manifestation of packaging may also be allowed trademark status provided that it is not a form dictated by function (of which the most famous case is the Coke bottle). Similarly, decorations and ornamental details that appear on a product which are neither fully functional, nor represent the trademarks of the company can be protected as industrial designs, provided they are original and have not been previously registered by another company. Industrial designs like trademarks may only be reproduced with the registered owner's explicit permission. Both trademarks and industrial designs, while requiring some form of regular (re)registration, unlike other IPRs can remain property in perpetuity.

Trade secrets – a special case

Trade secrets are seldom recognised as a form of intellectual property. Usually reproduction of knowledge covered by IPRs is allowed and often encouraged as a way of securing an income. Conversely, trade secrets are retained by their originators and not disseminated. While trade secrets may be bought and sold, stolen or discovered, they retain their full value only while they remain secret. Unlike other forms of intellectual property which exchange disclosure for control over reproduction and thus allow competition to emerge, trade secrets are specifi-cally anti-competitive denying competitors the means to reproduce the company's knowledge-based advantage. More exactly, they deny the secret to those companies unwilling (or unable) to invest in reverse engineering programmes, an activity not generally prohibited by common law (Friedman *et al.* 1991: 70). However, once revealed or stolen, trade secrets are worthless and reproduction uncontrollable: it is an all-or-nothing strategy for knowledge ownership. A trade secret is kept out of the public realm altogether but when revealed can enjoy no subsequent protection from unauthorised reproduction whatsoever.

Unlike other forms of intellectual property which are clearly defined by international conventions, trade secrets defy generalised description. Thus, laws used to protect them are concerned with the methods used to obtain trade secrets, not with the secrets themselves. Ranging across employment, commercial and contract law, differing forms of non-disclosure agreement are the most common method for protecting trade secrets. The way a secret is secured may also be covered by criminal law. The sale of stolen goods embodying trade secrets (documented recipes, plans or manuals, for instance) or industrial espionage are illegal in most if not all countries. Furthermore, some employers have started to claim that knowledge developed by their employees during their working practices may be covered by this sort of protection, as some of the cases I discuss in Chapter 4 reveal.

Between private and public

In some celebrated cases a trade secret is relied on to maintain a massive and continuing competitive advantage (again the example of Coca-Cola is apposite), but usually a more formalised intellectual property approach to protection is adopted. Indeed, for most knowledge industries it would be counter-productive, impossible even, to function on the basis of knowledge being secret, given the importance of reproduction and transfer to generate income and profit. Intellectual property constructs a balance between public availability and private benefit which allows wider access to knowledge than trade secrecy but restricts use none the less within specific legal limits, allowing a price to be taken.

Patent law in particular reflects the widespread recognition that monopoly rights of ownership in innovations require some dilution by political authority. This is to ensure that certain social needs are fulfilled, most notably the prompt use of technical advance in the economic realm. Legislators in Britain during the seventeenth century (the legal dawn of intellectual property) swiftly realised that society needed to be able to utilise new methods more widely than a single owner with a monopoly might allow. Patents are therefore an explicit bargain between the idea's originator and the state, balancing ownership and disclosure, allowing both individual reward and social use. The state protects the originator from unauthorised use of their ideas provided access is allowed on agreed terms. And finally, ideas enter the free public realm when patents expire, no longer having their scarcity enforced by the state.

The return of intellectual property to the public realm is one of its key defining qualities. Unlike material property which is usually owned in perpetuity, intellectual property only exists as property in a temporary sense. In some cases this period may be much longer than in others: from the need to renew trademarks on a regular cycle of between five and ten years, through patents which may last for twenty or so years, to copyrights which can last for a period of fifty years after the death of the original creator. Intellectual property is a continuing and explicit balance between the private ownership of the fruits of intellectual labour and the social benefit of the distribution of useful ideas or knowledge. It is this distinction between private and public, and importantly where the line separating the two might lie (both in the sense of what is protected and the period of protection in any specific case), which is the central issue of intellectual property encompassing its legal existence and its political economy.

Property, intellectual property, political economy

What interests me in the following chapters are the issues that stem from assuming a metaphorical relationship between property and intellectual property. For critical theory the question of why certain outcomes have come to pass is a central concern. It is also necessary to identify how interest has been mobilised to support specific forms of institutionalisation. As I noted above, a critical theory 'does not take institutions and social power relations for granted' but seeks to examine how and why particular origins led to current manifestations. Indeed, it is not my intent to suggest how the current arrangements might work better, but to ask how these arrangements reflect power mobilised over political and legal relations. I therefore offer a critique of the current legal settlement which has been global-ised through the Trade Related Aspects of Intellectual Property Rights agreement (TRIPs) under the auspices of the World Trade Organisation (WTO). I suggest that rather than being a technical issue of legal refinement, the current global regime for intellectual property serves quite specific interests. Furthermore this is not the only alternative, intellectual property need not necessarily be like this.

In considering intellectual property in this manner I am examining a particular manifestation of the generalised triangular interactions Cox sees between material capabilities, institutions, and ideas. Specifically, in the following analysis of intel-lectual property the significant material capabilities identified are those controlled through informational resources (including information-related technologies and innovations defined as intellectual property). The central institution the study identifies is the legal construction of intellectual property, allied to the complex institutional arrangements of modern capitalism. And the ideas which are accorded analytical significance are those that identify: what is considered to be intellectual property; who has the right to claim ownership of intellectual goods; and more general concepts of ownership rights in a market-based society.

I am interested in the power that stems from the ownership and control of particular innovations and technologies, established through the institutions of intellectual property. This may allow certain agents to maximise their influence through the control of specific knowledge-based resources, but also allows these preferred actors to enhance their advantages by the legitimisation of their interest through law. These actors bring political resources to bear to defend and extend their legal rights, by utilising and defending the arguments for a labour desert, expression of self and economic efficiency. These justificatory schemata, identify-ing 'owners', justifying the protection of owners' rights and arguing for the efficiency gains from treating knowledge as property, inform the legal arguments which resulted in the current settlement. This leads me to highlight the conflict between arguments for the protection of private rights of owners and a notion of the general interest represented by a wider public domain.

At the centre of many of the issues that will be discussed in the following chapters is the question of the commodification of knowledge. It is commonly recognised that capitalism has widened itself geographically (usually discussed under the rubric of globalisation). However, it has also deepened its penetration into previously non-commodified social relations. While dependent on the construction of alienable property to separate labour from its product and to allow products to be exchanged in a market, under capitalism forms of property are not unduly limited except for their legal existence *qua* property. As I will suggest in the next chapter, there is little that cannot in one way or another be rendered as property. This process is driven by the need to earn a profit, for capital to be reproduced, and not by the 'natural' existence of particular *forms* of property. Intellectual property rights are the key method to assert ownership over knowledge resources. Where these knowledge resources were previously part of a social reservoir, IPRs are a tool of commodification or enclosure.

During the period from the fifteenth to eighteenth centuries vast areas of common grazing land were enclosed by landlords and made private property. Land previously held in common by local communities and used by villagers on a shared basis was rendered private property by erecting fences and securing title deeds through the courts. Once land became private property its use could be mediated through the market, by charging rent for use or selling to those prepared to pay most for it. Given the organisation of capitalism is firmly rooted in the recognition of property rights, those areas of social life that capitalists wish to profit from must be rendered as property. This may not involve physical boundaries but does require the construction of a legal scarcity relative to a previous commonalty. In one sense the dynamic of enclosure is the expansionary dynamic of capitalism itself (Heilbronner 1985). In the realm of knowledge this has led to the enclosure of genetic resources, of scientific knowledge, of folk forms or of the skills we might regard as our own. Indeed, the recognition of such commodification as enclosure has become more than a merely spasmodic polemic. Many environmental groups regard the commodification of knowledge resources as a direct parallel to the enclosure of common land three hundred years ago (*The Ecologist* 1992).

Though intellectual property has its origins at least as far back as the seventeenth century (the time of the original enclosures), it is only relatively recently that the wider implications of property in knowledge have become an issue that might be a site for major contention. Earlier debates regarding copyrights and patents have been swamped by the flood of discussion in the last twenty years. However, this has largely been limited to issues of efficiency and productivity, rather than the underlying justification of property in knowledge itself. I will argue throughout the following chapters that the justificatory schemata of intellectual property are neither natural nor self-evident and most importantly they are not the only possible ways of thinking about valuable knowledge. The limitation of the mainstream debate to these alternatives, I suggest, has been supported by the mobilisation of power over knowledge. The knowledge structure has limited the recognition of alternatives to IPRs in the service of particular powerful groups in the global political economy.

Intellectual property is located at a particular nexus of historical forces – the development of technology, the development of law, and the development of conceptions of individuals as knowledge creators. Technology, law and ideology come together to support the current settlement and acting on each other none should be considered exogenous. Developments in any of these three areas are contingent on the others. The actuality of the global development of IPRs is not some historical accident but the result of particular histories and processes.

However, given the complexities of intellectual property I have chosen not to present an overall history of patents, copyrights, trademarks and other intellectual properties. Rather, I take TRIPs as a watershed in such a history. I relate some recent intellectual property disputes to further locate the specificity of the current settlement under the TRIPs agreement, but I do not examine previous controversies and the contested history of intellectual property. An international history of intellectual property remains beyond the scope of this study, though such a history would be of great value to the continued critical study of the subject.

The argument in outline

In Chapter 1 I set out three justificatory schemata underlying the social institution of property: the instrumental or labour-desert argument; the self-developmental justification; and the economic or pragmatic justification. I then suggest that social institutions are subject to power within the knowledge structure, an approach I adapt from the work of Susan Strange. Thus, I identify agenda-setting ability as a major site of power over institutional practices and outcomes. I also develop the approach to the incidence of change in social systems which informs my treatment of intellectual property in the rest of the study. This is founded on a dual-dialectic as the mechanism of change – the continuing interaction between ideational and material elements of the political economy, alongside a central role for the revelation or obscuring of contradiction.

In the second chapter, I discuss the justificatory schemata as they have been mobilised within the political economy of intellectual property. I also note that despite superficial similarities, the current settlement of intellectual property does not resemble the holding of leasehold property. The proposal that all knowledge flows from an author, or at least that there is some form of authorial function, is widely accepted. Therefore I make an initial exploration of the role of the knowledge worker *vis-à-vis* their employers and discuss some of the arguments which are used to dispute the possibility of intellectual property. Having explored these general issues, in Chapter 3 I focus on the global settlement represented by the TRIPs agreement during the Uruguay Round of the General Agreement on Tariffs and Trade. I take this settlement to be a watershed in the debates over the emerging global importance of IPRs and as such explore its emergence and content at some length.

Once I have outlined the TRIPs agreement I examine the benefits and costs of the current settlement given the increasingly globalised institutionalisation of this particular system of intellectual property. In Chapter 4 I look at areas where there has been considerable criticism of various elements of intellectual property and the industries which it supports – specifically the pharmaceutical and bio-technology sectors. I also look at the broader issues of technology transfer (or lack thereof) and labour relations under intellectual property laws. These deliberations lead me to conclude that though intellectual property formally allows a balance or bargain between public and private rewards generally it over-emphasises private benefits. Users of the justificatory schemata accomplish this by limiting very narrowly their conception of social utility, and by allowing corporations the same rights in this area as individuals. In the last part of the chapter I re-focus on individuals as they actually exist rather than their idealised counterparts in the justificatory schemata.

In Chapter 5 I take this treatment of real individuals further and examine some of the paradigmatic knowledge industries – publishing, music, computer software – where individual knowledge workers and creators have benefited significantly from the incidence of intellectual property in their creations. However, once again I conclude that while the individual is theoretically well served by intellectual property in the real world their benefits are both contingent and partial. In this and the previous chapter I examine these issues by utilising an immanent critique – I take the justificatory schemata that I laid out in the earlier chapters and compare them with what happens within intellectual property relations. This leads me to identify a number of contradictions which suggest that the schemata are kept in place to obscure such tensions. The revelation of these contradictions is, as I argued earlier, the way that political economic shifts can emerge. Thus, at the same time as the knowledge structure tries to obscure these tensions, the exploration of contradictions can lead to new political economic possibilities.

In the final chapter I explore two ways in which intellectual property might fit better with its justificatory schemata: by expanding the formalised notion of social utility, through an 'environmentalism of the net'; and by ending the direct correlation between real individuals and companies' legal characterisation as individuals. I also return to the issue of whether it plausible to treat knowledge objects as property. I conclude not by dismissing intellectual property, but by suggesting a reformation which would recognise and value social utility more widely. Specifically I suggest a reformulated intellectual property right which supports both the individual knowledge creator, and the global society in which they are located. Though this is a reformist argument rather than revolutionary, it will still require considerable political will to enact such changes. This study is intended to act as a resource for such actions and a spur to further engagement with both the reality and the rhetoric of intellectual property.

1 On institutions and property

At the centre of this study is the question of a particular set of property rights, and so it is useful to be absolutely clear at the outset: property is not protected by the state's legislative apparatus because it is property but rather vice versa. Writing in the 1930s Professor Walter Hamilton summed this up succinctly, noting that it was 'incorrect to say that the judiciary protected property; rather they called that property to which they accorded protection' (quoted in Cribbet 1986: 4). Or as Ely stressed when discussing the role of the state in property relations: the state has 'the power to interpret property and especially private property and to give the concept a content at each particular period' (Ely 1914: 207). Property *qua* property does not pre-exist the apparatus of government (or the state), waiting to be recognised legally; rather, the legal recognition of property constitutes its existence in a form we can identify. Only when there is some form of government and legal apparatus can property be thought of in a way other than merely possession by those with the physical ability to protect themselves from dispossession. As such, rather than thinking of property as a physical thing, it is better to think of it as a social institution, one that can change in response to social and political requirements. It is constructed and reproduced by state legislation to protect not something previously existing, already recognised as property, but rather to protect certain current interests and in doing so codify their protection as 'property'.

The control of things by humans is not a sufficient basis for the emergence of property; it is rather their interest in the differential control of things that encourages a legal construction of property (with linked rights). The key right that extends to the owner of property is the right to 'control the actions of others in respect to the objects of property' (Ely 1914: 132). Property rights are held against others and the state itself (in most cases). It is these rights that form the institution rather than the specific stuff to which a property right is attached. And though the institution of property is established enough in modern societies that the sanction of the state to support or enforce this control is seldom needed, once a thing has been accepted as property by those conducting social relations, behind such acceptance lies the legal strength of the institution. In the last analysis any property rights are dependent on the support of the state in its role as authority over legal process.

If modern law is 'a body of enacted laws; . . . *positive* law, willed, made and given validity by the state itself in the exercise of its sovereignty', then we can assume that laws do not develop spontaneously (Poggi 1978: 103). Laws may recognise non-state activities or traditional practices but can only be law in the sense of a society-wide legal code through the existence of state authority. Indeed, the development of a legal code is one of the foundations on which the modern state's authority and legitimacy rests. Furthermore, 'Integral to the law is a moral topography, a mapping of the social world which *norm*alises its preferred contours – and, equally importantly, suppresses or at best marginalises other ways of seeing and being' (Corrigan and Sayer 1981: 33). By coding certain outcomes and practices as legal and others not, the state (and its government) affects certain outcomes and legitimises coercion against those practices not consistent with such an agenda. The state cannot be removed from the institution of property; without it there would be no institution of property.

The presence of the state in the relationship between property owners is rooted in two contradictory dynamics, each of which has played a general role in the development and expansion of property rights. Part of the history of property rights has been the ability of the powerful to protect their particular interests through the mobilisation of a legal apparatus that cedes to their interests the characterisation of property, to which are attached specific rights. But in a contrasting dynamic, the history of property is also related as a history of the protection of the individual's interests from the intervention of the state. The property rights derived from the state-sanctioned legal apparatus are also held against the state, provided certain conditions are adhered to relative to the rest of the legal code. Property rights may be dissolved in light of certain criminal activities, for instance. Therefore the interests that are protected through the incidence of property rights can be potentially under threat both from other individuals and from the state itself. The history of property rights is often presented as the manner in which individuals have developed legal protection from this dual threat, from the danger of theft and state appropriation or confiscation (Reeve 1986). However, these rights could not have been normalised without a further element. Law needs some form of social justification if it is to be successfully legitimised. A continuing recourse to force does not a society make.

When thinking about the incidence of property and property rights there are two issues that need to be explored. First, there is the actual appearance of property as an institution which protects certain interests in society in a specific manner. And second, though by no means less important, there is a parallel history of the ways in which the institution of property has been legitimised and justified within the social relations in which it appears. However, it is by no means always the case that this analytical distinction is made, and much of the power of justificatory schemata stems from their appearance as 'just history' (both in the sense of *merely* history and in the sense of a history that has produced an equitable outcome). Indeed, the present conceptual resolution of the character and applicability of 'property' implicitly denies its contingency on the current *political economic* settlement: it is characterised as having 'always been with us'. I shall examine possible explanations for the emergence of the institution of property before returning to the issue of justification and legitimisation below.

Property as an institution

At their most basic, social institutions are 'the humanly devised constraints that shape human interaction . . . they structure incentives in human exchange, whether political, social or economic' (North 1990: 3). In this sense the notion of an institution brings together the formal and the informal. Rules can be those which are legally constituted by the state, but alongside them are the informal modes of behaviour, the norms of society, which make such rules effective without the constant need for positive enforcement. Equally, laws related to traditional practices codify and formalise certain, but by no means all, previous patterns of social interaction. Enforcement of legal rules, then, is both dependent on their incidence as law and their basis in accepted ways of proceeding within socially legitimated parameters. These rules or institutions facilitate activities by reducing levels of uncertainty, producing layers of patterned behaviour which can be easily understood and followed. The duplication of effort that would be required constantly to re-negotiate bi-lateral co-ordination between social actors is dispensed with on the basis of the shared rules governing the particular area of social interaction being undertaken at any time. In this view, then, institutions arise to ensure a more efficient co-ordination of society. The risks of the breakdown of social exchange are lower, which frees the extensive reserves (of food and fuel for instance) which it might be prudent to hoard when the risks of 'dishonest dealing' are higher. This is to say, the emergence of social institutions serves a particular function – the efficient co-ordination of social, political economic activities.

If some form of social efficiency is the motive force behind the emergence of institutions, how does the particular institution of property emerge? In the first instance it might have emerged between individuals whose activities required some form of co-ordination, due to their competition over scarce resources. Institutions, and in this case property rights, structure the expectations which individuals have regarding the behaviour of others towards them. Thus an important reason for the emergence of property rights is the internalisation of external costs and benefits – all activities have costs and benefits to those who indulge in them. Property as an institution seeks to attach those costs and benefits to the 'owner' of the property which produces them (Demsetz 1967: 348–350). Part of the continuing fluidity in the legal constitution of property rights has been the widespread attempt by 'owners' to secure benefits while keeping costs externalised. Social efficiency might be best served by costs accruing to the property that delivers the benefit; however, for individual owners it is more 'efficient' to have the costs met by others. This tension between the public or social and the private interest will be a recurring theme throughout this book.

Property rights (and therefore intellectual property rights) do not just emerge, however; they are constructed to serve particular interests. As will be discussed below, the logic of efficiency has often been utilised to both justify and to explain the incidence of property rights within economic justifications. But efficiency cannot be the whole picture; goals are more ambiguous than a single end that can be achieved in a particular and efficient manner, and power relations are never absent from social relations (Lukes 1974; Oberschall and Leifer 1986). Indeed, power manifests itself in whose efficiency is prioritised, society's or the individual actor's. Though there may be a need for efficient operation of economic transactions, this is only one and not necessarily the most important aspect to the history of property as a social institution.

Therefore while the gains from co-operation and co-ordination can be explained and located as part of social development in an abstract sense, in the history of social relations the emergence of particular institutions may be more difficult to explain. As North points out:

> Institutions are not necessarily or even usually created to be socially efficient; rather they, or at least the formal rules, are created to serve the interests of those with the bargaining power to devise new rules. In a zero-transaction-cost world, bargaining strength does not affect the efficiency of outcomes, but in a world of positive transaction costs it does.
>
> (1990: 16)

The assumption that the social location of an activity is neutral, as it costs nothing to transfer the product from one 'owner' to another produces a different result from that which is found in the real political economy. Thus, though in an abstract sense the location of activities might be decided by the efficient use of resources, the ability of some actors to extract a transaction cost for transfer (either monetary or social) may shift the location on grounds other than efficiency. The same is the case for the emergence of institutions – while in the abstract world of zero transaction costs, institutions will emerge that produce an efficient co-ordination of social activities, when power differentials are taken into account, the sorts of institutions that actually emerge may well serve different purposes (Williamson 1985: 26ff.). The emergence of particular institutions is tied up with the need to reduce costs of certain behaviour and to maximise the benefits obtained by specific (which is to say, powerful) social actors.

The institutions that interest me in this study are those providing the structures in which economic exchange can take place. Usefully for this purpose North suggests three historical types of exchange. Each has different levels of transaction costs and thus different needs relative to the emergence of particular institutions (North 1990: 34–35). The first is small-scale interpersonal exchange which is characterised by repeat-dealing, a substantial amount of cultural homogeneity, and the lack of incidence or need of third-party enforcement. But while transaction costs are low, the development of the division of labour and specialisation are also rudimentary, and therefore the costs of transforming inputs into goods are relatively high. The next type of exchange emerges as the scope and extent of exchange expands. In this second type, exchange becomes impersonal by virtue of the increasing quantity of individual exchanges between clients and contractors.

However, here behaviour is regulated through kinship ties, bonding, merchant codes of conduct or in extreme cases hostages. This sort of development underpinned a geographic expansion of trade along international trade routes and at the fairs of medieval Europe. It led to an increased role for the proto-state in protecting merchants' interests and to the use of such merchants as a revenue source through taxation and the sale of monopolies.

In this second stage, in certain respects the predecessors to the state increased rather than decreased transaction costs. As protectors and enforcers of property rights they intervened in transactions which were being concluded through informal links and ties. However, in the third type of exchange (which might be termed modern) enforcement no longer relies exclusively on informal links (through guilds or families) between contracting parties, but is enforced by a third party. An even greater proliferation of exchange(s) is allowed as there is no longer a need for any sort of personal link between parties. On the other hand, third party involvement, by virtue of its imprecise and generalised nature is more costly in any particular circumstance relative to first and second stage exchanges. Where the returns for cheating and opportunism expand through the anonymity of the market, third party enforcement is necessary. If enforcement was entirely dependent on active policing and force, the advantages of complex economic exchange would be unlikely to arise. Thus 'effective third-party enforcement is best realised by creating a set of rules that then make a variety of informal constraints effective' (North 1990: 35). This leads to efforts to produce a legitimised and socially embedded set of norms and principles which will in most cases ensure behaviour accords with the formal rules without being policed: legislators build on rather than contradict broad patterns of traditional practice.

The sorts of institutions required and supported in each of these types of exchange are somewhat different. For property this is the history of the move from the common understanding of property as *physical things held for the owner's use* to the more modern conception of property as assets, which can be used or otherwise sold to another potential user. However,

> while this transition was hardly noticeable as long as the merchant, the master, the labourer, were combined under small units of ownership, [it] becomes distinct when all opportunities are occupied and business is conducted by corporations on a credit system which consolidates property under the control of absentee owners. Then the power of property *per se*, distinguished from the power residing in personal faculties or special grants of sovereignty, comes into prominence . . . When to this is added the pressure of population and the increasing demand for limited supplies of mineral and metal resources, of water-powers, of lands situated at centres of population, then the mere holding of property becomes a power to withhold, far beyond that which either the labourer has over his labour or the investor has over his savings, and beyond anything known when this power was being perfected by the early common law or early business law.
>
> (Commons 1959 [1924]: 53)

It is this move from holding to *withholding*, the ability to restrict use, which is of crucial importance. When the resources required for social existence are scarce, then the distribution of the rights to their use (property rights) becomes a central, if not *the* central issue of political economy.

If property is to be something more than possession then the rights accorded to possession (or under property law 'ownership') need to be embedded within a legal framework that can be enforced by the state. Thus, as the Supreme Court of North Carolina made clear in 1872

> Property itself, as well as the succession to it, is the creature of positive law. The legislative power declares what objects in nature may be held as property; it provides by what forms and on what conditions it may be transmitted from one person to another. The right to give or take property is not one of those natural, inalienable rights which are supposed to precede government, and which no government can rightfully impair.
>
> (cited in Ely 1914: 189/190)

Property, while being related to pre-legal practices, can only be recognised *qua* property to which rights are accorded by the intervention and sanction of the state. Legitimate disputes therefore will not be concerned with the actual institution itself, but rather with boundary issues (what is and is not property) and ownership issues (the control and legitimisation of sales and rents, alongside the punishment of theft and other infringements of the rights of owners, such as damage by third parties).

This retelling of the history of property carries with it the implicit notion that property rose as an institution, to fulfill a certain function. And therefore justifications founded on the emergence of property as a support for the efficient operation of markets relate the function of property as the efficient allocation of scarce economic resources. Even if it is accepted that this allocation may not be 'optimal', property markets are still presented as, though less than perfect, the most efficient method of allocation available. However, as I will discuss when I turn to intellectual property, there is a complementary function which may equally well be seen as the root of certain developments. The emergence of property furthers the interests of specific groups in society: those in possession of such resources that can be utilised to accumulate more resources, the nascent capitalists. While the institution of property may further efficiency of allocation there is a need to remember exactly what such efficiency means and whose benefit it serves. In the pragmatic or economic justifications I discuss below, it is exactly this functional history that is appealed to to legitimise the institution of property.

This returns us to the problem of property's emergence in the first place. As with many social institutions it is difficult to pinpoint a moment of transition and so part of the problem in justifying property has been to construct not only the legitimated rights accorded to ownership but also a legitimated (philosophical) history, a myth of origin. And it is to these histories that I now turn.

Justificatory schemata of property

Throughout the following chapters I explore the way intellectual property is currently justified and legitimised. There are three groups of justifications which are mobilised to support the institution of intellectual property. I call them 'justificatory schemata' to capture their purpose – the justification of (intellectual) property – and their complex nature. Each schema is mobilised in stronger or weaker versions, with different aspects of their arguments stressed at different times. The claims which are made are often included almost subconsciously as the common sense of (intellectual) property. Using the term schemata emphasises that these arguments are used to achieve a certain end, the continuity and reinforcement of a particular understanding of property in knowledge. Also, in its popular usage scheming is seen as something that is partially hidden from those its machinations effect. As I suggest the knowledge structure attempts to obscure and hide alternative ways of treating knowledge in the global political economy, this implication seems appropriate. The term 'justificatory schemata' will be deployed throughout as a shorthand for the ways of constructing a 'common sense' of intellectual property. First, however, I will examine their more widespread use supporting the institution of material property.

Under communism there might be, and perhaps in pre-modernity there was, some form of possession that could be conceived of as property, and could be held socially by a group without rights being explicitly accorded to an owner. However, in the modern period of which most writing on property is concerned, the existence of property rights is seen as having an axiomatic link with ownership. Though modern, 'property' is seen as essentially trans-political. Such a view enables Macpherson to argue that as 'soon as any society . . . makes a distinction between property and mere physical possession it has in effect defined property as a right' enjoyed by a sovereign individual (Macpherson 1978: 3). Thus, the tendency in theories of property is to focus exclusively on individual ownership and this is certainly how Macpherson presents his influential history. But while the history of property in Anglo-Saxon capitalism *has* taken this road of conceptual development, it is a teleological argument to see this as self-evident. Many of the international disputes over intellectual property rights discussed later find their cause in the contrasting views different socio-legal traditions accord to the ownership of property. There are specific rather than general reasons why the institution of property in Western states looks as it does today.

The seventeenth century is usually depicted as a period of major disjunctures in the recognition of property and its attendant rights (Ryan 1984). And while there is a history of property that goes much further back than this period, to Roman juristic tradition and its recognition of rights in 'things' (Burch 1998: 23), here I will concentrate on the histories that have been constructed on the basis of the reformulation of property that took place during the seventeenth century. The intellectual ferment of this period was not a sufficient cause of the disruptions of the meaning of property, but the questioning of what could justify the ownership of property stimulated an engagement with prevalent and accepted notions of

ownership (Hill 1972). The roots of conceptual reformulation lie in this engagement
with the dominant understandings of property.

There are two significant changes in the concept of property which arose in the
seventeenth century (Macpherson 1978). First, property began to be treated as
things to which rights were attached, not rights by themselves and second, there
was a move to conceive of property as something that could *only* be owned privately
(by someone or some organisation). Until then property had been a set of limited
rights of ownership. An individual's ownership of land gave him (and usually it
was 'him') certain limited rights to its use, and such rights were not often freely
disposable or transferable. They were held conditionally by the individual
concerned: property was not fully alienable. Property also included the right to
revenues from monopolies, tax-farming and other State (or proto-state) authorised
activities. The concept of 'property' was concerned with rights to benefit from
certain things or relations (but was not absolutely linked to the things or relations
in themselves). After this period property became things that were owned and the
linked rights flowed from the ownership. The rights themselves *were not* property.

Second, there had been previously a recognition of both private *and* common
property. However, during the seventeenth century while private property
remained, common property 'drops virtually out of sight' being treated 'as a
contradiction in terms' (Macpherson 1978: 9). After this period everything had to
belong to *someone*, where that (legally constituted) someone could also be the state,
the local community when organised, or other legally constituted organisation.
This led to the acceptance of the possibility of common property being treated as
a *critique* of the legitimate existence of any sort of property, and Proudhon's famous
assertion that 'all property is theft' (Proudhon 1994 [1840]: 13). However, the
problem with such a statement is that to recognise the concept of 'theft' is to
recognise the prior validity of the notion of property. Even if 'all property is theft',
to be stolen something needed to be owned in some form, and thus perhaps
Proudhon's critique of property is better seen as a critique of a certain *distribution*
of property.

Reeve argues that despite such simplifications, the multiplicity of different *actual*
material constructions of property makes a singular parsimonious theory of
property unlikely (Reeve 1991: 112–114). Indeed, the tenacity of such a position,
that there is one theory of *all* property (*including* intellectual property), is a product
of political economic power. The idea of comprehensive private property (and
therefore its promotion as a legitimate conceptual construction) which began to
dominate considerations of property after the seventeenth century enabled all
property to be transferred (alienated) and enter a system of exchange. This was an
extension to the rights of *owners* of property: an extension of the right to protect
an interest; the ability to recover its value from a despoiler; and an extension of the
right of disposal (especially of land) (Reeve 1986: 50). In extending the interests of
certain social actors, which is to say property owners, there is a need to recognise
the incidence and mobilisation of political economic power.

To exchange property in a market, all parties to the exchange must see both
property and market as legitimate institutions. To explore the main ways of

justifying or legitimising property (and its attendant rights) I shall utilise Ryan's taxonomy of an 'instrumental' perspective and a 'self-developmental' perspective (Ryan 1984). These justificatory schema are often utilised in discussions of property as accepted precedents, which is to say they are taken as largely accurate views of the social emergence of property. While political positions on property rights may also appeal to other arguments, they usually rely on one or other as the underlying justificatory position. Mediated positions are not necessarily more, or less, coherent, but they usually seek legitimisation or claim warrant by invoking one or other of Ryan's two philosophical traditions, alongside a third which I shall refer to as the pragmatic or economic schema.

First, it is necessary to be clear that arguments that rest on 'first occupancy' are only of secondary importance here. These are responses to the 'common-sense' enquiry: 'who had it first?' While being a plausible element of any discussion of *particular* property rights this cannot form part of the overall justification of property. The acceptance of a notion of legitimate property against which chronology is set bars it from a role in the justification of such property in the first instance. The legitimacy of ownership is seen as unproblematic, it is accepted as *a priori* to the rights of 'first occupancy'. When a regime of legitimisation has been settled, such temporal issues may be of major import, but only after such regimes have been settled can they assume any justificatory role (Becker 1977: 24–31; Waldron 1988: 284–287). Thus, prior to any temporal claims, how is the institution of property generally justified?

Instrumental justification

'Instrumentalist' justifications draw on arguments rooted in the work of John Locke, whose perspective on property is laid out in the Second Treatise of his *Two Treatises on Government* (Locke 1988 [1690]). And while he founded his conception of property on the 'labour of the first occupier', as I have noted, the key issue is not the temporal, but the notion of 'labour'. Property for Locke is the reward for the conversion or 'improvement' of nature, taking place *within* a society of men into which the individual is born (Ryan 1984: 28–29). This includes an individual's use of one aspect of nature to improve another (a man using a horse to crop grass) but more importantly assumes that property is a social phenomenon through its relation to other claims. Ownership of property is held *against* other claimants: the deployment of labour establishes a particular individual's ownership within a particular society. Others who have not laboured on this particular piece of nature are excluded from the benefits this work brings. Property in this sense can only appear within social relations, it makes no sense to talk of the property rights of a castaway on a desert island, as there is no-one *against* whom the rights could be held.

For Locke, the initial relation to Natural Law is important, unlike Rousseau who thought only the recourse to a legal constitution enabled the recognition of legitimised property (Ryan 1984: 54–55). In this sense Locke sees the emergence of property pre-dating its institutional development. First there was something which was socially recognised as property, with a legal form following later. Property is part of the customary practice on which the more formal (legal) institution rests. While Locke maintains that there may be things that are *not owned* (the property of God existing in nature), the utilisation of labour to improve these previously un-owned things brings them into the realm of property. The mixture of the individual's labour with naturally existing resources, adds a certain value. Property is not merely the product of mixing labour and nature but the result of the 'value' added by this operation. This labour theory of property is therefore based on two central premises: individuals have property in their own exertion; and the reward for utilising this exertion to add value is ownership of the result. Equally, the promise of ownership of property inspires individuals to labour in the first place. Only by ownership of the product of labour can human endeavour be encouraged. This is 'instrumental' inasmuch as it is meant to encourage and facilitate profitable human activities.

Locke initially sets some limit to the application of such a regime for property accumulation:

> As much as any one can make use of to any advantage of life before it spoils; so much he may by his labour fix a Property in. Whatever is beyond this, is more than his fair share, and belongs to others.
>
> (Locke 1988 [1690]: 290)

But, at what point does the property owner overstretch the needs and satisfactions that are represented by property? What do we understand by 'spoils', and what is 'his fair share'? The normative element of Locke's position is very interesting when intellectual property rights are considered. Under copyright for instance: when does a copyright holder's interest in restraining all (or some) uses of their intellectual property reflect a 'spoiling' of that resource? Or with patents: what level of profit is fair from the monopolisation of an innovative idea? And in either case: should there be a maximum licence charge for other users? But for Locke this issue of 'fair use' is compromised by subsequent developments.

Locke believed that the 'Invention of Money' led to the extinction of previous natural limits to the fruits of labour represented by property, as he argues at some length in the second treatise (sections 36, 37, 47 and 48). With the commodification of property moral (or Natural Law) limits to the ownership of property were removed. The utilisation of money as a medium of exchange (and store of value) enabled 'over-accumulation' of property. Those with money at their immediate disposal (through careful husbanding in the past) could buy more property than they might actually 'need'. But as property reflected an application of labour (which was financially rewarded when purchased from the first owner), over-accumulated property could still be considered legitimate under Locke's schema. As Macpherson argues: 'Locke's astonishing achievement was to base the property right on natural right and natural law, and then to remove all the natural law limits from the property right' (1962: 199). By removing the moral limitation on the extent of property ownership, but retaining its justification based on the strictures of Natural

Law, Locke established a more permissive realm of property ownership, founded on the exchange relation mediated by money, rather than by *direct* labour.

Despite some questions regarding the overall coherence of Locke's position (Becker 1977; Ryan 1984), I want to stress the notion that labour's application is rewarded through property (and its rights) in the object worked on, as this is a position widely recognised today. Crucially this position does not require the current owner's labour to be that which is rewarded by the recognition of property rights, only that labour took place at some point. Therefore, for the instrumentalist position ownership accrues to the expenditure of effort, in whatever manner that effort may be defined, and effort is encouraged through the prospective rewards to be gained. Property rights accrue to those who have worked on the 'improvement' of any particular object, even if the object has subsequently been transferred to another owner along with its attached rights. This requires both the ownership of one's own efforts as well as the alienability of their product.

Self-developmental justification

The question of how the ownership of one's own efforts can be conceptualised leads me to the second perspective – the 'self-developmental'. This draws on the work of Georg Hegel, laid out in *Philosophy of Right* (1967 [1821]) and elsewhere. Hegel argued that the legitimacy of property was intimately tied to the existence of the free individual, and the recognition of that free individual by others. Property was how the free individual was identified, 'since the respect others show to his property by not trespassing on it reflects their acceptance of him as a person' (Avineri 1972: 136). The individual has a will to control and master nature, and this is expressed through the ownership of the fruits of such control, reflecting the individual's personality. The individual's freedom is expressed through the ability to control relations with nature, as ownership protects the individual from the 'unreasonable' rights or interests of others in society, and from state intervention in their lives. As with Locke, property rights are seen as held against others and as existing only by virtue of their place in social relations or 'civil society'.

But for Hegel, civil society is 'essentially the market and its legal framework' and thus property is not absolute, in the sense that it can be used without limit, but is legally constrained by the laws of the society in which it is owned (Ryan 1984: 134). Unlike Locke, this property is entirely a legal construct. There may have been prior customary practice but property *qua* property is a legally constituted right. For Hegel property is part of the individual's appropriation of things needed to support the self, sanctioned through the practices of the state. However, as Avineri points out, only Hegel's division between individual moral life and a wider ethical universe enables him to support the system of private property while recognising its denial of property to the poor (which would seem to largely rob them of the possibility of individuality) as 'one of the most vexing problems facing modern society'. By separating out the family from contractual social relations Hegel allows that individuals might be able to establish personality through their relations with other members of the family group even if they are propertyless in the wider society

(Avineri 1972: 135–141). This is a useful step to make as it allows the individual's expression of self (which should be controlled by the individual) to remain the centre of justification while also allowing for property-based inequality of distribution of property rights.

For the self-developmental perspective, the important question is possession, rather than the actual application of labour (though this is by no means excluded). In the hands of Marx, however, this conception of property becomes the mechanism for *removing* the self from the individual through work (through *alienation*), rather than its reflection. As Ryan notes 'Marx's strictures on property entail that Hegel's positive claims for private property, work and the market are all of them the reverse of the truth' (1984: 161). Property denies the individual's self through an act of alienation. For Marx, under capitalism, the creative worker cannot enjoy the fruits of his production due to the division of labour in industry and alienation of effort that is required to garner the exchange value of his labour. This reward is required by the worker to socially reproduce his labour (his life) but robs him of the property which enables the development of self-worth. Through commo-dification the worker's labour is robbed of its self-developmental potential for the individual (no act of creation produces a finished article reflecting Hegel's 'self', controlled by its creator). The worker is alienated both from the product of labour and the productive activity itself (McLellan 1973: 118–119, 128–129).

Whether an expression of self is alienable is a pivotal question for notions of (intellectual) property.[1] If it is acceptable that there is something of the self invested in the interaction with that which the individual's 'will' seeks to change (or mingle with), then should the expression of that 'will' always belong to the sovereign individual (in perpetuity)? But if alienation takes place, can the idea of the sovereign individual still stand? This investment of self might better be described as the act of creation. By mixing themselves with the world about them individuals are able to claim the resulting processions as their own. The outward manifestation of the self must be the property of the self to ensure that the self is protected from being dissolved into some form of collectivity – where the individual is not separate from society. This reflects the second of the two dynamics I suggested underlay the development of property rights – the protection of the individual from the intervention and power of the state. The justificatory schema that draws its sustenance from Hegel emphasises this role for property rights. The Lockean stream, on the other hand, emphasises the protection of the rights of owners, not from the state (though this might also be the case) but from other individuals.

Property is linked to human endeavour in both perspectives, but they are divided about the character of this endeavour and what it might produce. Broadly speaking, effort and its material reward are contrasted with possession and the subsequent development of self. Waldron, making the same distinction refers to these two broad streams as the special right and the general right theories. He highlights the need for some specific action to be taken in the instrumental justification (labour's desert) making it a special right. In the self-developmental approach there is no necessary expenditure of effort to enjoy the right to property as it is part of the recognition of individual citizenship making it an unconditional right to private property, and therefore a general right (Waldron 1988). This distinction based on the requirement or otherwise for some notion of effort is a key element in the debates about a number of intellectual property issues, in the biotechnology sector's desire to 'patent nature' and in the copyrighting of collated material, for instance.

My brief account of the distinction between these perspectives is by no means meant to represent a comprehensive discussion of the theories of property that might be proposed, but these two perspectives will be useful in drawing together seemingly disparate arguments regarding intellectual property. Indeed, both justifications lie behind most arguments over the incidence of intellectual property rights, what differs from position to position is the relative weight allocated to either aspect. However, once property has been justified in one way or another there is still the question of the boundary to be addressed – where is the line drawn between property and not property?

Recognising active and passive property

Within the potential field of private property that can be owned and transferred (to which theories of justification are applied), the expansion of potential 'items' *for* ownership is a crucial issue. The line over which the shifting notion of property has moved can be conceived as the division between active and passive characterisations of property. While property may be 'active' or 'passive', each is historically specific (and socially constituted), and as I argue below, the result of power distributions in the structure of knowledge.

Active property can be defined as anything that an individual 'can use to produce an effect in the world and include[s] everything from productive capital to personal characteristics'. Active property produces measurable change in the world (an 'improvement') and is what the 'self-developmental' perspective would understand as 'will' or 'intended action'. Passive properties 'are simply attributes or possessions not of a will, but of a person', which includes identity, appearance, ideas (which have yet to be acted on). This is a residual category including those things or attributes which are referred to as property but which at present are not ownable. This distinction, then, is 'not one between actual things in the world, but merely between different human attitudes, or uses of things' (Minogue 1980: 13–14). It is the difference between property which has been used in some way and property that awaits use, potential property.

However, there is little in the world that cannot *become* active property, if the technology exists to utilise it. This means it is at least possible to render anything as a commodity given the right conditions. In the realm of intellectual property as technology becomes able to use aspects of knowledge for economic intervention in the world of objects, more knowledge becomes active (and in the terms of the World Trade Organisation, 'trade related'). There is little if any knowledge which may have no potential effect on the material environment. Under capitalism this might be reformulated to conclude that there is little socially existing knowledge that is potentially unable to be treated as a commodity. Indeed, Heilbronner argues that 'much of what is called "growth" in capitalist societies consists in this

commodification of life . . . the continuous search of business for areas of social
activity that can be subsumed within the capital-generating circuit' (Heilbronner
1985: 60, 118). Therefore the field of property is not fixed by its justificatory
schemata, there is always the possibility that new things can be thought of as
property, which is to say commodified and subjected to market exchange.

The links between the justification of property and its institutional existence
revolve around the construction of history. Lockean justifications stress that
property emerged as the necessary social reward for those far-sighted enough to
invest their labour to 'improve' the natural resources with which mankind was
provided. The Hegelian justification suggests it is man's spirit that has encouraged
him to express him/herself through the mixing of self with nature to produce new
possessions or creations, which are owned by the sovereign self, and act as a check
on the intrusions of the state. These imaginary histories underpin the institution
of property, responding to its emergence by portraying it not as the reflection of
particular interests but as an institution which has social worth. At the centre
of these considerations has been the issue of the existence or property as a set of
socially accepted rules of conduct, governing not the relations between owner and
property, but rather those between owners and others, which is to say social
relations. As an institutionalised set of rules, property is socially constructed and
thus subject not only to power over material resources (and their distribution) but
as importantly to power over the construction of knowledge, the legitimisation of
a particular understanding of what rights accrue to the property owner.

Institutions as structures of knowledge

Institutions are constructed through the production of specific knowledge. Rules
which are both the product and the substance of social institutions are not natural,
they are the products of society expressed as knowledge about social reality,
knowledge of possibilities and constraints. These rules are reproduced by use; they
may shift as social relations bring new pressures to bear on the institution as a whole
(or in part), but at any time the rules of an institution also appear fixed, which is to
say they appear as the structures of society. Though the generation of knowledge
produces institutions which appear as structures, it also allows for shifts as
rules react to changes in the social relations over which an institution presides.
The operation of forms of power over such knowledge generation is crucial to
understanding how certain justificatory schemata are utilised to support particular
institutional settlements in the political economy of intellectual property, and why
these settlements emerge.

Susan Strange suggests that knowledge as a source of power in the international
political economy is seldom accorded sufficient weight in analyses. It may be hard
to analyse because what is believed, what is known (perceived as understood or
'given') and the channels by which these beliefs, ideas and knowledge are
communicated or confined, are not easily quantifiable. This lack of materiality she
suggests, has led to a mis-recognition of the importance of knowledge, but is also
a result of the way the power of (and within) the knowledge structure manifests

itself. Strange argues that as power derived from knowledge is often based on acquiescence, authority may flow from a socialised belief system, or from the status conferred by possession of knowledge (Strange 1988: 115–118). There is seldom a clear power relation based on the utilisation of material resources in the distribution and use of knowledge derived power. Thus there is often some difficulty recognising and allocating importance to the role of knowledge in any particular instance.

This leads Strange to identify three sorts of change which should be accorded some importance within the knowledge structure: changes in the provision and control of information and communication systems; changes in the use of language and non-verbal channels of communication; and changes in belief systems (Strange 1988: 116). The first group of changes are concerned with the control of the conduits of information and knowledge – the ability to constrict or alternatively facilitate the flow of knowledge around the global system. The second is concerned with the representation of knowledge and information. Issues of education and the ability to utilise information are crucial here – access is only part of the problem, there is a requirement for intellectual tools and training as well. The third area of change is more fundamental and includes the sorts of issues I am concerned with when I discuss institutions.

For intellectual property these three aspects of change can be regarded as: changes in the distribution of (and access to) data and information sources – in a sense technical issues of infrastructural development and technological diffusion; changes in the distribution and availability of the theoretical or symbolic knowledge required to make full use of information – including the availability of expertise and scientific methods, for instance; and changes in the rules governing the ownership and characterisation of property in knowledge resources. This last aspect of change in the knowledge structure, I will suggest in the rest of this book, has a major impact on the first two aspects. Not least of all as the use and benefits that might flow from knowledge and information depend on the rules of distribution; on intellectual property.

The key to this approach to thinking about power in the international political economy, power that is mediated through a knowledge structure, is that for Strange this structure is only one of four structures which act on each other. The other three structures that complete her overall characterisation of structural power are: security; production; and finance (Strange 1988). However, the distinction between the knowledge and production structures to some extent starts to break down with the commodification of knowledge. As the 'production' of knowledge objects itself becomes an economic activity (locating it analytically within the production structure) it erodes the formal distinction between Strange's structures as ontologically separate spheres of activity. However, Strange's taxonomy of structures is not meant to identify hermetically sealed realms, quite the opposite: they are interpenetrated, and coexistent within a coterminous realm of political economy (ibid.: 24–28). Indeed, they are meant as an aid for identifying lacunae in political economic analyses rather than a closed ontology. Thus, the elision between the knowledge and production structures within an information society reveals the commodification of information and knowledge, while reinforcing the point of the ultimate inseparability of the four structures.

It is within the interactions of all four structures that specific 'bargains' between authority and market as a mechanism of control will be struck. In any particular case there is a settlement, produced by the mobilisation of power, between the use of political authority to pattern the distribution of benefits and the use of the market mechanism. This settlement is never absolute; there is always an element of both mechanisms but the bargain made in a particular instance will allocate either authority or market as the lead distributional device. To adopt this analytical approach a mechanism of interaction between the structures which results in this settlement must be identified, and it is to this question I now turn.

Structural interaction and change

The central question which any analysis utilising the idea of the knowledge structure needs to address is: *how does knowledge interact with and affect the other structures?* For Strange, it is the control of information and know-how that enables structural power to set the agendas in the other dimensions – security, finance and production. Broadly conceived, these other structures respectively set the agendas: in the realm of social welfare (stretching from local law and order, including national security, to the threat of war in the international system); in the realm of provision of credit and the economics of fiscal relations between state and non-state actors; and in the realm of productive relations, which is to say the distribution of benefits and profits from productive activities. One of the main purposes of this sort of power is the transfer of risk from the powerful to the relatively powerless and the retention of benefit by certain groups at the expense of others (May 1996). So, for Strange, structural power is agenda-setting power – the power to circumscribe choice in such a way that the limitation of choice is not perceived as such by the actors in social relations (Lukes 1974). This ability to set agendas also acts to obscure the particular political economic interests which certain rules and limitations on social action may serve. But to carry this to its apparent logical conclusion, is to place the knowledge structure in a foundational role. If the manipulation of knowledge is how agendas are set, and agenda-setting is a central role of structural power (in that it shapes outcomes by ruling some as impossible and others as feasible), then knowledge issues must shape structures. This would require the knowledge structure to act as the primary structure; the foundation of the other structures.

Neither Strange nor myself want to make this analytical move, indeed, her argument is that the four structures interact, with none being necessarily prior in any particular situation. Therefore to understand how structural power over knowledge reproduces social institutions the links and exchanges between materiality and knowledge – between the world and how we conceive of it – are of central importance. Thus, while it is acceptable that knowledge or information can be a direct influence on specific actions, this is not the only aspect of its influence. As Bourdieu has argued: 'The theory of knowledge is a dimension of political theory because the specifically symbolic power to impose the principles of the construction of reality – in particular, social reality – is a major dimension of political power' (Bourdieu 1977: 165). The ability to establish warrant for truth claims enables power to define the social agenda of possibilities, within which resistance and opposition are mobilised. It sets the limits within which acceptable social practices can take place. Institutions such as property, which produce sets of rules for social relations, based as they are on the mobilisation of knowledge and the claims for their legitimate depiction of social relations need to be examined as sites of structural power not merely accepted as the structure *in which* power relations are arrayed. A critical theory needs to reveal those social forces which support particular settlements and suggest alternatives that may be currently portrayed as *implausible* by the dominant set of institutional rules.

If knowledge plays an important role in the agenda-setting processes of structural power, then *the knowledge structure is itself subject to this agenda-setting process.* The social institutions which set the agenda of social relations are themselves subject to structural power over knowledge. Equally, and importantly, with the commodification of knowledge, aspects of the knowledge structure are subject to power in the production structure. The distribution and circulation of knowledge have become partly structured by a wealth effect rooted in productive activities. This leads me to ask: how does change in a material structure produce change in the knowledge structure?; how do shifts in the knowledge structure produce changes elsewhere in the political economy?; and thus how does differential power change social institutions?

Towards a theory of change

A discussion of change is dependent on knowing that there has been a change in the observed field of study. Thus, there is an epistemological question concerning what is entailed in claiming warrant for such a recognition. But there is also an ontological issue to be surmounted: what is recognised as change and how is this to be divided off from things that have remained the same (Maclean 1981: 48). A critical theory must address the issue of *why* certain outcomes have come to pass. And, when all around appears to be changing (the continual movements of socio-economic relations), there is a requirement to develop an ontology that can be used to throw subjects for analysis into relief. By doing so, significant changes can be identified (and thus the theory in which this particular change *is* significant and meaningful can be constructed). Once this has been outlined there is the important question of why these particular changes, why not others? And it is here that my central concern with the structural power over the construction of institutions is rooted.

Change stems from new or repeated bargains in the field of social relations. But these changes are *not* naturally occurring phenomena, nor do bargains between actors over outcomes take place in a vacuum. Bargains are the 'trade-offs' between different possible outcomes (which includes the possibilities of the renewal of previous outcomes) within the agenda of choices recognised by actors making decisions. This will involve an assessment of costs and benefits (economic, political and social) accruing to the parties and the strength of their interest in supporting potential outcomes. And given that bargains will in all likelihood be between unequal actors, power differentials will play a role in the outcome (Strange 1988: 39). The agendas in which bargains are constrained are those of social institutional rule-making. The discussion of the forces of change needs also to recognise the forces of institutional reproduction. This needs to be understood incrementally, but there is always the danger of allocating too much weight to a specific bargain. Thus, an historical sensitivity must be reflected, both in the identification of particular changes and of the overall *context* in which such changes are embedded.

This suggests two distinct conceptions of analytically significant change. The first category of changes occur when the ability or capacity of actors to produce desired outcomes in their political economic relations alters. When one actor's power to bring about outcomes changes relative to another's in the relationship under analysis, there is a shift in the balance of power. Investigation needs to focus on such a change and suggest its causes. This may be indicated for instance, by the ability of previously weak actors to have more impact on bargains in a particular context, or perhaps the success of previously side-lined groups in resisting certain imposed outcomes. Indeed, analysis may reveal shifts in the importance of certain types of resources for the settlement of bargains over outcomes, changing effective resource endowments relative to effective power. However, this dimension of change is essentially within the extant institutional settlement, and reflects the choices among possibilities set and reproduced through the knowledge structure. Particular institutions may encompass shifts of power without the overall rules of social interaction being effected.

This leads me to also identify a second sort of change, that which occurs to the institutions themselves, within the structure of knowledge: changes in what might be termed the 'rules of the game'. These changes are the shifts in the recognisable options available to power holders or social actors, the agendas from which their actions may be chosen. This may happen at the same time as the first sort of shifts, but also may act as a precursor to such shifts – changes in the rules may change the effectiveness of particular power resources without any positive action by their holders. This second sort of change is implicated in the shifting structures of meaning utilised to make sense of the world of social relations. These are subject to the knowledge structure's (re)production function but also the material reality to which they relate. Crucially these are the changes that take place within social institutions themselves. Though at any particular moment such institutions are portrayed by the knowledge structure as fixed, they are subject to change, and a historical sensitivity reveals as much.

Finally, bringing these two groups of significant changes together, a third key concern emerges. How do they interconnect in specific instances? They may reinforce each other, or they may be in tension. Changes in effective resources may still have little impact due to a strong and unchanging structure (or agenda). Shifts in the structural agenda may not overcome the distribution of resources in power relations as such resources may be used in new ways within the changed structure.

Alternatively change in one may reinforce changes in the other, or stasis in both may support the status quo. Therefore analysis must be concerned to ask *why* this particular change, why did actors make these particular choices, why did changes interact in a certain manner at a certain time? Any understanding of these changes needs to be rooted in an historical narrative, rather than an abstract (or modelled) account of the field under investigation. My understanding of a mechanism for identification of change and causality specifically does not aim to suggest any conclusions that are not rooted in particular investigations. While this approach will aid my investigation of intellectual property rights, it does not fix specific conclusions prior to such an investigation.

Moving back to my concern with why such change happens, this can be under-stood as the result of a continual action of 'contradiction' and 'complementarity'.[2] Where institutions contradict emerging changes in power distributions they become possible sites of contestation and tension. However, where institutions continue to reflect social power distribution (that is, they are complementary to them), then continuity will result and the status quo will be reinforced. Equally, institutional change may bring institutional structures into line with the power distribution between the actors whose relations are governed by the institution's rules. Resistance to such changes may stem from previous sites of power wishing to keep reproducing their preferences through the institution. The recognition of when such contradictions and complementarities are actually manifest is of major importance. Indeed, the structure of knowledge, by producing institutionalised rules does not necessarily aim to promote change or stasis, but to ensure that social relations remain within the parameters that benefit the actors or groups who enjoy power over the structures in the first place.

The knowledge structure may at times obscure the contradictions between the pattern of rules and the distribution of effective power resources, or at other times may emphasise such contradictions to produce institutional shifts. There is a substantive link between contradiction and knowledge in the realm of social institutions. And, following Cox, I identify contradiction operating on two levels:

> At the level of logic, it means a dialogue seeking truth through the exploration of contradictions . . . the continual confrontation of concepts with the reality they are supposed to represent and their adjustment to this reality as it continually changes . . . At the level of real history, dialectic is the potential for alternative forms of development arising from the confrontation of opposed forces in any concrete historical situation.
>
> (Cox 1996: 95)

As the second sentence reveals, Cox is actually concerned here with a notion of the dialectic, and this leads me to suggest that to deal with change in the knowledge structure as it is related to the other three structures Strange posits (which is to say, material reality), a notion of dialectical social forces is useful.

Components of a dialectical theory

Developing a dialectic theory of change for a study of the knowledge structure holds some promise as such a theory 'absolutely requires *both matter* (phrased as social relations, simple activity, mode of production, or whatever) *and mind* (whether seen as cognitive process, psychoemotional states, and so forth) in interaction with each other. They are inseparable . . .' (Murphy 1972: 84). A dialectic approach 'negates the opposition between materialism and idealism' by producing an understanding of the chosen subject based on the analysis of the *whole*. It is not possible to wrench an account of change out of social relations in which it appears, and as such the approach presented below is meant to identify the key issues for an account of particular social relations.

There are two distinct and opposite ways of describing the operation of an historical dialectic: the first as formulated by Hegel; and then the second, as (re)formulated by Marx. And in that Marx was a 'young Hegelian' before he stood Hegel's dialectic 'on its head' there is a clear and important link between the two writers (Marx 1974a [1887]: 29). Here I will present brief and rather general characterisations of these opposing views on the dialectic to establish the dynamic of social movement, before bringing them together in what I have termed, for ease, the 'dual-dialectic'. While I have called these the Hegelian and Marxist dialectics this is merely a shorthand for identifying the two directions a uni-directional causal relation between existence and essence might be proposed to run. And though I use these writers to illustrate these arguments in the following section, this is due to their familiarity and influence rather than any necessary direct link between my arguments and theirs.

For Hegel and those who have adopted some form of Hegelian position, the dialectic is a process that would finally lead to the 'unity of essence and existence'; history is essentially teleological. Hegel did not accept the final separation of the realms of essence and existence – the division of ideas and materiality – rather, unity is the object of historical process. However, while not accepting this division, Hegel *does* claim that the 'only necessity in historical development is that of freedom's progress towards self-realisation in human consciousness' – essence is given historical and therefore causal priority (Avineri 1972: 221). Hegel makes it quite clear that the 'Idea is the inner spring of action', which is then realised through material existence (Hegel 1956 [1899]: 38). He argues that:

> Spirit . . . consumes its own existence; but in this very destruction it works up that existence into a new form, and *each successive phase becomes in its turn material*, working on which it exhalts itself to a new grade.
>
> (Hegel 1956 [1899]: 73, emphasis added)

There can only be historical development in the world of objects, once the idea (the essence) of such existence has been remade through the destruction and reconstruction of the Spirit. But this presupposes a uni-directional development, a belief in the notion of 'progress'. In Hegel, it is the idea of history (and its progress towards the actualisation of Universal Freedom) that conditions material existence. Historical shifts are moving the structure of social relations towards an ideal settlement – Universal Freedom. While the material world is by no means dismissed it is subject to the operation of the dialectic of Spirit, essence or ideas.

Essentially a Hegelian dialectic represents the priority of ideas over materiality in locating historical causality, the direction of the dialectic can be summed up as an account of change where *change stems from the realisation of contradictions within the thought of individual social actors*. Essence precedes existence, in the sense that the construction of the world of the 'spirit' is then compared to the 'real' world and the real world is found wanting, driving progress and change forward. Or using different terms, institutional rules and changes within those rules produce the actions of social actors. Thus, though there is a clear and necessary link between essence and existence, it is essence or ideas that are the root of changes. Famously Karl Marx took Hegel's ideas on history, and while agreeing that undoubtedly the key historical drive was some sort of dialectical movement, disputed the Hegelian location of this dialectic in the realisation of the spirit.

Like Hegel, Marx did not suggest only one side of the essence/existence distinction had any importance. Though Marx reversed and modified Hegel's dialectic, this is not to claim that Marx was a material determinist, arguing that existence was all, indeed the suggestion that Marx was crudely deterministic is essentially a caricature of a more subtle account of political economy (Bimber 1995; Hoffman 1975: 71–108). The aspect of the dialectic that I wish explicitly to draw on here is the process that is related as the material dialectic of history. Marx's construction of the dialectical process of history is concerned to locate the mechanism in man's material relations and specifically in the production of the socio-economic environment which is the history of man's 'escape' from nature. Marx argues:

> as everything natural has to *come into being, man* too has his act of origin – *history* – which, however, is for him a known history, and hence as an act of origin it is a conscious self-transcending act of origin. History is the true natural history of man.
>
> (Marx 1974b [1844]: 136, emphasis in original)

This claim that history transcends the self, in as much as it exists outside the perceptions of such history does not involve the claim that man has *no* reflexive self, only that such reflection is related to an already extant materiality. This contributes to and informs man's essence, and while such essence may feed back into material relations (through their recognition and/or valorisation), the existence of specific social relations is prior. Man's ideas have a role to play in the dialectical processes of history, but they cannot blithely reconstruct the social relations produced in man's material history as they see fit.

In much the same manner as Hegel accorded essence priority over existence, but did not wish to remove the latter from his analysis, Marx wished to do the same, but as a mirror image. For Marx:

Consciousness can never be anything else than conscious existence, and the existence of men is their actual life-process . . . The phantoms formed in the human brain are also, necessarily, sublimates of their material life-process, which is empirically verifiable and bound to material premises.

(Marx and Engels 1965: 37–38)

This leads to a conception of the dialectical process as material contradictions in man's existence and crucially the social relations that such existence brings in to being, with the ideas about such social relations following on from their existence. Marx can then assert in the sixth thesis on Feuerbach that 'the human essence is no abstraction inherent in each single individual. In its reality it is the ensemble of the social relations' (Marx and Engels 1965: 660). Where for Hegel history is a teleological process reaching its final realisation in Universal Freedom, for Marx history is concerned with the social relations of material production. And within these social relations of production the dialectical opposition is that between classes. This might be summed up as *change stems from the emergence of contradictions within the material relations between social actors.*

This element of Marx's wide-ranging analysis is the second component of the dialectic I wish to propose. One way forward in the analysis of the interaction between knowledge and materiality is to synthesise the opposing positions drawn from Marx and Hegel.[3] Indeed, outside a specific historical juncture a crude claim for the necessary priority of either ideational or material forces may be a mistaken reading of the movement of social development. Specifically, while at definite points (at particular times) ideational or material forces may be established as causal, it can never necessarily be the case that one or other is prior. Social man lives an interpenetrated ideational and material existence – with both continually acting in consort to produce both change and continuity.

A dual-dialectal analysis of change

Utilising these two dialectical dynamics suggests that causality actually flows in two directions. In no particular or fixed order, change flows from material existence to the concepts that represent that materiality, and from those concepts to material existence. Thus, as the concepts that social actors have about a material 'reality' increasingly do not fit that reality, their ideas of the material reality shift. But because these material actions are driven by conceptions, this change will also cause their actions and interventions in the material realm to alter, which then changes the material reality itself. This then sets off another change in concepts, and so on. Change enters conceptual-material relations through a continual process of contradiction and (re)construction.

Current institutions shape social acts and thus may maintain social relations even where there may be pressure for change from other areas. Changes may be resisted, attempts may be made to hide contradictions (or influence the conceptual changes taking place), but equally they may be embraced and encouraged. Both dialectics operate simultaneously and are interpenetrated. This 'dual-dialectic' is mediated through the four structures that Strange (1988) proposes – security, finance, production, knowledge. The changes that flow through the dual-dialectic are potentially changes in social (or political economic) relations *and* in the structures (or institutions) within which such relations are played out. Emergent contradictions in power relations may impact on the mobilisation of resources to affect outcomes, and contradictions within structures may shift agendas. Changes in one will be brought into tension with tendencies to stasis in the other, or where there is broad complementarity between both dynamics continuity of settlement will be the likely outcome.

An *a priori* direction of change should not (indeed I would argue, cannot) be established. In a particular case an analysis might suggest one or other direction of the 'dual-dialectic' is determining but there is a need to be aware of the opposite movement, even if it is to be given less weight during a specific investigation. Thus, while causality might be established, from the material side to the conceptual, or vice versa, this can only be established for specific instances. In every case a previous point on the circular movement of this dual-dialectic could have been chosen as the starting point rather than the one picked for a particular investigation. Differing analyses may start from different segments of the dual-dialectic process. In this circulatory process I resist strongly the imposition of a starting place or the notion of a 'foundation'.

What this implies is that any final postulated temporal origins of such processes are lost to investigation, as they must by definition pre-date recorded history. For every idea there is a material instance against which it may be located, but equally for every materiality, there is a prior idea of its existence. I could keep tracking back round the process to the point where information (or a 'trace' of an idea) is no longer available, but this does not mean that finally at this juncture knowledge had no role to play, merely the means for the recognition of such knowledge are not available to the contemporary investigator. It is the concentration on material artefacts that has limited the recognition accorded to the historic role of the knowledge structure. Ideas, by leaving few direct material traces, have been discounted in most historical analyses, which have only stressed their material manifestations (Mumford 1967: 23). Before writing, there were ideas, but they were not fixed in a form that could be recovered by research, while the material products of such ideas have some chance of surviving to be discovered.

This is explicitly a rejection of the previous priority given to the material over and above the ideational, which is to say I reject a technological deterministic account of the rise in importance of intellectual property, typified by much of the literature on the emergence of the information society. But this is also a rejection of an 'idealism' that locates thought prior to materiality, especially prevalent in the more legal-philosophical accounts of the history of intellectual property rights. I propose an acceptance of the interpenetration of materiality and ideas in social relations. This relation can be cut at a temporal point and a directional flow identified, but at another point such an account might be reversed. Any speculation regarding the links and relations between structures at a specific point must be based on an historical understanding of the relations under analysis.

A model of change in the global political economy

The linking of Strange's idea of structures of power to a dual-dialectic account of change can be expressed as a simple diagram, representing one 'slice' of the continuing process I have proposed. The circuit of the 'dual-dialectic' should be imagined as the shape of an infinite spring, where the third dimension is that of time. This can be thought of as producing a historical movement like an induction motor: the current (contradictions – dialectic) flows round the two-way circuit (material–ideas–material–ideas) producing movement in the core (the four structures) over time (see Figure 1). The speed of movement is determined by the balance of contradiction and complementarity. Where complementarities are preponderant, the movement caused by the dual-dialectical dynamic will be slower if not completely stalled. Where contradictions predominate, then change will be at a more frantic pace. However, this is not to suggest a mechanistic understanding of these process – this should only be viewed as an illustration, nothing more.

In this general model the knowledge structure functions as a material/ideational gateway. Interactions (contradictions and complementarities) in all the structures influence and inform the knowledge structure. Changes then feed back into the other structures through their interaction with the knowledge structure, most significantly through their impact on institutionalised rule-making. Material changes are refracted through the knowledge structure and pass back into either the same or different structures. But it is also crucial to recall that there is a power element within the knowledge structure that causes these refractions to be modified. The knowledge structure distorts the outcome of interactions between the structures when they appear in the relevant social institutions.

Changes within political economic relations and institutions are caused by the contradictions within these dual-dialectic flows as well as across them, and when in particular historical circumstances causality is sought, both ideational and material elements play a role. Therefore the analysis that I will develop in the following chapters will be concerned with immediate (relational) causality and the construction of 'available' alternatives through institutional rule (re)making. I will

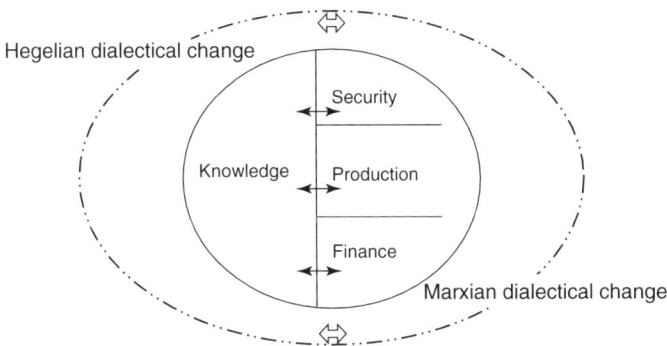

Figure 1 The dual-dialectic account of change

look at bargaining between actors in political economic processes as well as the way the 'rules of the game' are established and reproduced to reveal the knowledge structure's role within the institutional settlement of intellectual property rules within the global system. The key institutional settlement in this regard is the TRIPs agreement which I explore in Chapter 3. But, having outlined this understanding of change and its implications for my method, there is still the important matter of how the knowledge structure actually interacts with it co-structures.

Structural interactions

With the knowledge structure, it is necessary to understand not only how aspects of 'recognised reality' inform 'knowledge', but also how the knowledge structure informs what is recognised in other structures. This needs to go beyond (but without dispensing with) the conception of a knowledge structure affecting the other structures through the utilisation of information, and establish the mechanisms (or processes) that allow the knowledge structure to mediate the inter-action between the other structures. The role of the knowledge structure is central to the interactions between other structures but does not exclusively determine the outcomes.

The key role of the knowledge structure is the attempt to keep potential issues out of politics altogether: structural power controls the agenda to obscure and hide conflict. Though potential conflicts (and contradictions) will still exist, they may never be actualised. There may be a '*latent* conflict, which consists of a contradiction between the interests of those exercising power and the *real* interests of those they exclude' (Lukes 1974: 24). This involves a counter-factual argument: a particular settlement is recognised and it is suggested that this settlement is obscuring aspects of social potential social conflict (which is to say, expected conflicts are not manifest) and thus the absence is explained by the operation of structural power. This positing of absent (though analytically expected) conflict, leads me to suggest the way the structures interact.

The prevailing authority or power, through intervention in institutional practices, aims to define problems and by doing so, the choices of solution. By controlling the agenda, the decision-making process may be presented as fair and equitable because unpalatable or unacceptable solutions never reach the agenda for consideration; they are ruled nonsensical or 'uninformed'. In this way, language can be crucial: illogical, 'extreme', idealistic, outdated, opinionated, 'political' alternatives may all be stigmatised and below them there is a sub-strata of positions that are irrational or 'stupid'. The agendas which are formed are not just explicit lists from which social actions are chosen, but the implicit (sometimes hardly conscious) choices among perceived alternatives made by social actors: their world-views. The formation of agendas through the 'prism' of the knowledge structure informs the choices (and the perception of *available* choices) made in the other structural dimensions of the global political economy. But the power relations within the other structures (and the changes therein), also feed into the process of contradiction and elaboration of alternatives.

The recognition of legitimate alternatives can be constricted by power relations. Expectations about the results of social actions are needed to make decisions as to their possibility or viability, but the recognition of what can be done at a particular juncture is subject to knowledge structural agenda formation. This agenda of possible alternatives is itself related to the pattern of power resources elsewhere (in the security, production or finance structures). Thus, materially existing (and therefore possible) options cannot be marginalised indefinitely. The contradiction between the existence of the resources to produce particular outcomes and the representation of their non-existence will lead to pressures for change at the level of social relations. The conflicts within material social relations – the competition for scarce resources, for security, for the limited provision of credit – feed into the continual (re)construction of agendas within the knowledge structure.[4] Where these conflicts imply different settlements from those which currently shape outcomes, resistance to such change may be possible through the knowledge structure and the reinforcement of institutional rules. But where legitimised alternatives do not satisfactorily reflect changes in social forces it is unlikely that resistance to change through the knowledge structure can prevail for ever.

Through the recognition of contradictions and complementarities within interactions of the actors in the global political economy, power within all the structures is constantly being both challenged and reinforced. Material resources appear in different guises in different structures, and trans-structural resource use leads to changes in agenda setting in the knowledge structure as the potential for new resources to impact on particular structures is either resisted or utilised. The historic ability to set or police agendas may be challenged by those enjoying some emerging material resource advantage in a particular structure. Through changes in agenda setting, there may be attempts to reconfigure conflicts to lend more weight to different resources, an example being military conflicts which started out as trade disputes. Therefore, in the complex social relations of the global political economy the different structures of power interact through the agenda-setting mechanism. The power within each structure – security, production, knowledge, finance – is the product of its interaction with the other three by virtue of the resources needed to maintain a legitimate agenda setting ability. And while this might imply some priority for the knowledge structure, this is not the case. The structures cannot be finally separated or prioritised, each needs resources only available in other structures. Power is produced through combinations of ideational and material resources.

The relationship between power relations and power structures is located in the ability to mobilise resources to establish and reproduce the agendas of possible outcomes in any particular instance. This process may reproduce the existing power distribution or may produce challenges and shifts in the distribution of power, and with it changes in the benefits flowing from political economic outcomes. Thus, if we take the security structure as an example, the ability of an authority to mobilise sufficient resources (which will include financial and production elements) to guard against specific threats enables it legitimately to define the nature of future (unknown) threats on the basis of its past successes in providing security against agreed threats. Thus, relational power feeds structural power, though as time passes perceptions of threats may change in a manner that does not sit well with the resources that the power holder is able to mobilise to support security. This may then lead to a changing notion of security that sits better with another authority's resources, or alternatively may lead to an attempt to reconceptualise security in such a way that the original resources can once again be related to the new agenda of security issues. The 'history' of threats itself may be rewritten in an attempt to reinforce an agenda that reflects the current availability of material resources. The rewriting of histories and traditions is a fertile, though by no means uncontested area, for the revelation of contradiction.

As there is a two-way relation between material and ideational factors over time ideas have an impact on material relations *and* material relations have an impact on ideas. If material relations remain unchanged but ideas about them shift, then there will be pressure for change. And equally, if material relations change but ideas about those relations remain fixed, a similar pressure will build up. Structural power uses the weight of history and the ideological armoury of knowledge construction to limit or avoid these possible challenges. The distribution of power within social relations may be the basis of the historical construction of structural power, but also through the material aspect of the dual-dialectic offers the ground on which contradictions are revealed and turned into sites of resistance or potential change. The structures of the global political economy continually interact through the mechanism of agenda-setting and its relation to the patterns of resource distribution. Change over time does not 'just happen' but is the result of the emergence, recognition and accommodation of contradictions within the dual-dialectic and is related to how the structures of power react to such challenges.

A critique of intellectual property rights

In light of the discussion above, the critique I develop of intellectual property seeks to link its conceptualisation (legal and philosophical) and its actual use (technological and economic) in the global political economy. These two elements impact on each other: use and conceptualisation are both changing but are also sites of considerable contestation regarding such changes. The political economy of intellectual property is subject to significant political conflict, is the source of economic effects and is also a site for the mobilisation of power resources.

The contradiction that lies at the heart of the political economy of intellectual property is between the low to non-existent marginal cost of reproduction of knowledge and its treatment as scarce property. The metaphorical treatment of 'knowledge objects' as material objects is the root of conflicts over intellectual property. Intellectual property rights construct scarcity to ensure market relations in 'knowledge objects' can be undertaken. The metaphorical link between property and knowledge is supported not by acknowledged utility but by the partial and specific interests of certain groups. It is these groups who mobilise their power resources to guard and reinforce their benefits by continual maintenance of the justificatory schemata. Though knowledge may be unlike property, this is discounted in the contemporary institution of intellectual property and its attendant rights. Knowledge objects, a generic term I use to refer to the various forms of intellectual property, are treated as scarce things, and this myth is perpetuated through the use of powerful justifications drawn from the history of material property. This is the outcome of the mobilisation of structural power over knowledge.

Throughout this book I argue that intellectual property is a method of commodification. Intellectual property rights enable the expansion of capitalism into areas hitherto regarded as a realm outside direct exchange relations. Though hardly unprecedented, the enclosures of common land from the fifteenth to eighteenth centuries were essentially an act of commodification, only in the last half century has the commodification of knowledge moved to the centre of capitalism's expansionary logic. Thus, given the new areas into which commodification is reaching, the products of intellectual effort and creation, the information society is a new period of enclosure. The argument that the global information society represents 'something new' is predicated on the claim that its use of a new resource – knowledge/information – fundamentally differentiates it from previous systems of capitalism. However, the actual economic and social organisation of the posited information society is working to maintain and expand a wide spread recognition of the legitimacy of *intellectual* property.

The intent (explicit or implicit) is to rein knowledge in to a set of property relations which are an adjunct to those found in 'already existing' capitalism. Thus the claim that the new uses of knowledge within capitalism have produced a fundamental transformation are undercut by capital's clear, and mainly successful, project of commodifying knowledge through its characterisation as property. If the claim for the disjuncture between industrial society and information society is based on the differences between their respective social relations of resource use, that knowledge is a different sort of input from material resources, then this claim is fatally compromised by capitalism's ability to treat both in the same way – as property. In the following chapters I examine the way the process of commodification (and legitimisation) is taking place from the global level to the individual. The legal rules encapsulated within the TRIPs agreement represent the triumph of the knowledge structure's agenda of metaphorical links between knowledge and property. These rules not only act as legal constraints on the flow of knowledge in a formal sense, they also limit and shape the discourse that can be mobilised to criticise intellectual property rights.

This study is intended to reveal the structures of power which have produced the contemporary settlement regarding intellectual property. I suggest that this settlement can only be understood as a direct result of the structural power of certain groups within the global system. However, drawing on Cox's notion of the purposes of critical theory and the above analysis of the role of emergent contradictions in the dual-dialectic, through an immanent critique I show that the current settlement actually does not produce the ends which it claims. Thus, utilising the methodology I have set out above, contradictions can be revealed and, as such, a plausible alternative and critical political economy of intellectual property rights can start to be constructed. The TRIPs agreement and other legal formulations of intellectual property are not technical solutions to emergent problems but are rather manifestations of structural power within the global political economy.

2 Developing intellectual property

Ideas, like wild animals,
are yours while they continue in your possession; but no longer.
(Justice Yates in *Milar v. Taylor*, 1769 cited in Grosheide 1994: 220)

Having suggested that property is a social institution and is subject to power in the knowledge structure, I now move to the central subject of this book – intellectual property. The three justificatory schemata outlined in the last chapter, which have been used to legitimate property rights since the seventeenth century, have also been used to justify and support intellectual property. It will become evident as I discuss various aspects of the global political economy of intellectual property rights that some combination of these three justifications is appealed to in most if not all debates and disputes about the protection and transfer of knowledge. However, there are some important problems with such a philosophical importation into this area.

The paramount problem with importing justificatory schemata used for material property into the realm of knowledge lies in the contrasting character of these two different subjects of ownership. Material property is by definition in any particular case formally scarce. Material objects cannot be in two places at once and, as such, parallel use is limited to shared use in a single location. However, the use of knowledge is not restricted in the same manner. Whether it is information about something, or a technique, whether it is a depiction of a pattern of material artefacts or a learnt skill, use by one person does not preclude simultaneous use at the same level of intensity by someone else. Thus the marginal cost of an extra user of any specific piece or form of knowledge approaches zero. The development and use of the institution of intellectual property, however, aims to return knowledge from this possible ubiquity. The aim is to establish some form of constructed scarcity which is achieved through the use of the previously legitimated justificatory schemata of property.

Characterising property

The contrast between property's material character (linked to the rights to use singular and therefore scarce things), and the features of intangible forms of property, is seldom developed at any great length in treatments of the legality and theory of property rights. For instance, Waldron in what is otherwise an extensive and elaborate discussion of the rights to private property recognises no need to analyse separately forms of intangible property, except to assure the reader that these can be dealt with in the same manner as material property because this is where the practices relative to other forms of property are drawn from (Waldron 1988: 33–37). The transfer of justificatory schemata is thus rendered unproblematic; intangible property and therefore intellectual property can be satisfactorily dealt with by analogy with material property. But at least Waldron mentions this issue; in some other standard treatments (Reeve 1986; Ryan 1984) the notion of intellectual property is notable by its absence. This silence on intellectual property would seem to indicate that the authors of these standard accounts believe that *all* property is subject to similar treatment without regard to its actual characteristics once it is deemed property. This accords with the desire to justify property in knowledge, which in its simplest form relies on the argument that knowledge *can* be seen as property, and is in effect no different from other resources and commodities which are recognised as property.

Where intellectual property is recognised as presenting a problem it is seen as a minor issue, which can await some future discussion (Becker 1977). The characterisation of property and its justification may need some adjustment to cover knowledge objects, but this is not a major issue. Munzer deals with the problem by arguing that:

> property must, at some point, involve material objects . . . , however, the qualification 'at some point' is important. This transcendental feature does not mandate either that all property be material or that all property rights be rights in material objects. Intangible property, such as copyrights and patents, is a counterexample to these putative requirements . . . [But] Intangible property is not property in abstract things or ideas *tout court*. Copyrights and patents, for example, traditionally require some writing or drawing or model through which rights are claimed.
>
> (Munzer 1990: 72–3)

Through the inevitable material manifestation required to exercise intellectual property rights the scarcity of knowledge objects can be asserted and its treatment as property assured. Control of licensing and reproduction are dependent on the documenting of the intellectual property object to establish its status *qua* property and so it has a material existence, like other property. The implication of Munzer's position therefore is that the relationship between 'owners' of knowledge and those desirous of its use can be legitimately patterned as a normal property relation. That is, the necessity of fixing intellectual property in some form of material manifestation produces a similar set of rights to those accorded to material property. Differences between property and intellectual property are therefore illusory, both can be treated in the same way.

My contention is that *this most certainly is not the case*. Due to its character intellectual property cannot be unproblematically brought into economic and social relations on the same basis as material property. By attempting to ensure that intellectual property is understood in the same way as material property, and similar 'common-sense' protection is afforded these knowledge objects, legitimisation is asserted rather than established. The institution of intellectual property is strengthened by the appeal to the more naturalised institution of material property, an institution that has become so accepted as to be part of our everyday lives. The agenda which is used to discuss the use and ownership of knowledge is limited to how particular knowledge can be best discussed as property, not whether it should be in the first place. Property in knowledge is asserted and then only the areas of applicability become contentious.

In the following exploration of intellectual property rights (IPRs) I stress power over the material relations in the realm of knowledge (ranging from technological and production issues to the control of finance and security) impacts on the way intellectual property relations are understood and patterned. Equally, through the knowledge structure conceptual developments affect the agenda of acceptable outcomes from which bargains between authority and market in the realm of IPRs may be constructed. Thus, knowledge (in the sense of acceptable agendas of inclusion) defines the character of the knowledge that can be commodified as intellectual property. The character of intellectual property is not fixed, but is the function of the needs of powerful economic actors to exploit new resources made available by new technologies. Simultaneously changes within the agenda of the knowledge structure redefine those objects recognisable as intellectual property, engendering the development of innovative technologies to affect their capture and the consolidation of new sites of economic power. Thus the social institution of intellectual property is intimately connected to (and indeed gains much of its power over social relations from) its legal element, but cannot be divided off from the development of technologies that make its (re)production possible.

From property to intellectual property

The notion of intellectual property at its simplest suggests that ideas and knowledge can be parcelled into separable and transferable knowledge objects which enjoy similar characteristics to material property. Within the debates over intellectual property the justifications of particular positions are familiar. The author's idea is an expression of herself and as such an aspect of her free intelligence. It should be protected and theft of such expressions (their unauthorised use or reproduction) should be subject to the sanction of the law. The singularity of the author tends to emphasise the scarcity of the knowledge object produced. However, this cannot be asserted too stringently, as the need to transfer or exchange such property in a market is the way the intellectual producer earns a living – the knowledge object must also be alienable. Thus, Lockean justifications are utilised to establish that new ideas will only be produced if the labourers of such creations are duly rewarded by receiving the benefit of such initial ownership when intellectual goods are exchanged. The originator should be able to transfer the knowledge object to someone of their own choosing for a negotiated reward. Where these arguments seem problematic for one reason or another, justifications fall back on the need to ensure the efficient social use of innovations. The protection of intellectual property ensures that those who can use knowledge objects most efficiently can secure an appropriate reward for such usage. And by ensuring the transfer of knowledge to the most efficient users, the public good is maximised along with the totality of social welfare. If it is suggested that commodification still produces a less than optimal outcome, a comparison is drawn between IPRs and no protection at all to suggest that the alternative is unthinkable (North 1981: 165). While there may be problems, this is the best method available for the reward and stimulation of knowledge production.

Though there is much discussion of the rights of authors and inventors as knowledge creators, modern justifications for intellectual property rights concentrate on the economic incentives and protections needed for producers to (re)produce knowledge objects. As in the Lockean tradition, the producer (of intellectual property) needs to be guaranteed the reward from its exploitation to ensure that such work is carried out. If there was no system to transfer IPRs then knowledge could not be passed to those who would value (meaning 'value economically') it most and who have the means to make the most efficient use of such knowledge. Thus, in the case of the sole inventor, or author, IPR regimes allow that their original rights may be alienated for a reward (payment of a fee, or if employed, as part of the contracted work relationship). Where this work is undertaken by an employee, the creator is usually legally defined as the company (or employer), allowing this legal entity to enjoy the same rights as the individual creator (Vaver 1990: 104). These rights are transferable, residing with the intellectual property concerned and not with the author/inventor. Ideas have become things which have rights linked to them, they have become transferable active property.

Once property has been deemed active, it is possible to secure rights to it and appropriate it for profitable enterprise. Intellectual property rights bring 'ideas' across the line from passive to active property – once a passive property can be defined in intellectual property terms it has become active, it has become a commodity. Passive intellectual properties were part of the public sphere of recognised but unowned knowledge. It may not be an exaggeration to suggest that the appropriation of knowledge in this manner is 'analogous to the enclosure of common land in England in the Eighteenth Century'(Farrands 1996: 175). The institution of property is concerned with the expectations that owners of property can form regarding their relations with others. But the expectations of those who held common land (inasmuch as they had traditional rights of use and exploitation, and projected these forward in their anticipation of the future) were not respected by the move to enclose land before and throughout the eighteenth century. The expectations of the private owners, as they managed to include common lands within their holdings were, on the other hand, supported and reinforced. However, if the logic was shifted to consequences rather than expectations then it could be (and frequently was) argued that the overall good was best served by the most efficient use of land in general (Horne 1990: 156). The expectations of certain social groups were deemed more likely to produce a beneficial outcome than those of other groups. The group who was privileged in this conception were the owners of private property, who unsurprisingly were also those who had most influence over the social expectations in which policy was grounded.

Similar arguments regarding the efficient use and transfer of knowledge are made in defence of the increasing inclusion of different types and forms of knowledge object under a rubric of intellectual property. This process of 'enclosure' explicitly does not recognise (or accept) that knowledge can be used without depleting its intrinsic value to society as a whole: IPRs are defined *against* the notion of (economically) freely available knowledge. While it may be possible to argue, as many critics of IPRs do, that to commodify knowledge 'makes ideas artificially scarce and their use less frequent – and, from a social point of view, less valuable' (Vaver 1990: 126), this claim is for the most part ignored. Rather, the construction of scarcity in knowledge is one of the chief aims of knowledge entrepreneurs. Only when a commodity is scarce and therefore treated as property can it be accorded commodity status, allowing it most importantly to command a price. And only when it commands a price will users really 'value' knowledge. By ensuring users recognise the costs of knowledge objects, their interests will lie in maximising their (and society's) benefit from the use of such knowledge.

Publishers and/or manufacturers wish to protect knowledge objects from unlicensed reproduction, reinforce their scarcity and maximise returns from the constructed monopoly rights. The interests of the economic exploiters of intellectual property have been grounded in the philosophical justification regarding property as alienable, drawing its line of development from the Lockean or instrumentalist perspective. The self-development justification of property, which would not allow full alienability was not nearly as attractive: it would require a continuing right for the originator to limit use, which compromises the rights of the *new* owner of their intellectual property (Hettinger 1989: 45–47). But, on the other hand, such a justification could not be completely disregarded as one of the key reasons that intellectual property could be regarded as scarce was on the basis of the idea having its genesis with a singular author or creator. The most scarce of all physical resources is one's own body, from which in the forms of thoughts and ideas intellectual property flows in the first instance (Palmer 1990: 856). Thus, to maintain that the author's creation is singular and worthy of protection from unauthorised copying is supported by the self-developmental justification. If any specific knowledge object was not singular, then the notion of copying or reproduction would be compromised and the logic of protection undermined.

Nevertheless the overall reliance on instrumental justifications produces a paradoxical logic in which limiting the diffusion of intellectual property is regarded as a method for increasing the quantity of intellectual property available for diffusion or as Joan Robinson has put it: 'The justification of the patent system is that by slowing down the diffusion of technical progress it ensures that there will be more progress to diffuse' (quoted in Hettinger 1989: 48). This might also be said to apply to the system of copyright but to a lesser extent – without the ability to protect the reward from their creations why would artists be prepared to allow multiple reproductions? But in both cases, it is the rights of the owners who exploit the knowledge object which are seen as being of most importance, rather than those who might originate intellectual property in the first place.

Of authors and markets

As has been the case in the history of property, there has been a diminution of the possibility of a public domain of knowledge. The conception of intellectual property solidified for copyright with the rise of the romantic notions of individual creativity (Geller 1994: 168–170). With the need for patents to be lodged by a legally constituted individual, a similar norm has operated for patentable ideas since the earliest patent monopolies were awarded (Boyle 1996: 206). At the centre of intellectual property discourse is the notion of the individual creative individual, the 'author', acting in solitude to produce a new piece of knowledge. I call this act of creation the 'authorial function' so as to include the authors of texts and artists of other sorts alongside the inventors of patentable ideas and others. The authorial function produces the knowledge object and in this 'empire of the author' all knowledge objects have a moment of genesis which justifies the IPRs attached to them (Aoki 1996: 1323, 1330). The scope of the authorial function has spread from its original limited coverage (under both patent and copyright law) which sought to protect only innovative knowledge and the expression of individual's ideas to more recent moves to include patterns of collected information as well as acts of discovery and codification. Intellectual property rights may attach to particular knowledge objects on the basis of the identification of the organisation of extant knowledge *as* new knowledge.

This leads to a key question for any justificatory schema for intellectual property: how valid is the single author as the paradigmic creator of intellectual property? New knowledge is the result of the manipulation of previous knowledge, with some further marginal elements added: innovation is largely incremental. Though insights and new knowledge will have novel elements, they fundamentally rely on the overarching context of previous knowledge. Focused specific expertise which has been learnt and the socialised knowledge that is part of our general intellectual equipment feed into a 'new' idea. However, the paradigm of the autonomous author as intellectual producer is still strongly held and defended by the entre-preneurs of the knowledge economy (Boyle 1996: 175–176). The identification of the individualised authorial function lies behind the justification of IPRs based on the author's encouragement and motivation to continue production. This is easily located within the instrumentalist notion of the required reward for the creator represented by property rights. The individual labours within his or her own intellect and produces a novel knowledge object which attracts property status.

But some intellectual property is not really created in this way, rather it is collected from public sources and its arrangement while novel and possibly useful merely organises previously available publicly available information (street maps and telephone directories, for instance). Equally, the information may represent a codification of something that already exists in nature (i.e. genetic material). It is the collecting work which is to be rewarded by a right over the pattern produced by such collection, based on the effort expended to produce the work. However, if the process of collection is duplicated to a similar end by some other 'author' then neither can have exclusive rights with regard to the patterned collection of information.[1] The temptation to cheat where two authors are collecting the same information has historically been quite significant; why duplicate work already done if the end is the same? This has led many directory publishers to deliberately introduce false entries and small errors to prove that a parallel work *has* been copied from their work rather than reproduced in parallel through the efforts of another 'author'. But, while the patterned or collected information may attract protection, the underlying information remains in the public domain. In most cases the easiest way of accessing such information remains through the collection which has become intellectual property.

Knowledge creation is incremental. All knowledge must be *largely* extant by virtue of the extent of knowledge needed to have the insight or creativity (call it what you will) to add something to any field. If the provision of the building blocks of knowledge involves no necessary diminution of utility to previous users/owners when (re)used to create or invent, then the rationale for charging for inputs is not particularly robust. The marginal cost is nil – once an idea has been had there are no extra costs in others rethinking it. Neither is it clear why protecting a particular creator (the idea's current possessor), over and above the creators who contributed earlier through their ideas is legitimate. Even if many others know our ideas (which may have implications for our privacy) this does not detract from them as expressions of self. Is it ever possible to identify the part of the knowledge product that is completely the labour of the rights-owning individual (who is enjoying labour's desert)? Neither of the more philosophical justificatory schemata of property (self-developmental and instrumental) can resolve these problems with intellectual property as both are essentially based on the scarcity of any particular property. To deal with knowledge both need to treat knowledge objects as monolithic rather than being composed of a complex of knowledge elements, none of which are necessarily used exclusively within a particular knowledge object.

This shortcoming has resulted in IPRs being defended on the basis of their support for the maximisation of economic utility. This encompasses the liberal view that economic organisation through markets is the most efficient manner to govern society's allocation of resources, whatever those resources may be. By assuming that the market is the best method of allocation (in *all* circumstances), IPRs can be justified on the basis of bringing this tried and tested method of resource allocation to the use of knowledge through commodification. To introduce the market into the products of the mind, an artificial scarcity (property-ness) must be constructed (Palmer 1990: 864/5). In itself the argument that the market is the most efficient allocator of resources requires a certain world-view to be adopted, one which is neither natural nor transhistorical. The market is embedded within the institutions of a market society, and while it is now difficult to imagine other methods of allocating resources it does not follow that the market form was not socially created

(Polanyi 1957: 56ff.). That said, once the market has been identified as the best way of dealing with useful resources, a certain agenda of choices in the realm of knowledge allocation is established. The next step is that to take advantage of markets knowledge must be rendered as property.

However, only the view that intellectual *property* itself is plausible in the first place allows the arguments for efficiency/utility to support specific IPR regimes. Thus, the operation of the knowledge structure maintains a circular argument: efficient allocation depends on markets and so a market must be created; this requires knowledge to be treated as property because without formal scarcity there is no requirement for market exchange; and if knowledge is property then the most efficient method of allocation is through the market. The agenda of choices from which plausible and acceptable arguments can be developed is strictly limited to those which draw explicitly on established property *and* market efficiency themes. Thus the possibility that it only makes sense to propose a market for knowledge if knowledge is *already* conceived of as property is hidden by the assumption that knowledge *needs* to be thought of as property to enjoy the benefits of market allocation. The possibility that the two elements of the argument might be mutually interdependent is obscured by the utilisation of claims drawn from the other two justificatory schemata – the need to recognise a reward for effort made, and the need to allow the author to have property in their creations. Anything outside these choices remains unrecognised as an argument and as such is deemed outside the knowledge of 'knowledge', being coded as opinion or worse still irrational. This is especially ironic in the realm of copyright as 'even in the heyday of absolutist notions of "private property" copyrights were an exception: They were limited rights promulgated pursuant to public regulation, a mapping that is obscured when viewed through the occluding lens of romantic authorship' (Aoki 1996: 1338). While in the past the authorial function was of strictly limited application to property in knowledge, the rights of the individualised knowledge creator have gradually risen to become the defining element in intellectual property's rationale. The doctrine of the authorial function has enabled a widening of the exception accorded to the author to the point when it is no longer an exception but rather is the rule.

The remaining disagreements over intellectual property are conducted in the main between the three justificatory schemata imported from the realm of material property, leaving the boundaries of discussion broadly in place. It is hard to find any discussion of IPRs which does not allude in one way or another to these positions. This is not to say there is no disagreement, but the criticisms of 'informed' observers have centred on the issue of market failure, and in particular the problems of awarding monopoly rights. Thus,

> [the] advocates of intellectual property laws prefer to speak about property, and the opponents prefer the word monopoly. Even if the word monopoly were justified, the adherents of intellectual property rights argue . . . that such rights are created in furtherance of competition on a higher level of economic activity, and not to impede competition.
>
> (Quaedvlieg 1992: 389)

On both sides of the argument the logic of economic allocation is accepted: the economic utility argument is presented not as an argument from particular cases but from the need for efficiency in the market for knowledge; the argument concerning monopoly rights accorded to IPRs is embedded in an overall argument about how markets work not whether they are appropriate to knowledge in the first place.

Despite a tradition of such arguments within the economic literature, there is little to suggest that intellectual property protection alone aids the 'production' and dissemination of ideas and knowledge. Innovation and new ideas have produced human progress throughout history with little requirement for IPR regimes of any sort. In particular as Vaver points out:

> if the British patent law of 1624 really did encourage greater inventiveness, why did the Industrial Revolution take some 150 years more to arrive? A [social science] law with this time lag suggests a lack of, or at least a serious discrepancy between cause and effect.

(Vaver 1990: 100)

The causal effect of patents may play some role but cannot be the fully determining role claimed for it by the more strident promoters of intellectual property. For there to be such a lag from its introduction would imply at least some intervening factors. The acceleration of innovation quite possibly also argues against the role for intellectual property. Technological innovation reached a critical mass *because* ideas were widely available, not because they were scarce, expensive and well protected.

It is more likely that IPR protection, and its role in technological developments are rooted in the capitalist organisation of productive endeavour. The economic justification of IPRs is a product of the needs of certain groups in the (global) political economy. As technologies have been developed they are able to (re)produce new forms of knowledge object, and the control of these items has become of paramount importance to knowledge capitalists. For instance, as technologies have increasingly been able to utilise the thoughts of their users and their clients (in the case of customer databases) the ownership of these ideas (both in the sense of patterns of consumption, and how symbols are interpreted) that might have previously been seen as unownable has become not only a contentious issue, but one around which significant global actors have organised substantial resources (Poster 1990). Alongside the encouragement to innovate has been the development of technological methods for profiting from knowledge objects' reproduction, and capitalism's pattern of reward for such exploitation.

A major element of the history of the justification of intellectual property has been the interlinked dynamic of technological development. Contemporaneous with the legal history of intellectual property, and the evolving philosophical justification of authorship's reward has been a history of technological advance in the use and distribution of knowledge and information for profit. As technologies were developed that would allow for the reproduction and dissemination of knowledge (the printing press, broadcasting, the Internet) so legal regimes reacted.

But, recognising the dual-dialectical nature of such changes, the social milieu in which such technological advances took place was also patterned and structured by the emerging legal framework of intellectual property. And as it became clear that it was possible that knowledge and information might be valued over and above the material method of delivery, pressure for intellectual property rights in new sectors, and their subsequent widening, emerged. The argument that an 'essential precondition for price-making markets is the existence of well-defined and enforced property rights' in the commodity or service which is to be the subject of exchange (North 1977: 710) has become a constitutive element of the knowledge industries' position. The prospective exploiters of knowledge objects needed to be assured their 'ownership' would be respected and protected, to enable them to act within a market. But the market itself could only emerge as technology for reproduction became available. The technological means for reproduction and exploitation of intellectual property, however, were seldom held by the authorial functionary. In the age of the global knowledge industries this continues to be the case, which leads me to stress that it may be mistaken to assume that intellectual property can be directly related to the individualised freeholding of material property.

Leasehold as a model for intellectual property?

Another way of making a connection between material property and intellectual property is to focus on the issue of the time-limited character of intellectual property. Intellectual property is not only summoned into existence by the authorial function, it has a limited temporal existence. This varies from quite short patent periods of twenty years to copyright periods that are increasingly harmonised as extending for fifty years after the original author's demise. This divergence under economic justifications is related to the limitations put on others by such rights. The constriction of other artists caused by the protection of a specific expression of an idea is not onerous (they are still free to express themselves through the authorial function) and thus longer protection seems acceptable. Conversely, patent protection of important and innovative ideas may have severe social costs if overly extended. A much shorter period of protection represents the greater perceived social need to have such ideas in the public realm to stimulate further socio-economic development. But in any case, once these periods expire, the knowledge objects cease to be intellectual property and become part of the public realm of knowledge and information. This limitation on the basis of time elapsed since recognition of intellectual property-hood is one of the chief ways in which it is conventionally supposed that intellectual property manages to balance the private reward accorded to the creative process with the public interest in the dissemination of knowledge. This temporality suggest a possible similarity between leasehold property and intellectual property.

Leaseholds as regards land and leases concerning commercial goods used in production by firms, split the ownership of the relevant property into at least two parts. There is an underlying set of rights to the property which are held in perpetuity and as such are alienable (or transferable) without regard to the status of the lease – the freehold. The lease is a time-limited contract which transfers the right to use the property or part thereof in certain and clearly defined ways from the freeholder or owner to the leaseholder. Leases include conditions on mandated use alongside responsibilities for the maintenance of the property or leased item and may limit the class of party to whom unused segments of the lease may be transferred or sold. Most importantly for the comparison with intellectual property, the lease is also limited as regards the period to which the rights to the use of the property or item it concerns can be enjoyed. Once the leasehold agreement reaches its maturity the ownership of the right to use the property reverts to the freeholder, the primary owner. The lease is a purchase of particular rights over a specific property rather than the property itself. Leasehold, as with other forms of property, is concerned not with the relations between the property and the owner, but with the relationship between the owner and the non-owner.

The lease agreement enables the owner of a property to grant to the leasee certain, but not all, rights that accrue to the owner in their position as freeholder. It would be mistaken to assume that the division this represents is between the rights accruing to ownership of the property and the property itself. It is more accurate to say that leaseholders are able to purchase for a limited period a subset of the rights which the freeholder enjoys. That these rights are significantly less than those enjoyed by the freeholder is emphasised by the lease agreement's limitation of the rights of ownership, over and above those national legislatures might put on the freeholder. Thus, the leaseholder is subject to the legal structure of property ownership as defined by the state which is further curtailed by the leasehold agreement. For instance, the leaseholder clearly does not retain the right to destroy the property whereas the freeholder is able to dispose of property in such a manner if he or she sees fit to do so, within the legal limits imposed by the state. Indeed, in the leasing of equipment, the transfer to another leasee is usually proscribed by the lease contract and thus, the rights accorded to the leaseholder may be very limited *vis-à-vis* the actual owner. On the other hand, what rights the leasee has purchased are rights against the freeholder – the leaseholder holds certain rights which preclude their enjoyment by the freeholder, immediate residence or use being the most important.

There are clear parallels here with the transfer of the rights to exploit the idea, or knowledge object, from its creator. The ability to transfer the right to exploit intellectual property while the author, inventor or creator is still able to think through this idea resonates with the idea of leasehold. In this regard, a 'true property right in an idea or an expression would constitute a right of exclusion from that idea or that expression itself' once it had been transferred from the originator to another agent for exploitation (Penner 1997: 119). However, this is not the reality of intellectual property. Though the right to exploit and benefit from such exploitation may be transferred, it is the nature of knowledge that the creator or author of that knowledge will retain the idea, even if the right to use it in the economic realm no longer resides with them. Thus, the copyright of this text may reside with the publisher, but the ideas it represents and indeed the words with which I have expressed these ideas, remain part of my intellectual repository; I still think and work with these ideas and ways of expressing myself. Thus while the publisher holds certain rights against me – the right to publish this book and reproduce it – I also retain the rights to use my intellectual property in the ideas this book represents in other works, as long as their expression, the pattern formed by those ideas, is different.

Is it possible that the use of a model of leasehold may help resolve the problem of incommensurability between material and intellectual property? Making an argument that intellectual property could be seen as leasehold property might serve to support IPRs in two ways. First, it might enable the distinction between intellectual and material property to be located as part of an already existing set of distinctions enjoying the legitimacy of property. Second, and perhaps more importantly, such an argument might add support to the treatment of knowledge and information as property through the utilisation of precedent. If leasehold is acceptable why should intellectual property not be so?

The first argument, that leasehold is a useful model for recognising the distinction between material and intellectual property relies on two strands of argument: that the time limitation is the key defining issue for intellectual property; and that the limited rights of intellectual property are similar to the division between leaseholder and freeholder. While the periods may be changed (and are to some extent arbitrary), it is clearly true that both leaseholds and intellectual property are property rights that cannot be enjoyed in perpetuity; there is some legal limit to the lifespan of such property. At some point in time, the legal rights that are accorded to ownership of such (leasehold or intellectual) property cease and are no longer owned. Thus, there is a reasonable parallel between these two forms of property. However, this is undermined when the situation once such rights are dissipated is examined. The rights that were transferred to the leaseholder revert to the freeholder, which is to say they are transferred for a limited time, but remain exclusive rights which can then be transferred again to another subsequent leaseholder. But, the rights accorded to intellectual property cease to be exclusive at the end of their term and are not restored to their original owner. Rather, the rights evaporate and the intellectual property enters the public realm. Additionally, where material property can become the subject to lease at any time, which is to say the period from which the transfer of rights is not necessarily linked to the temporal existence of its freehold (indeed, there may be a series of successive lease agreements with the leaseholder), intellectual property's temporal existence is completely dependent on its moment of creation or (for patents) its official recognition. Once recognised as intellectual property, its residual life is being depleted.

The second argument, that the relation between intellectual property and material property is analogous to that between leasehold and freehold, falls on the basis of a simple point. The rights that are transferred with the lease are still rights to the benefits and use of a materiality and therefore they are held *against* the freeholder. The freeholder agrees for the duration of the lease not to exercise the rights which are transferred, though they have been divided for the duration;

the rights to the property that accrue to the leasee are still exclusive, even if such exclusivity is hedged around with particular conditions. It is this exclusivity which is the key area in which the difference (and justificatory problems) between material and intellectual property are played out. The scarcity of the leased object is unaffected by the leasehold – it remains as scarce as before. For IPRs, however, the scarcity under property law has had to be legally constructed. Thus, though attractive in the sense that it draws a link between a legitimised form of property and intellectual property, any justificatory claim built on a link with leasehold would fail to recognise that the differences between the two forms of property still compromise the analogy between material and intellectual property.

Trade secrets, contracts and tacit knowledge

Trade secrets are different from other forms of intellectual property inasmuch as they involve no legal requirement for dissemination. While trade secrets cannot be protected against reverse engineering by competitors, their unauthorised revelation or transfer through other means (industrial espionage, theft) is usually regarded as illegal. There is a trade-off for companies in deciding to keep something as a trade secret, between risking its disclosure through competitors' ability to work out what the secret is and retaining a competitive advantage based on a novel aspect to the product. This trade-off will be linked to an assessment of the expected period of product life, the expense of the secret's duplication, the contribution of the secret to the product's input costs and the competitive environment in which the company finds itself. Given the costs of patent registration, for short-term innovations there may be no economic logic for patenting small and cheap 'secrets'. Conversely, trade secrets that form a small but crucial part of the productive process may need to be kept secret because mere knowledge of the character of the secret might shift the balance of advantage between competitors. It may be reasonable to expect that formulas and engineering fixes may be regarded as trade secrets (and thus as intellectual property) based on the right of any actor to control the initial disclosure of their ideas (Paine 1991). But the remit of the trade secret has been widened in recent years through employment contract law to include some ideas that might be less clearly acceptable as intellectual property.

As Braverman pointed out, the principles of scientific management revolve around the capture of information about, and important to, the productive process:

> if the first principle is the gathering and development of knowledge of labour processes, and the second is the concentration of this knowledge as the exclusive province of management – together with its essential converse, the absence of such knowledge among the workers – then the third is the *use of this monopoly over knowledge to control each step of the labour process and its mode of execution*.
> (Braverman 1974: 119, emphasis in original)

This would initially suggest that there is an increasing absence of useful knowledge in the workforce. In Braverman's factory there is a move to deskilling and the capture of knowledge by capital. Though there has been an extensive literature which has critically engaged with Braverman's analysis of the extent of deskilling (for instance, Elger 1979; Knights and Wilmott 1990), I want to draw on one aspect of this argument regarding scientific management. Management is concerned to control and develop a monopoly over the knowledge of the functioning of the productive process. Thus while the knowledge (or skills) may still reside with the worker, it is becoming less clear that they are able to control its dissemination for their own benefit.

Companies increasingly wish to define the knowledge of important workers, not as the workers' skills and abilities, but as the trade secrets of the employer, through the use of employment contracts with intellectual property provisions. A recent article by an intellectual property lawyer writing with an employment lawyer advised companies with 'valuable intellectual property assets' that

> the purpose of well-drafted contracts between employers and employees (and independent contractors) is to establish the employer's ownership of intellectual property valued by the corporation. The contract language should operate first to convey to the employer any rights the employee or independent contractor may have in specific copyrights, patents, trade secrets or trademarks.
>
> Second, contracts may expand the rights of the intellectual property owner beyond those otherwise provided by law . . . an employee who agrees not to use certain trade secrets at any time after the end of his or her employment may face a greater restriction than one who signs a one- or two-year non-competition agreement. Such a confidentiality agreement may also protect information that is not otherwise protected from disclosure under the [US] Uniform Trade Secrets Act.
>
> Third . . . a carefully drafted contract can make the often arcane defences raised in intellectual property litigation irrelevant.
>
> (Little and Trepanier 1997: 67)

This advice has been quoted at length to illustrate the possible use of contract law to submerge the logic of the individual author or creator's rights beneath the rights of the 'owner' where that owner is the employer not the creator. The second clause is especially interesting in this regard: 'contracts may expand the rights of the intellectual property owner beyond those otherwise provided by law'. Thus, the historically constructed (and legitimised) balance between public benefits and private rights can be distorted or even overturned through the use of contract law. Included within such contracts are the ideas and innovations that individuals may produce while they are contracted to said employer, not just the more formalised intellectual property in the form of copyrights and patents. Furthermore, such 'arcane defences' as an employee's right to work elsewhere using their skills for another employer can be short-circuited by well-drafted employment contracts.

Presented as the danger of 'inevitable disclosure', the problem of employees revealing the organisational trade secrets of their previous employer to their new employer (which might have previously been coded as 'transferable skills') has become an important concern for multinationals (Di Fronzo 1996; Spanner 1996). This issue was at the centre of the dispute (which I discuss at more length in Chapter 4) between General Motors and Volkswagen over the employment of a high-level manager by the latter, who was using an approach to cost-cutting developed while employed by the former. The dispute was finally settled, but not before accusations of espionage and theft were aired in a German court, and though the executive had to resign his post with VW, he was amply compensated. Interestingly it seems that in any case the cost-cutting approach which the executive had developed at GM was little more than an adaptation of Toyota's low-cost production system (*The Economist* 1993b). If this is so, the question of the origin of intellectual property, and the proportion that might be novel, is once again apposite. It would be a mistake to regard this merely as an issue at executive level, as the tightening of many standard employment contracts' intellectual property clauses indicates.

Intellectual property laws may be justified on the basis that they accord protection to the individual knowledge creator, but the effect has been to facilitate the transfer of intellectual property from these creators to those in the global political economy who control the means of production which can take advantage of such knowledge for the accumulation and reproduction of wealth. The creators may be outside the company and only transfer their intellectual property after its creation: having created it they sell the rights for a price which allows the knowledge capitalist full scope for further gain. Or the authorial functionary may be under contract to the company in the first place in which case any intellectual property than is created is generally *already* the property of the employer. Payment *vis-à-vis* the individual knowledge object is an exception, no special value is put on such creativity over and above the retaining price of the employment contract.

Much tacit knowledge (such as know-how or organisational memories) can still flow with ease through the economy, through the movement of its holders and through their social communication with colleagues. But, as this sort of knowledge is increasingly valued, there are more attempts by employers to retain such knowledge in one way or another. Management literature (both descriptive and prescriptive) has recently stressed the usefulness of knowledge, especially that which is resident in the workforce (Kay 1993; Nonaka and Takeuchi 1995 and surveyed in Micklethwait and Wooldridge 1996: 134–158). It is unsurprising that such knowledge, representing a valuable resource, is of interest to companies wishing to fully own and control their productive assets. Given that many of the aspects of knowledge that are now accorded value are not necessarily the traditional stuff of intellectual property regimes, it is also unsurprising that the characterisation and scope of intellectual property should have become a site of acute interest and contest.

A set agenda

In the recent negotiations over the formation of the World Trade Organisation which I discuss in the next chapter, the inclusion of intellectual property into its remit has been cast in terms of calculations of the losses incurred by the Western knowledge industries as a result of 'piracy' and 'theft'; but these calculations rarely attempt to get to grips with the conflict of definitions of what should count as 'property' in the first place.

(Frow 1996: 90)

The dominant discourse of intellectual property has been accepted and its boundaries were defined by the dominant actors in these negotiations. Given the pervasiveness of the justificatory schemata of IPRs, it is not only important how intellectual property is justified overall but also where the boundary between intellectual property and not-intellectual property is supposed to lie, and how movements across this line are legitimised. This line is not static, and thus the knowledge structure works not only to justify intellectual property but to amend the shape of the field (its inclusiveness) on an ongoing basis, it continues to justify new areas of commodification.

An account of intellectual property needs to be concerned with the question of intellectual property's posited borders as well as its justifications, especially where the borders are most difficult to settle. Samuelson suggests that in the legal debates over information law

[a] world in which all information is its discoverer's property under all circumstances is unthinkable. Before we start labelling information as property, we need a coherent theory about when information should be treated as property, and when not. This is a task to which little thought has been given, but must be.

(Samuelson 1991: 19)

This importance of this distinction (the borderline) stems from the need for ideas to draw on a raw material, which historically has been the result of socialisation or at least socially available knowledge. New knowledge emerges from the vast resources of social and public knowledge. If this knowledge is being 'enclosed' (knowledge scarcity is constructed through commodification) then the boundary between public and private is not only shifting but will be illustrative of the distribution and pattern of political economic power within the emergent knowledge economy. Indeed, some groups have already successfully restricted access to previously (at least potentially) freely available social knowledge.

Therefore while the central issue in a political economy of intellectual property is whether the products of the intellect can be considered property at all, there is also a substantial secondary issue of the way in which the inclusiveness of the field and what lies beyond it is continually (re)constructed. If neither the overall justification nor the shape of the field of knowledge objects are self-evident (or 'natural'), this suggests the knowledge structure plays a major role in supporting any current settlement of these issues. And if there is a disjuncture between the arguments that might be applied to IPRs and those that are actually mobilised in disputes in the global political economy, again a role for the knowledge structure can be proposed. Where intellectual property is discussed, the knowledge structure limits discussions to the three justificatory schemata obscuring a further alternative, which is that there is *no* justification for intellectual property. Where there is a need for new knowledge objects to be included or excluded from the IPR regime, the knowledge structure shapes the arguments presented to support such re-negotiation of the borderline.

The alternative to these regimes, that there can be no property in knowledge, is based on the assertion that knowledge does not conform to an understanding of property that is acceptable, which is the central claim of much of the material on Internet copyright issues. The pragmatic (though circular) nature of the economic justification of intellectual property recognises this case has some potential merit. This is further emphasised by the differences in the duration of protection both nationally and internationally for different classes of intellectual property (Nance 1990: 758–9). The economic justification of intellectual property is both the most vulnerable and the most subtly rigorous. It is vulnerable as in any particular case the argument that intellectual property does not maximise social utility might be possible. It has great rigour because it appeals to a dominant and broadly accepted claim about the efficiency of the market as a method of distribution, and economic motivation. And thus market failure is depicted as a special case, an exception needing state intervention, not as revealing a flaw in the overall organisational arrangement. Where intellectual property is 'trade related' or economically defined as 'value added', there is a vast body of work to appeal to for the usefulness and applicability of property relations undertaken within market exchange. And by using the notion of utility, linked with changes in technologies of reproduction, this argument also serves as a methodology of enclosure and widened commodification, as well as consolidation and support.

Disposing of intellectual property?

Before moving on to the debates on specific issues within the global political economy of intellectual property rights, I want to briefly outline the shape of the arguments which see any claim to justify intellectual property as essentially illegitimate. Perhaps the most popular criticism of intellectual property *qua* property, which I have referred to a number of times above, is based on its 'non-exclusivity'. Indeed, the most frequent maxim in the debates over the availability of intellectual property on the Internet has been that 'information wants to be free'. Underlying this claim is the supposition that the current beneficiaries of IPRs are not individual creators but large media and drug companies who control large banks of intellectual property. For those arguing against intellectual property in this manner, individual creativity needs to be recognised outside a marketised property regime. This is to say that the division that is drawn between the creator and the intellectual property in law (which enables its alienation) should be dissolved. Though this initially might be presumed to be similar to the self-developmental position, it proposes no protection against intellectual 'trespass' or unauthorised reproduction, leaving the only protection as non-expression (or secrecy). The reward for intellectual activity should be reputation or fame of some sort or another, rather than the ability to restrict the spread of the idea itself.

Those who need access to knowledge but are unable to afford it would likely benefit from this disappearance of intellectual property, with the proviso that currently known knowledge continued to be available and was not simply hidden as trade secrets. With knowledge's increased importance in complex societies, for critics there can be little justification for infinitely reproducible resources being hoarded through a constructed market scarcity. As Hettinger asks: 'Why should one person have the exclusive right to possess and use something which all people could possess and use concurrently?' (1989: 35). To establish the historical continuity of such a position, Barlow quotes Thomas Jefferson:

> If nature has made any one thing less susceptible than all others of exclusive property, it is the action of the thinking power called an idea, which an individual may exclusively possess as long as he keeps it to himself; but the moment it is divulged, it forces itself into the possession of everyone, and the receiver cannot dispossess himself of it.
>
> (Barlow 1993)

This position is centred on the difference between material and ideational existence, the 'natural' character of that which would be accorded the status of property. It points to the difference between property and intellectual property, and the gulf of conception that justificatory schemata have to bridge. For critics of intellectual property this gap is unbridgeable.

The other major line of criticism which I have also alluded to above, might best be described as the 'non-labour desert' argument. Though Locke's justification has a good common-sense feel, in intellectual property this is not particularly robust. Again, Hettinger sets this out well:

> Given the vital dependence of a person's thoughts on the ideas of those who came before her, intellectual products are fundamentally social products. Thus even if one assumes that the value of these products is entirely the result of human labour, this value is not entirely attributable to *any particular labourer* ... [and so] this market value should be shared by all those whose ideas contributed to the origin of the product. The fact that most of these contributors are no longer present to receive their fair share is not a reason to give the entire market value to the last contributor.
>
> (Hettinger 1989: 38, emphasis in original)

If knowledge is a vast accretion of incremental additions, then why should the person who adds the most recent marginal addition receive a vastly disproportionate reward? In a knowledge product, the language it is expressed in, the underlying previous discoveries, the contextual knowledge that guided the 'discovery' are all as much part of the product (and thus should see their 'originators' logically rewarded) as the most recent knowledge worker (Martin 1998). This sort of reward allocation is hardly practical, especially given the difficulty of locating the estates of long dead innovators, and the difficulty of according weight to each share of the reward generated by the knowledge object. The impossibility of producing a system that approaches a just distribution requires the abandonment of the fatally flawed compromise that has been constructed in its place.

It can also be argued that one person's enjoyment of property in an intellectual item can obstruct another's use of that same intellectual item (the same knowledge) to achieve desert for their own labour: 'while property in tangible objects limits actions only with respect to particular goods, property in ideal objects restricts an entire range of actions unlimited by place and time' and thus goes directly against the notion of liberty at the centre of Locke's arguments *for* property rights (Palmer 1990: 830, 833–4). This contradicts certain aspects of the economic justification of IPRs, given that they should encourage productive activities likely to enlarge social utility. Should a property regime restrict the ability of the free individual to labour and receive a just reward, where such labour consists of the utilisation of previously developed knowledge? As no loss of utility is necessarily caused to the original thinker, such a limitation seems to go against the argument that property is labour's just reward. Though property is held against others, it should not prevent them from earning their own reward where the means to labour do not represent a diminution of the first labourer's utility and reward for their labour. The complexity of trying to decide whether the utility and reward for the first labourer might be lessened by the use of the knowledge elsewhere (due to the advantage gained by its first use, for instance) suggests a simple labour desert argument is not supple enough to deal with intellectual property.

As I have already suggested, any criticism of the economic justification of intellectual property is grounded in the counter-factual claim that social utility would be enhanced without IPRs. While this might be possible on a case-by-case basis it is less easy to establish such a general argument, against the dominant ideology of the market. Where there is 'market failure', it is argued, states can step in and for instance fund basic science research. This leaves applied science to utilise scientific knowledge to produce new intellectual properties, even though basic scientific breakthroughs might not have been produced within a comprehensive intellectual property regime due to their lack of immediate utility. But the immanent critique that IPRs actually constrict the 'free trade' in knowledge is never present in economic justifications, not least of all as the trade in ideas is dependent on them *not* flowing freely through the economy. This paradox is dissolved in the construction of the circular argument regarding the initial proposition that knowledge *can* be property – to assert a 'free' trade in knowledge would immediately disrupt the constructed scarcity on which intellectual property rests in the first instance and therefore the efficiency argument. This near silence on a free trade in IPRs is the result of knowledge structural power hiding the restrictions required for the trade in ideas to exist in the first place.

Whatever the arguments to suggest that no intellectual property can be justified, in the global political economic relations of the knowledge economy an acceptance that property in knowledge can be justified remains 'common sense'. This leaves argument to centre on the boundary question, what is and what is not intellectual property (IP). The view that there should be some reward system for the developers of knowledge 'has achieved broad consensus in the industrial countries, wherein reside the bulk of IP consumers and the overwhelming majority of IP producers' (Maskus 1990: 387). This acceptance is the result of the knowledge structure's ability to rule certain items off the agenda for those who wish to be seen as presenting 'acceptable' and 'plausible' arguments in debates about IPRs.

The strength of the knowledge structure is such that one of intellectual property's most eminent critics from the developing world still only argues that there must be a line drawn between public and private intellectual property. The possibility that there might be no justification for intellectual property is left unarticulated. Martin Khor's position accepts that some knowledge should be privately owned, and then makes a moral argument based on where the line between public and private should be drawn, thus:

> The benefits given to an individual or company for the invention must be *balanced* by the public good or to the public's right to benefit from technological innovation or knowledge.
>
> Without such a *counter-balance*, the intellectual property privileges granted to the inventor would become purely monopoly rights to collect rentier income. In effect they constitute a form of protectionism, the protection of the inventor's benefits, which curbs the diffusion of technology or knowledge and thus prevents technological development.
>
> (Khor 1990, emphasis added)

Khor requests only a 'counter-balance' to a prior set of privileges, which should be lessened not abolished. And this actually fits well with the economic justification of intellectual property, as these rights are accorded to ensure the continued production of intellectual property. The only issue around which political efforts can be mobilised is this issue of boundaries, between public and private benefits, and between intellectual property and not-intellectual property. Commodification can only be criticised in light of a clear market failure.

The analytical question that needs to be returned to is, therefore, who benefits from the structured agenda that persists and is elaborated within the global political economy of IPRs? The overwhelming weight of discourse presumes that ideas can be owned in a parallel way to property, and that there is a need to allow sufficient flexibility in the field of knowledge objects to enable the introduction of new areas for ownership: the enclosing dynamic, the commodification of knowledge. The group who benefit directly from this settlement are those who own the knowledge being coded as property and the technology to exploit it. Importantly these groups are the current owners, not owners of socialised knowledge, nor of (say) language or other intellectual resources in the public domain, from which such property has been fashioned. Any need for public or social benefits is insufficiently strong to compromise this group's private rights.

The thin line between public and private

The issue of balancing private reward for the creation of knowledge objects against the public interest in their diffusion is conventionally related to the time limitation on intellectual property. The limited temporal enjoyment of intellectual property rights is seen as the recognition by public legislative authority of legitimate rights which should in the first instance be accorded to the authorial functionary in regard to their creative act(s). However, these rights are circumscribed in temporal terms by the weight of public or social benefit likely to result from the knowledge object's free dissemination. As I have noted, these rights are sometimes referred to as monopoly rights for their duration. But it is necessary to be careful how the term monopoly is used here. The monopoly rights attached to a specific knowledge object do not necessarily restrict competition in the area in which such knowledge is important. The restriction of action represented by copyright does not necessarily severely harm competitors where that particular copyrighted knowledge is exploited – others may still express themselves in books or songs or art objects. This may also be the case for some industrial, patented ideas; however, given the importance of a crucial and ground-breaking idea, there is always the possibility the supposed limited rights may become monopolistic if they represent a sufficiently innovative development.

The agent of authority in this matter is the state, even where the state is responding to international treaty obligations, such as those under the Trade Related Aspects of Intellectual Property Rights agreement. Only through legislation can intellectual property be subject to this trade-off between public and private benefits. Unless kept absolutely secret, knowledge's scarcity (unlike material property) needs to be enforced alongside ownership rights. The state agrees to support the recognition and protection of a particular intellectual property in exchange for limiting its existence as intellectual property. Outside this bargaining arrangement, there is no time limit on how long a knowledge object might be a trade secret, but its revelation does not bring with it intellectual property rights. Once revealed, the trade secret's value as intellectual property is dissipated, rather than retained through the licensing that is possible under both copyright and patent. But even for patents and copyrights there comes a time when protection (which is to say the very existence of the intellectual property) finishes and use or diffusion is no longer limited.

The following examination of the global political economy of intellectual property rights is essentially concerned with this issue: when is the right to benefit from the creation of an intellectual property outweighed by the public good? As will become apparent, there is no fixed or easy answer to this question. The debate takes place at the nexus of technology, legality and ideology. Debates about intellectual property can only make sense when and where technologies have been developed that enable its dissemination and reproduction in such a manner that can induce some form of market relations. Such market relations presuppose that the commodification of knowledge is possible in the first place, and these two streams of development – the legal and the technological – are intricately linked as will become evident. But as I have been discussing in these first two chapters, underlying the legal regimes of intellectual property, and the use of technology to maximise the return on such property, are the justificatory schemata that have previously been utilised to justify material property.

While the nexus of technology and legality is vital for an investigation of intellectual property, there is also a need to examine the workings of the knowledge structure in supporting and reproducing these socio-economic aspects of intellectual property relations. As I look at various issues within the global political economy of intellectual property rights I will constantly return to the importance of this three-way nexus, which is in itself a particular instance of the general dual-dialectic I described in the previous chapter. In the next chapter I will examine the agreement under the auspices of the World Trade Organisation in the realm of Trade Related Aspects of Intellectual Property Rights. This is the background against which all contemporary debates regarding IPRs are played out.

3   TRIPs as a watershed

For the first time since the General Agreement on Tariffs and Trade was originally launched in 1947, the Uruguay Round of multilateral trade negotiations included an attempt to harmonise international intellectual property rights protection. At the end of these negotiations in 1994, the Final Act signed by the negotiating states included an agreement to regulate and protect trade-related aspects of intellectual property rights (TRIPs). This incorporated much of the Paris and Berne Conventions previously administered by the World Intellectual Property Organisation (WIPO) bringing intellectual property into the trade regime over-seen by the new World Trade Organisation (WTO). Once the agreed transition periods extended to the developing countries and ex-communist states pass, the TRIPs agreement will harmonise signatories' intellectual property rights regimes with respect to regulations covering eligibility for protection, its duration and enforcement.

The incorporation of the regime for the protection of intellectual property into the WTO recognises that widely perceived threats to the rights of owners of intellectual property are not only caused by differences in the legal construction of intellectual property in different national legislations, but also by the (non-) inclusiveness of such legislation and the impact this has on the trade in intellectual property. Previously, in many jurisdictions formal legislation had been devised to emulate the main aspects of the protection that owners might enjoy in the developed states. However, WIPO did not have the power to address international enforcement issues in any effective manner. Therefore, one of the major shifts that the TRIPs agreement represents is a move to a more effective and stringent dispute resolution mechanism for intellectual property within the organisational structure of the WTO.

First, I will briefly outline the shape of the actual agreement and explore its importance as an extension of the previous global system of intellectual property legislative co-ordination. I then outline some possible implications of this new agreement, most importantly in terms of the allocation of social and economic benefits between developed and developing countries, often portrayed as a North–South issue. In the last part of the chapter I return to the issues I presented in the first two chapters, how a particular settlement regarding intellectual property emerges. The TRIPs agreement is an important illustration of the intersection of legal, technological and knowledge structural streams that I highlight throughout this book.

tline of the TRIPs agreement

 April 1994 in the Moroccan city of Marrakech the negotiating states formally brought the Uruguay Round of negotiations to a close by signing and adopting the Final Act. This established the World Trade Organisation as a formal institution incorporating the legal structure of the 1947 General Agreement on Tariffs and Trade, as well as the subsequent additions which were agreed in the successive rounds of negotiations. As part of this Final Act intellectual property rights (IPRs) were included in the international trade regime for the first time and, as such, the agreement 'is probably the most significant development in international intellectual property law this century' (Blakeney 1996: v). The WTO included 111 states in its initial membership who became signatories to the TRIPs agreement, rising to 128 in 1995 with some 20 further prospective members waiting to join. The previous governance structure for intellectual property overseen by WIPO included 135 states, though of the 18 conventions administered, the Paris Convention had the most signatories standing at 108. With the exception of the Berne Convention (95 signatories) other agreements overseen by WIPO had between 20 and 50 signatories. The membership of the United Nations, which is a reasonable proxy for the number of states in the global system, is currently over 180 states. Joining the WTO automatically involves accession to the TRIPs agreement and so the scope of intellectual property governance will be widened considerably.

The World Intellectual Property Organisation replaced the United International Bureaux for the Protection of Intellectual Property (known as BIRPI, its French acronym) in 1970 and became a specialised agency of the UN in December 1974. However, it traces its legal history back to the Paris Convention for the Protection of Industrial Property enacted in 1883 and the Berne Convention for the Protection of Literary and Artistic Works from three years later. And while there had been national protection for intellectual property for at least two centuries prior to these agreements, these conventions were the first attempt to further the harmonisation and protection of intellectual property internationally. The TRIPs agreement incorporates most of the provisions of both these treaties into the WTO's trade regime and by doing so considerably enhances their legal enforcement mechanisms. The TRIPs agreement formally covers intellectual property in: copyright; patents; trademarks; geographical indications (for wine, predominantly); industrial designs; integrated circuit topographies and 'undisclosed information' (trade secrets), all of which have been subject to separate agreements under WIPO. The main aim of the agreement is to bring all member states' legislation into harmony and thus to bring the same level of protection to intellectual property that was previously only available in developed states to all states in the global trading system.

The preamble to the TRIPs agreement which itself was subject to some considerable negotiation was finally agreed on the basis that the signatories desired

> to reduce distortions and impediments to international trade, and taking into
> account the need to promote effective and adequate protection of intellectual

property rights, and to ensure that measures and procedures to enforce intellectual property rights do not themselves become barriers to legitimate trade,

would adopt the provisions of the TRIPs agreement (GATT 1994, A1C: 2). The recognition that 'intellectual property rights are private rights' was only balanced by an allowance of the need for the 'public policy objectives of national systems for the protection of intellectual property, including developmental and technological objectives' rather than any provision for a formalised public realm of knowledge protected by law. The historical problem of WIPO's largely ineffective ability to sanction states or their domiciled companies who did not observe the formally adopted agreements is reflected in the desire to promote 'adequate' protection.

The keystone of the TRIPs agreement is the adoption of the principles that are central to the WTO (like the GATT before it) in the realm of intellectual property: national treatment; most-favoured nation treatment (MFN); and reciprocity. Though they do not dissolve specific agreements within conventions under the auspices of WIPO, in the main these principles will be effective across the various elements of the TRIPs agreement (Verma 1996: 337–338). National treatment requires signatories to accord the same rights and protection to both nationals and non-nationals in their jurisdiction. Though there are some exceptions these are only allowable 'where such exceptions are necessary to secure compliance with [national] laws and regulations which are not inconsistent' with the TRIPs agreement itself (Blakeney 1996: 41). The TRIPs agreement explicitly extends national treatment to cover performers, producers of 'phonograms' and broadcasting organisations, where such treatment was ambiguous under the WIPO supervised conventions.

As with the WTO overall, the application of most-favoured nation (MFN) status to all members requires that 'any advantage, favour, privilege or immunity granted by a Member to the nationals of any other country be accorded immediately and unconditionally to the nationals of all other members' (GATT 1994, A1C: 4). And while there are again several exceptions linked to the previous conventions which some members of the WTO have acceded to, in the main these do not compromise this requirement. Reciprocity as a principle has a long history within international agreements and its formal inclusion in the TRIPs agreement does little in itself to change the intellectual property regime. The introduction of MFN, however, does shift the ground for intellectual property governance somewhat and is directly the result of its inclusion within an institution concerned with international trade law. Whereas, under the auspices of WIPO there were many smaller-scale treaties and conventions on various aspects of intellectual property, under TRIPs all such specialised agreements if entered into would immediately apply to all the members of the WTO. So most importantly, where there has been resistance to incorporate particular sectoral legislation covered by limited conventions in the past, these now by virtue of the membership of the WTO become as wide in scope as the main conventions. Most-favoured-nation treatment is the key tool for expanding trade agreements and is therefore in one sense the most important innovative aspect of the TRIPs agreement.

The TRIPs agreement is a detailed international agreement and I do not intend to go through its clauses in detail here.[1] However, I will outline its main elements before I discuss their implications and where specific issues are important for the arguments I make in this study they will be dealt with below. The central intention of the TRIPs agreement is to provide a legal framework for a single intellectual property regime throughout the international system. Through its articulation to the WTO, intellectual property has become part of the trade regime which has been progressively widened since the original GATT-1947 agreement on trade and tariffs was concluded. Though the international regime for intellectual property pre-dates GATT its institutionalisation under a single administration, WIPO, was delayed until the 1970s. Even then this organisation was little more than an administration agency for a diverse number of multilateral agreements with varying memberships. Thus, the TRIPs agreement presents WTO members with a single framework for dealing with the diverse aspects of intellectual property, replacing WIPO's more fragmented set of treaties and sectoral agreements.

The TRIPs agreement, however, does not represent a direct legal structure for the recognition of intellectual property. It is not a model piece of legislation that can be incorporated directly into national law. Rather, it sets the minimum standards that should be reflected in the national legislation of all WTO members. It does not preclude members setting more rigid or stronger protection for IPRs except where such extensions above and beyond the minimum standards represent an infringement of the agreement's articles in some way. By incorporating the previous agreements (the Berne and Paris Conventions, and other specialised treaties) into a single framework, the agreement aims to homogenise membership and extend its coverage to all states who wish to become members of the WTO. Within all member states the intellectual property owner should have recourse to a prescribed set of procedures and remedies that will be legislated in national laws to protect their rights. The agreement is concerned with the effects of legislation not the legislation itself. National legislatures are required to ensure IPRs are protected but the method for this protection is only important as regards its consequences, not its form. But national legislative enaction of the TRIPs agreement's principles are subject to the WTO's dispute-settlement mechanism under the agreement. Therefore, unlike the WIPO's stewardship of previous conventions, the WTO offers a considerably more robust mechanism for states to appeal to where the national laws of a particular state are seen to impede the rights of other nationals.

While the character of intellectual property, what is actually to be protected, is modified to some extent by the agreement, the main area of discontinuity with prior practice is in the enforcement of IPRs. By bringing intellectual property under the purview of the WTO, the TRIPs agreement stipulates that 'procedures shall be applied in such a manner as to avoid the creation of barriers to legitimate trade' central to intellectual property law (GATT 1994, A1C: 19). The enforcement of intellectual property rights (or more often their non-enforcement) should not be used to disrupt trade flows. For instance, if only nationals are protected this would act as a barrier to non-nationals who would receive no protection for the IPR element of goods or services they wished to export to that jurisdiction. Non-discrimination must be explicitly part of a clear and fair registration procedure for IPRs where they require registration to be recognised (the exceptions being copyright and trade secrets – 'undisclosed information'). The agreement provides a set of conditions which national legislation for registration must fulfil, broadly based on the requirements of openness and prompt enacting of procedures.

The perceived lack of robust enforcement procedures available under WIPO's stewardship of the existing conventions was one of the main underlying motives for the inclusion of intellectual property in the Uruguay Round and its subsequent inclusion in the WTO. The members of the WTO are required to enact suitable procedures to ensure the 'effective action against any act of infringement of intellectual property . . . including expeditious remedies to prevent infringements and remedies which constitute a deterrent to further infringement' (GATT 1994, A1C: 19). These procedures must be fair and equitable and available under civil law. In the section of the agreement covering Civil and Administrative Procedures and Remedies there are a number of requirements which national legislations should include, ranging from the need for courts to have powers to obtain evidence of infringements to the need to produce fair settlements with regard to damages. The agreement's significant departure from previous international legislation is encompassed within its adoption of precedents developed in British law to grant applicants access to the premises of the defendant to seize and discover materials that might potentially represent an IPR infringement (Blakeney 1996: 126). This represents a major extension to the manner in which the rights of intellectual property owners can be protected prior to formal infringement through actual sale and is based on the 1976 *Anton Piller v. Manufacturing Processes* case under the Court of Appeal in Britain. This ability to act prior to an act of infringement of rights (the legal acceptance of the likelihood of infringement) had previously been available in only a small minority of jurisdictions.

The last general element of the TRIPs agreement which represents a change to the previous IPR regime is the enacting of stricter border controls with regard to goods with IPRs attached. This was perhaps to be expected given the centrality of the rhetoric of international intellectual property theft that permeated the negotiations which led to the agreement. Blakeny points out that

> as a matter of practice, although a number of countries had provided for the seizure by customs authorities of goods bearing infringing trademarks, this was more symbolic than real. The priorities for customs authorities had been the collection of trade-related revenues and the control of the trade in weapons, drugs and noxious substances. Their resources and expertise did not equip them to deal with the trade in intellectual property infringements. The identification of intellectual property as a trade-related issue has *obliged* the customs authorities to reorder their priorities.
>
> (Blakeney 1996: 133, emphasis added)

One key practice this is meant to halt is the parallel importation of licensed goods from other jurisdictions. However, the border issue is further expanded under TRIPs to cover not only trademarked goods but also 'pirated copyright goods . . . [and] goods which involve other infringements of intellectual property rights' (GATT 1994, A1C: 23). This therefore requires legislation to deal with parallel importation and the international sale of pirated intellectual property of all kinds, from trademark infringements to the importation of goods produced through the unlicensed use of patented processes. Therefore, with the inclusion of the requirement for border control authorities to be aware and responsible for policing intellectual property, the protection to IPR holders is strengthened by the TRIPs agreement both inside particular national legislatures where before protection had been weak or ineffective, and between national jurisdictions where many of the problems for consumer goods manufacturers lie.

The importance of the agreement

While it is corporate rights that are infringed by foreign nationals' disrespect of IPRs, disputes are mediated at the WTO through the agency of inter-governmental diplomacy. Some (though not all) states are able to further the corporate interests of their nationals through the WTO's dispute settlement mechanism and ultimately, where there is no satisfactory conclusion, economic sanctions can be brought to bear on the miscreants. This extension of the protection of intellectual property in the international realm as well as the harmonisation of law within WTO members represent a major triumph for the 'US pharmaceutical, entertainments and informatics industries that were largely responsible for getting TRIPs on the agenda' of the Uruguay Round (Hoekman and Kostecki 1995: 156). These corporations have sought and gained the support of certain developed states to protect and further their particular interest in the protection of IPRs. Interestingly where international trade effects groups other than corporations, say, workers in the area of minimum labour standards or disparate local populations subject to environmental degradation, the willingness to include such problems within the remit of the WTO and inter-state diplomacy, or even agree to consider them in the future has been less than forthcoming.

The TRIPs agreement is significant in the extension it represents for the rights of the owners of intellectual property. Burch contends that this expansion of ownership rights 'also extends an essentially liberal conception of social life as relations organised and understood by reference to exclusive property rights . . . [it] promotes the vocabulary of rights and property and the liberal conceptual framework they help define' (1995: 215). The TRIPs agreement is therefore important at two levels:

* as an extension of the rights accorded to the owners of intellectual property;
* as part of the extension of a property-based market liberalism into new areas of social interaction, previously outside market relations.

To some extent the second issue of widening global commodification is one th
underlies much of the discussion in this book. For now I want to discuss the first
level of importance, the extension of the rights of ownership.

If there was any doubt that the TRIPs agreement is about ownership rather than
creation, it is crucial to immediately note though moral rights are recognised in a
number of jurisdictions in continental Europe, where those rights come into conflict
with rights mandated by TRIPs, they are disallowed. That said, the agreement
does not mention the question of moral rights directly (Worthy 1994: 196). It only
alludes to them in Article 9 which notes that 'members shall not have rights or
obligations under this agreement in respect of the rights conferred under Article
6*bis* of [the Berne] Convention or of the rights derived therefrom' (GATT 1994,
A1C: 5). This clause of the Berne Convention is the 'moral rights' clause. Thus,
though it does not actually preclude the recognition or moral rights (only noting
that they are not conferred by the TRIPs agreement itself), elsewhere in the text it
does require that no protection of rights over and above the minimum laid down in
the agreement should conflict with the rights held to constitute the minimum. The
retention of moral rights by the creator of the particular intellectual property after
its reproduction rights have been transferred enables the creator to retain some
control of the use put their particular creation. But the TRIPs agreement favours
the holder of the transferred rights over the moral right of the creator and therefore
if such a matter were to come to a dispute, the moral right would be identified
as an impediment to the rights of the current owner. Or to put it more simply,
the rights of knowledge capitalists (and owners) are favoured over the rights of
knowledge producers.

Another area which has been extended not so much by omission as by dilution
is the compulsory licensing of innovations. In the past, it has been argued by
developing states' representatives that the refusal to grant patent licences for
particular innovations, or the failure to work them in a national economy (relying
on imports for the fulfilment of demand), has impeded important aspects of
technology transfer. In the TRIPs agreement, while it proved impossible to render
such compulsory licences illegal, the developed states' negotiators did manage to
put some limits on the legal recourse to compulsory patent. Thus while Article 31
of the agreement allows for some level of compulsory licensing it requires that such
compulsory licensing for use should only be undertaken if 'prior to such use, the
proposed user has made efforts to obtain authorisation from the right holder on
reasonable commercial terms and conditions and that such efforts have not been
successful within a reasonable period of time' (GATT 1994, A1C: 14, emphasis
added). There are of course some circumstances which allow for the waiving of this
limitation, such as national emergency or 'other circumstances of extreme urgency'
but even then the 'right holder shall, nevertheless, be notified as soon as reasonably
practicable'. The original patent holder also retains the right to suggest that the
previously offered terms were not at a 'reasonable commercial' level, leaving the
compulsory patent at odds with the agreement's conditions.

There is also a provision for non-commercial use such as health care and national
defence, though again there remains a requirement of notification, and the

stipulation that prior negotiation has failed to be settled on 'reasonable commercial terms'. Furthermore, such compulsory licenses must be *non-exclusive*, un-assignable (which is to say they must be publicly and freely available, not handed to a particular national producer), and the decision to grant them shall be subject to judicial review. The intent is to maximise the difficulty of actioning a legal compulsory patent while minimising its benefit to the recipient. It is also required that the 'right holder shall be paid adequate remuneration in the circumstances of each case, taking into account the economic value of the authorisation' (GATT 1994, A1C: 15). The key issue here is that all of these conditions are hedged around with the terms 'reasonable' or 'adequate', and given the importance put upon the owner throughout the agreement, it would seem likely that it is the owners' interpretation of these terms that will carry more weight in any dispute. Additionally, the rights of these owners (most often in the richest states) are supported by the full might of the home state and its ability to bring pressure to bear on infringing state governments through the WTO's mechanisms.

The area which has been most widely perceived in the public discussions of the agreement concerns the criteria for patentability. The issue of what sort of 'things' can be considered as intellectual property is at the centre of the popular debates around IPRs and will be returned to frequently during this study. In the negotiations prior to the TRIPs agreement, this was one of the most divisive areas between, broadly speaking, the developing or Southern states and the developed or Northern states. Though the agreement carries the normal provisions forward – newness, usefulness and applicability – it does not expressly preclude a considerable expansion of 'patentable subject matter'. This extension is produced through the provisions of Article 27 which allow that members *may* exclude from patent provisions a number of classes of goods and materials such as diagnostic, therapeutic and surgical methods as well as plants and animals, and the 'essentially' biological processes for their production. These classes of objects and processes may be excluded, but they are not required to be outside patent regimes.

More importantly, to ensure that patents on genes and bio-technological materials are covered in all member states, these exceptions expressly do not include micro-organisms, non-biological and micro biological processes of plant and animal production, nor pharmaceutical products. Additionally, members 'shall provide for the protection of plant varieties either by patents or by an effective *sui generis* system or by any combination thereof' (GATT 1994, A1C: 13). These biotechnological provisions aim to ensure that though plant varieties may be treated differently, they will also be brought into the system of intellectual property, even while responding to the requirements of the International Convention for the Protection of New Varieties of Plants (UPOV). For the purposes of clarity the GATT always tried to reduce non-tariff barriers, even if this merely meant transforming them into actual tariffs. Here, the same logic is being applied – the reduction of difference in treatment to a variation in the same broad legislative method. This underlines Burch's claim that TRIPs is an extension into new areas of the construction of social relations as property relations.

In the other area that has been frequently raised in public debates, Article 10 of the agreement makes it clear that 'Computer programmes, whether in source or object code, shall be protected as literary works under the Berne Convention' (GATT 1994, A1C: 6). Not only does this extend the Berne Convention itself, but allows computer programmes to be covered by the longest period of protection available under the agreement, and subject to considerably less stringent conditions of recognition as intellectual property than other sorts of manufacturing/industrial processes covered by patents. The form of computer programmes (their existence as language) has been given precedence in their characterisation as intellectual property over their function as tools, again favouring owners over possible users. Given the importance of information technology and other forms of knowledge resources in the global economy, this raises profound issues over technology transfer which I will return to in the next chapter. The second clause of Article 10 also explicitly includes 'compilations of data or other material, whether in machine readable or other form, which by reason of selection or arrangement of their contents constitute intellectual creations', though such protection 'shall not extend to the data or material itself'. Thus, databases, directories and other electronically stored public knowledge shall be protected by copyright and as such brought into the intellectual property regime, at least in their particular patterning (or structure of compilation). As I noted in the previous chapter, this expands the characterisation of the authorial function recognised by intellectual property to acts of collation and collection in addition to the usual notion of original creation of some sort.

Much of the diplomatic communication that surrounded the negotiations towards the TRIPs agreement, on the other hand, emphasised the harmonisation issue. One of the most clearly identified areas of such harmonisation was the duration or term of protection accorded to different groups of intellectual property. Thus, for instance, in copyright the agreement carries forward the general term of protection from the Berne Convention of the author's life plus fifty years. Where there has been no authorised publication of works other than those covered by the Berne Convention, then the term is limited to fifty years from when such work was made. For photographic works and applied art the protection must be a minimum of twenty-five years. However, in international copyright disputes, one of the most important prospective harmonisations was in the protection for the 'performers and producers of phonograms' (to include CDs) which is mandated in Article 14.5 to extend 'until the end of a period fifty years computed from the end of the calendar year in which fixation was made' (GATT 1994, A1C: 7). One of the major concerns for the international music industry has been the importation of recordings from jurisdictions where the copyright had expired due to much shorter terms into states where such recordings where still under exclusive copyright. Though termed piracy by the affected companies, until TRIPs this sort of activity was difficult to control through intellectual property laws, as the exhaustion of rights was not fixed internationally, and no illegal act had occurred in the originating jurisdiction.

The TRIPs agreement has both harmonised and in many cases *extended* the duration of IPR protection. The harmonisation of patent durations was made quite rigid on the basis that there were a number of disparate durations from different points in the patenting process across WTO negotiating states. Thus, while other aspects of the agreement are quite complex, Article 33 on the term of protection for patents is a model of concise yet clear provision: 'The term of protection available shall not end before the expiration of a period of twenty years from the filing date' (GATT 1994, A1C: 16). This harmonises the patent duration provisions of member states in two ways: first, it ensures a minimum period of protection, above that which was available in many developing states, and second, it ensures that this duration is measured from a set point, that of filing for protection. Thus, the window of opportunity which was open to 'interlopers' when applications were published but protection was only available from the date of the grant of patent has been effectively closed (Blakeney 1996: 88). In other areas of intellectual property (such as trademarks) the aim of the agreement has also been to bring terms of duration up to a minimum standard that reflects the modes of practice in the developed states. Allowing that the duration of the protection accorded to intellectual property is the manifestation of the balance between private rights and public or social use of knowledge, then this move is again a strengthening of the rights of private owners *vis-à-vis* the public or socialised dissemination of useful knowledge.

Perhaps emblematic of the whole agreement, in the area of process patents, the burden of proof has been switched from the plaintiff (the owner of the patent) to the defendant. Thus if a product has been produced that is new, or it is likely that it has been produced by the patented process, it is up to the defendant to prove that the patented process has not been used. Thus, if the manufacturer is to prove that no infringement has occurred in circumstances where the patent's 'owner has been unable to determine the process actually used', the details of manufacturer will be forced into the public domain (GATT 1994, A1C: 16). And while there is provision for the 'legitimate interests of the defendant in protecting his manufacturing and business secrets [to] be taken into account', once again the balance of rights has shifted quite significantly to the owner of the patent (Verma 1996: 345–346). It may not be too far-fetched to imagine that when a new process to produce a particular product is developed in a particular jurisdiction, the patent holder of the previous process will find it possible through the courts to push their competitor into revealing the new process. Thus, where reverse engineering has failed there is now the possible recourse to law to force competitors to reveal how they are competing. Whether this provision will lead to this sort of case is hard to predict but even the likelihood signals once again where the benefits of TRIPs are to be enjoyed – it is an agreement for private ownership. The belief that defendants might be innocent until proven guilty has been eradicated where the interests of corporate intellectual property holders deem it obstructive to the benefits they enjoy from their property.

Likely implications of the TRIPs agreement

One of the chief implications of the TRIPs agreement is an expansion of corporate control of important knowledge resources. This is at the cost of the public or social availability of such knowledge; knowledge as property is now considered to be scarce and exclusive under the terms of the agreement. Thus, the balance between the realm of private rights and that of publicly available knowledge is where the impact of the TRIPs agreement is most significant. Though this underlies many of the specific legal changes outlined above, the key part of the agreement in this regard is Article 8 which sets out the provisions for the protection of the public interest in the area of intellectual property as part of the principles of the agreement.

1. Members may, in formulating or amending their national laws and regulations, adopt measures necessary to protect public health and nutrition, and to promote the public interest in sectors of vital importance to their socio-economic and technological development, *provided that such measures are consistent with the provisions of this Agreement.*
2. Appropriate measures, *provided that they are consistent with the provisions of this Agreement*, may be needed to prevent the abuse of intellectual property rights by right holders or the resort to practices which unreasonably restrain trade or adversely affect the international transfer of technology.
    (GATT 1994, A1C: 5 emphasis added)

As is clear, what public rights or needs that are recognised can only be accorded legal significance if they are consistent with the TRIPs agreement's overall provisions. But the bulk of the text of the agreement actually extends and expands the rights of private owners of IPRs. Therefore, this invocation of the need to recognise the importance of a public realm is of less real importance or significance than might be immediately presumed. The net effect of the TRIPs agreement is actually to critically reduce the area of public knowledge, especially in areas where new technologies and processes are important or even vital to socio-economic development.

One of the key functions of the justificatory schemata supporting intellectual property is to reinforce the necessity of regarding economically valued knowledge as intellectual property. The importance of the term 'trade-related' is that it makes explicit the central concern of the negotiators from the developed states: the need to legislate for this commodity form of knowledge. This means the line between public and private in the realm of knowledge in the agreement is the distinction between trade-related intellectual property (rights) and a residual category, presumably *non-trade-related* intellectual property, or knowledge that is not intellectual property. Thus where knowledge is related to trade in some manner it should be included within the remit of the TRIPs agreement's provisions. This notion of trade-relatedness brings knowledge across the line from passive to active property, from public/social to private. There is implicitly a moment when something that has previously been in the public domain (as non-ownable knowledge) is re-coded as trade related and thus amenable to the 'protection' afforded other trade-related (intellectual) property. This moment is when the (intellectual) property passes from passive to active, when its trade-relatedness is asserted. This movement, as a succession of such moments, is one that is broadly parallel to the enclosures of common land in Great Britain and elsewhere during the sixteenth to nineteenth centuries. What might once have been public or commonly 'owned' is rendered trade-related and thus private.

The international negotiators (at least from the developed states) who argued over the TRIPs agreement presented the notion of trade-relatedness as common-sense and unproblematic. Nevertheless the line represented by TRIPs/non-TRIPs, the line between public and private knowledge objects, is subject to constant reconstruction through the dual-dialectic – the reformulation of concepts of tradable knowledge working in conjunction with changes of the material technology that can utilise it. Though the form of the distinction remains fixed, as a binary division between non-tradable knowledge and tradable knowledge, the content of each sector varies with the development of technologies that enable the capture and profiting from different types of informational item or knowledge object. Equally, shifts in what might be intellectual property drive new attempts to capture attendant rights through trade-relatedness. Thus, the TRIPs agreement's text is careful not to prescribe definite limits to intellectual property; it is permissive of new forms of knowledge becoming property. Exclusions are allowed but not mandated, and there are no classes of knowledge that are expressly forbidden to IPR related legislation.

Whether 'trade-related intellectual property rights' is a better or even a different term to 'intellectual property rights' is unclear (Subramanian 1990: 509). The notion of rights as conceptualised within the TRIPs negotiations and the justificatory schemata utilised therein would indicate that the whole purpose of these rights is that they can be traded, that they are alienable. What other intellectual property rights might there be within the dominant justificatory schema? In these accounts IPRs are always trade-related. The use of the term trade-related is therefore somewhat redundant (or, as Subramanian's pun has it, 'counterfeit') and actually serves another function rather than of definition. But, what this use of the term does do is underline the economic aspect of the arguments being utilised to justify IPRs. To assert the trade-relatedness of intellectual property is to make a claim for it to be legitimately included within the legal structure governing world trade.

Another area where the TRIPs agreement is likely to have a considerable impact is in the transfer of technology to developing states. Dhar and Rao, in a detailed discussion of patents, suggest that historically the control of the process of patenting at the centre of particular industries has led to the establishment and maintenance of technological supremacy by developed states' corporations (Dhar and Rao 1996). Despite its origin in the state's wish to ensure that technological advances entered the public realm (and were disclosed), Dhar and Rao follow Joan Robinson in arguing that there is a 'paradox of patent': it actually limits the prompt dissemi-nation of new advances. There has been a speeding up of innovation, producing a shortened period in which the patent holder can effectively recover monopoly rents in developed markets before competing innovations appear. This leads to a disjuncture between the period of effective use and the protection accorded the monopoly rights of such use. The direct result is a technology gap reinforced by patents, which enables developed states' corporations to carry on profiting from first-generation patented technologies in developing states even if these have become out-dated in developed markets. New technologies only (re)enter the public realm long after a developing state's industry might be able to profitably utilise them in world trade or to compete with imports (or licensed production) in the domestic market (Dhar and Rao 1996: 310). In light of the harmonisation of patent protection towards longer protection the TRIPs agreement is unlikely to facilitate technology transfer, in the sense of making technology speedily available to developing states, despite pronouncements to the contrary. It may well expand the geographic locations in which monopoly rents can be earned within the patent's life, but this is not the same as technology transfer – it is essentially a widened control of technology and its uses. Thus, Dhar and Rao suggest that accession to the agreement by developing states will have the effect of making the technology gap more rigid. Far from freeing the flow of new technology to developing states the TRIPs agreement will limit and control it, ensuring that the technology gap is enforced.

This technology gap is not necessarily one of usage, however. One of the main intentions of the TRIPs agreement is to ensure that the rights of the patent owner are upheld in all jurisdictions. Therefore, technology usage may spread in the sense that corporations may be more inclined to license technology to developing state partners. However, as such technology remains protected as intellectual property, the technology has not been transferred and thus remains the property of particular owners, controlled by them. Furthermore, it is not unknown for licence agreements to include provisions that accord ownership of local improvements to the original patent holder. This either allows for the capture of innovation or discourages it. Nevertheless, it is a commonplace assertion that without some form of IPR protection patent holders will be unwilling to transfer technology at all. Thus even the limited leasing of technological innovations is an improvement where no technology transfer has previously taken place. Unfortunately it is also the case that often 'for the successful exploitation of a patent, technical know-how is essential, which is not readily available to the public and is usually not patented' (Verma 1996: 354). Thus, even where licensing is possible, it may not in itself ensure that processes which are a significant improvement on the current state of industrial know-how in a particular economy will actually be transferred. Additionally, patent protection has often been used to ensure that only imports of the patented product will be used to fill demand (that is, the patent is not being worked). Except within quite tightly drawn parameters, the TRIPs agreement has further limited the possibility of legal recourse to compulsory licensing in such cases.

It is difficult to be clear about the implications of the TRIPs agreement on issues of global trade, uneven development or technology transfer as much depends on the dynamic which flows from the agreement. States are not required to produce specific legislation but rather to ensure that the consequences of their legislation accord with the agreement's provisions. Additionally, technological advances may change the game sufficiently that IPR protection becomes impossible, which is certainly the expectation of some Internet utopians. However, a likely outcome in the short to medium term will be a redistribution of wealth from those who wish to use technologies, processes and other knowledge objects that are protected by IPRs to those who own the IPRs concerned.

Verma claims that the developing states 'own less than 6% of the world stock of patents, with about 84% of them owned by foreigners' by which he implies the developed states (Verma 1996: 355). Taking the figures for patents registered in the USA broken down by the residence of the first named inventor, in 1995, 57 per cent originated in the USA, with a further 25 per cent originating in Germany and Japan. Just under 3.5 per cent originated in fourteen 'late industrialising' states (Argentina, Brazil, Chile, China, Hong Kong, India, Indonesia, Malaysia, Mexico, Singapore, South Korea, Taiwan, Thailand and Turkey) leaving only 15 per cent from the rest of the world, of which the bulk would be taken up by other European originated patents (Amsden and Mourshed 1997: 354). And while this does not necessarily completely reflect the actual global patent distribution, it is a reasonable confirmation of Verma's claim about the likely geographical balance of intellectual property owners relative to non-owners. Thus, it seems likely that the TRIPs agreement will be redistributive towards developed states' corporations and other owners of IPRs. Given the background to the emergence of the agreement this should not be too surprising a contention.

The emergence of TRIPs

It was no accident that a major element of the Uruguay Round were the negotiations to establish an agreement on intellectual property and its protection. But its emergence as a major international trade issue was not merely the result of pressure by US knowledge-utilising companies. As I have argued in Chapter 1, to understand the emergence of particular intellectual property settlements, there is a need to consider material and knowledge structural issues as well. In 1992 the GATT produced a brochure entitled *The Uruguay Round: A Giant Step for Trade and Development and a Response to the Challenges of the Modern World*. Under the subheading 'Eliminating the wrongs', four reasons were given for the need to finally conclude an agreement on intellectual property:

> First, the protection of intellectual property has become a key element in international competition: creativity and inventiveness are major assets in competition between companies and countries;
>
> Second, the scale of trade in counterfeit products has reached alarming proportions and it involves a very broad range of products, from pharmaceuticals to auto parts and luxury goods;
>
> Third, the protection of intellectual property is a factor in technological progress: it can encourage technology transfer between countries, leading to investment and jobs;
>
> Fourth, the protection of intellectual property has become a source of trade tensions in recent years, owing to the differences in the levels of protection in competing countries . . .

In short, those who provide creative and inventive products and processes will be encouraged to share them and will get their financial return, while those who need such products and processes will have access to them.

(GATT 1992: 17)

As far as the GATT secretariat were concerned, the TRIPs agreement would be beneficial to all states because of the emerging global information society, the need to fight the widening incidence of piracy or theft, the need for technology transfer and the problematic disharmony of IPR protection.

This statement recognises that one of the key issues that has been raising the profile of intellectual property in the global political economy has been the emergence of the new economic and social relations of the prospective global information society. There would have been no TRIPs negotiation if the technologies that enable the profitable accumulation and use of knowledge resources on a global scale did not exist. Intellectual property itself may not be a particularly recent development, but the technologies that have allowed it to take on international commodity status are. The increasing speed of innovation and the expansion of the role for knowledge or information in the capture of economic value added have enhanced the importance of controlling knowledge resources (and by extension intellectual property) to national development. As the field of operations has expanded for corporations which accord significance to intellectual property, so their requirement to enjoy the same protection that has been institutionalised in their home markets has taken on an international dimension.

The Tokyo Round of GATT negotiations (1973–79), did not include intellectual property, and in any case, expansion of the GATT disciplines into new areas was being strongly resisted by developing states. At the time of the launch of the Tokyo Round information technology was still mainly characterised by mainframe computing, while other consumer technologies were still in their infancy. The personal computer revolution, which has driven the vast expansion of information technology usage was in the future, as was cheap video recording, CDs and perhaps most importantly the accelerating (non-academic) use of the Internet as a communications gateway. However, by the launch of the Uruguay Round in 1986, it was becoming clear to many governments that the issue of IPRs, their protection and use, was likely to be a major issue in future international trade relations (Primo Braga 1989: 245–246). The expanding possibilities for technical appropriation of intellectual property resources, alongside widespread 'pirated' reproduction and distribution of knowledge-based products emerged as issues requiring action by national governments on behalf of their home corporations. Thus, pressures started to build for some form of negotiations regarding intellectual property to be part of the round of negotiations which presaged the establishment of the WTO.

However, the changing diffusion and use of new technologies by itself would not necessarily have brought IPRs onto the negotiating agenda for this round if two quite divergent groups had not worked for revisions to the international IPR regime: the developing states; and a committee of US multinationals operating in various knowledge-related sectors. Corporations who control major intellectual property resources undoubtedly like to retain their technological lead *vis-à-vis* their (potential) competitors. While needing to allow use and distribution on the basis of authorised licence, as well as direct production or processing, unauthorised use of corporations' intellectual property eats away at their market position, and may undermine it totally where market access is pre-dated by counterfeit availability. Thus, there was likely to be pressure on the US government to work towards an agreement to include TRIPs in the WTO's treaties, and it was likely to come from the high technology, entertainment and luxury goods exporting sector of the US economy. In these sectors US corporations dominate the market based on their utilisation of knowledge resources. All sought to maintain their competitive advantage based on strengthening their control of the intellectual property elements of their activities internationally.

These US corporations formed the Intellectual Property Committee (IPC) which not only aimed to bring pressure to bear on the US government to get the issue onto the agenda for negotiation, but also provided considerable legal support to the negotiating team (Drahos 1995; Sell 1995). Crucially, the IPC's influence was not limited to the US negotiating team. As Sell sums up the process:

> The IPC began by pitching its proposals to the U.S. government and then pressed its case abroad. It worked hard to convince the industrial associations of Europe and Japan that a code was possible, and then mobilised them to support its quest to include intellectual property protection in the Uruguay Round. The three groups then worked together to produce a consensual document, rooted in industrialised countries' laws, on fundamental principles for a multilateral approach to intellectual property protection. This industry coalition presented its document to the GATT secretariat and Geneva-based representatives of numerous countries. *This process, in which industry played such a central role, was unprecedented in GATT.*
>
> (Sell 1998: 137/8, emphasis added)

While the IPC derived its influence from the economic resources and power it represented in the US domestic economy, its (self-)characterisation as representing the crucial sectors of the new information-based economy helped it establish the negotiating framework for the TRIPs agreement. Supported by the US, the IPC was able to broadly get the agreement on intellectual property it craved. Unlike textiles or the steel industry, these knowledge-centred industries are perceived widely to be the competitive and crucial sectors for the continuance of US economic strength and well-being, adding considerable weight to their protestations and submissions. Building on the discourse of transformation to an information society, these corporations were able to mobilise considerable political resources to further their particular interests. And given the specialised nature of intellectual property law, they were able to capitalise on their specialised knowledge to 'support' the negotiating teams. They essentially drafted the TRIPs agreement while the actual negotiations fine-tuned the text and made some concessions to the developing states.

Ironically the original pressure to amend the international system governing of intellectual property did not originate in the US or other developed states, but rather with the Group of 77 of underdeveloped states some years before. During the 1960s and 1970s, developing states' governments were worried about the problems of economic development and 'seized upon patent protection as a culprit behind import monopolies and patent abuse as a tool to prevent them from developing their own technology for the internal market and for export' (Sell 1998: 110). The institution of intellectual property was perceived not as an organ of free trade, as it would be characterised in the TRIPs agreement, but as the tool of protectionism for the owners of IPRs in the developed states. Through the institution of intellectual property the technology gap which underlay uneven development (or under-development) was maintained. This led developing states to be antagonistic towards demands that their national legislation should accord similar levels of protection to IPRs that were enjoyed in the developed states. During this period, the developing states argued for a dilution of international intellectual property law as it affected them, while the developed states merely supported the status quo.

The key distinction between the position of the Group of 77 and the developed states rested on the purpose of patent (and other IPR) protection. For the developing states the most important factor was their own development and the narrowing of the technology gap. The developed states' position, which in the end structured the TRIPs agreement, was that the rights belonging to owners (and therefore sanctity of property) were paramount. Only by ensuring the property rights of innovators and entrepreneurs were protected from theft could any national economy hope to develop and support economic growth. During the 1960s and 1970s the developing states used their national legislation to reduce the monopoly rights accorded to intellectual property. In this they received some support from the United Nations Conference on Trade and Development which was made most explicit in the 1975 report *The International Patent System as an Instrument for National Development* which was 'exclusively devoted to the question of revising the Paris Convention, sharply critis[ing] existing arrangements and urg[ing] reforms to improve the situation of developing countries' (Sell 1998: 116). Though there was some suspicion that the developing states' governments were using patents as a scapegoat for more difficult problems internal to their economies, in 1980 the Diplomatic Conference for the Revision of the Paris Convention was convened.[2] Unfortunately for the developing states' attempt to widen the public realm for intellectual property, the series of four conferences was deadlocked by the very different views of the purpose of IPR protection between the developed and developing states.

Having broached the subject of revising the international laws governing the protection of intellectual property, the developing states found that not only did the developed states resist any changes to the status quo, their governments slowly moved to a position that sought to strengthen the legal structure and 'give it some teeth'. To some extent the United States and the other developed states adopted this position in the light of pressure from the industrial groups mentioned above.

However, the growing recognition that the various conventions were both ineffectual and under-subscribed may have also influenced government negotiating teams who were already looking at co-ordinating other trade-related activities across the global economy. The pressure to further weaken international IPR protection regimes may well have alerted developed states to the actual problems caused by WIPO's stewardship of a mosaic of different agreements with some but not extensive overlapping memberships. Having opened the Pandora's box of intellectual property revision, the developed states found themselves overtaken by events, not least of all the increasingly high stakes involved in intellectual property related sectors. The changes in economic activities and organisation meant that intellectual property became a more important field of international trade as the 1980s progressed. While developing states still considered it a development issue, for the developed states' knowledge industries intellectual property was now an invaluable and crucial resource linked to competitiveness.

While technological theft between international competitors has always been a problem with the unlicensed use of processes or technologies, increasingly some industries have found that consumer goods markets in the developing states are being disrupted by pirated copies of products. This has been especially true in the case of computer software. One estimate suggests that in China and Indonesia pirated business-related software accounts for approaching 100 per cent of the market. However, even in the US over 25 per cent is pirated and in Britain the proportion is higher at around 35 per cent. Though rates of piracy may be slowly declining, the cost of lost revenue was estimated by the International Planing and Research Corporation to remain approximately $11.4 billion in 1997 alone (*The Economist* 1998c). Given the US corporations' leading role in this sector, their concern about these levels of non-authorised usage would be expected, though on the other hand the figures need to be treated a little carefully as they originate in industry estimates of lost sales as well as actual pirate copies located. Nevertheless, it seems clear that the 'theft' of software through unlicensed duplication is a significant factor in the profitability (or otherwise) of computer software companies. The same figures quoted above also show, interestingly, in the period 1994–97 a world-wide decline in the incidence of piracy as a proportion of business software being used. Whether this is linked to the TRIPs agreement, or shows the impact of more advanced anti-copying devices in software programmes is difficult to surmise, and it may well be a combination of both. Be that as it may, these sorts of figures are given wide credence in the software sector itself. Their portrayal of the extent of the problem of piracy suggests why the software sector was at the forefront of the IPC's lobbying activities as well as a major element in the successful attempt to shape the US position in the TRIPs negotiations.

In the final analysis, the role of intellectual property rights and theft is difficult to disentangle from other factors in the realms of technology transfer and economic development and indeed there are 'no definitive empirical estimates of the impact of the TRIPs agreement on developing countries' (Hoekman and Kostecki 1995: 156). There have been a number of assertions and suppositions regarding the welfare or economic benefits and costs of IPR protection mobilised by various negotiators during the emergence of the TRIPs agreement, but none enjoy widespread support. The broadly victorious US negotiating position was 'based on analyses and estimated loss reports provided by transnational corporate exporters and their industry associations' that were reproduced without verification or any real critical analysis (Sell 1998: 222). However doubtful these figures might be, they worked well with the property-based hypotheses that the TRIPs agreement finally embodied, and therefore conveniently supported the position adopted by the developed states. The arguments about the role of intellectual property have a certain familiarity about them.

Throughout its emergence as a major international issue, negotiators and diplomats have utilised the justificatory schemata I discussed in the previous chapter. Indeed, it is clear in the negotiations over the TRIPs agreement that the knowledge structural power of certain actors has progressively narrowed the agenda of possibilities in this area and has ensured that a certain sort of harmonised agreement was produced reflecting these acceptable justifications of intellectual property. While there were pressures on both sides from economic and social actors, the agreement that emerged from this process was constructed on a basis firmly rooted in the contemporary justificatory schemata of property as applied to the realm of knowledge and information.

The triumph of the knowledge structure

The TRIPs agreement included the developing states in a universalising discourse of knowledge as property, and de-legitimised competing methods of valuing or conceptualising useful knowledge, though there was some resistance during the negotiations to the imposition of this particular framework. The agreement aims to produce a singular globalised conception of the legitimate protection of intellectual property through the harmonisation of the effects of diverse legislation across members of the WTO. On the one hand, the developed states' negotiators stressed the justificatory schema which underlies their view of the worth of intellectual property – essentially, labour-desert arguments, the need for efficient allocation of resources implying the rights of knowledge owners and the codification of un-authorised use as theft. All of which they argued support further development and technology transfer. On the other hand, by articulating the TRIPs agreement within the WTO and therefore making it part of any general membership, the access to developed markets for developing states' other exports was made conditional on accepting such a regime of protection for IPRs along with this embedded set of justifications.

But there remains a disjuncture between the views of developing states and developed states concerning the role of IPR protection, despite the TRIPs agreement. This division is over the private and public benefits from the development of particular knowledge – or between private appropriation and social (re)distribution. One problem for developed countries trying to establish the more rigid and wide-spread protection of intellectual property which their knowledge entrepreneurs seek, is that when European countries (and the US) were at a similar stage of development governmental views of IPR protection for non-nationals were not dissimilar to the position developing states adopted prior to TRIPs (de Almeida 1995: 216). In the eighteenth and nineteenth centuries copyright and patent protection were seldom if ever extended to non-nationals. Indeed, much technology transfer and the adoption of innovation took place through procedures which would be codified as theft under TRIPs and the prevailing characterisation of the rights of knowledge owners. Introducing knowledge into an economy with no payments to intellectual property owners in another country, is exactly the developmental strategy which is illegitimate under the agenda set by the TRIPs agreement, despite its role in European and US development last century.

In addition, Reichman has captured another paradox underlying the negotiations:

> On the one hand, the industrialised countries that subscribe to free-market principles at home want to impose a highly regulated market for intellectual goods on the rest of the world, one in which authors and inventors may 'reap where they have sown'. On the other hand, the developing countries that restrict free competition at home envision an . . . unregulated world market for intellectual goods, one in which 'competition is the lifeblood of commerce'.
>
> (Reichman 1993: 2)

And a major cause of this paradox is that when the developed states' representatives think of intellectual property they are using one definition (one that given the history of property thinking, seems acceptable), while those in the developing (or under-developed) states only see the enclosure of what they think should be freely available, public knowledge resources, usable in their developmental strategies. However, the prevailing forces in the knowledge structure have sidelined and made nonsensical this second conception of intellectual property. The agenda set within the knowledge structure regarding IPRs has found its fullest articulation in the TRIPs agreement.

None the less, the negotiations included a number of interventions by the developing states to attempt to move the agenda towards the developmental properties their negotiators wished to stress. One of the issues in the early stages of the negotiations was whether the proposed development of substantive standards for IPR protection was actually part of the objectives of the negotiations laid out in the Punta del Este declaration at the commencement of the Uruguay Round in any case (GATT 1988a: 8). Brazilian negotiators also tried to get the negotiating group to consider:

> the extent to which rigid and excessive protection of intellectual property rights impedes access to the latest technological developments, thereby restricting the participation of developing countries in international trade; the extent to which abusive use of such rights gives rise to restrictions and distortions in trade; and the risks that a rigid system of protection of intellectual property rights implies for international trade.
>
> (GATT 1988b: 9/10)

Though this adopted the requisite language of free trade, in the negotiations over IPRs the prioritised discourse was not to be of development or technological transfer, but of the rights accorded to owners of (intellectual) property.

Despite the failure to move the early negotiations firmly in this direction, the developing states fought on, with India declaring that a number of GATT principles such as most-favoured nation and national treatment could not apply to IPRs 'since these obligations were related to goods and not to the rights of persons' (GATT 1989: 2). Such a contention struck at the heart of the arguments mobilised by the US and other developed state negotiating teams and was immediately rebuffed. For this group the question of whether intellectual property was property was no longer open to dispute. Indeed, as I have noted in the previous chapter, the idea that property in things might actually not be a useful model for knowledge is denied forcefully by the current justificatory schemata of IPRs. Had India's contention not been sidelined, the ground on which the developed states wished to negotiate would have proved rather unstable. Through the submission of a large number of multiple drafts from the developed states, differing in detail not substance, such arguments were relegated to the minority of texts to be considered by the negotiating committee – in a sense they were 'talked out', leaving the majority of drafts representing the developed states' position (within the set agenda of possible outcomes).

Once it was 'accepted' that the GATT principles were relevant to IPRs, the developing states moved in a different direction, to argue for an expansion of these principles to include 'the balance between rights and obligations, general interest, non-reciprocity, special and differential treatment, and the freedom of each country to determine the scope and level of protection' (GATT 1990a: 12). This cumulated in a draft text being submitted by fourteen developing countries (Argentina, Brazil, Chile, China, Columbia, Cuba, Egypt, India, Nigeria, Pakistan, Peru, Tanzania, Uruguay and Zimbabwe) during 1990. This text recognised the problem of counterfeit goods and included measures to address this issue. However, the second, more controversial section stressed that

> public-policy objectives underlying national systems for the protection of intellectual property, including those of development, transfer of technology and public interest, should be fully recognised and a maximum of flexibility be allowed for least developed countries in the application of this agreement. All states should have the sovereign right to ensure a proper balance between the rights and obligations of intellectual property rights holders.
> (GATT 1990b: 9)

And while this recognised that protection could be agreed in most areas, the Chilean team further argued that as not all these matters were trade-related, the TRIPs agreement should be administered outside the GATT system, staying with WIPO or a new body.

Nevertheless, late in 1990 the agenda of an agreement prioritising ownership rights had been essentially set in place, leaving only the details and concessionary delays of implementation by the developing (and ex-communist) states to be ironed out. The developing states were still expressing concern that the negotiations continued to treat IPRs exclusively as a commercial matter while insufficient account was being taken of national development priorities (GATT 1990c: 5). However, by this point the battle had been lost, with only sectoral concessions left to hold out for. In the end the staged dismantling of the Multi-Fibre Arrangement which benefits a number of developing states' textile and clothing sectors (by allowing market access to the previously protected markets of the developed states) may have played a role in securing their accession to the TRIPs agreement. If so, this horse-trading could in the end be more costly than the developing states' negotiators may have expected. The short-term gains that were secured will pale once the TRIPs agreement comes into full effect. Essentially the developing states have received concessions for the industries of yesterday while the resources and technologies of tomorrow remain in the hands of the developed states.

The knowledge structure has produced a discourse centred on the paradigm of property and theft, where the private rights of the intellectual property owner are given priority. Differences in national economies and their levels of development make it unlikely that the same protection afforded to intellectual property argued for by the developed states will benefit all signatories in the same manner or to the same extent (Primo Braga 1989: 251–258). Thus, though the broad argument of the developed states' negotiators and governments is that the TRIPs agreement will support and further development in the developing states, this is by no means certain. While the present agenda seems firmly in place, future challenges rooted in developmental issues may well arise if the proposed benefits of the protection of intellectual property fail to materialise. Thus, emergent contradictions between the knowledge structural view of the issues of IPRs and the development outcomes will be a site of contestation for IPRs within the WTO in coming years.

The linking of IPRs to developmental benefits has been supported by a number of economic studies (for instance see Gould and Gruben 1996; Mansfield 1988; Park and Ginarte 1997), and I will return to this issue in the following chapter. Here it is important to note that the TRIPs agreement will only be honoured in the sense of being upheld through enforcement as well as legislation if the promised benefits appear in one form or another. Debates about the success or otherwise of TRIPs will be less likely to be conducted in the realm of crude trade figures but more likely to be concerned with the sorts of knowledge that are being traded and protected. Though 'TRIPs is a concrete legal reality [and] represents hard law in every sense' (Drahos 1997: 201), there are a number of responses that developing states may make other than merely complying with both the spirit and letter of the agreement. It is in these strategies that further shifts and methods of resistance may emerge. Drahos discusses a number of ways developing states could react to TRIPs ranging from non-compliance, which is fraught with problems within a regime governed by the overarching dispute settlement process of the WTO, to the setting up of a TRIPs monitoring group to make transparent the costs to developing states of the agreement. The latter would enable TRIPs to be challenged on the basis of its own principles, if the predicted development inequalities of IPR protection did emerge as expected by its critics.

The most intriguing method of resistance suggested by Drahos, however, is what he refers to as the 'hard law strategy'. Here, allowing that much indigenous knowledge in the developing world (especially the resources that the bio-technological industry are increasingly interested in) is not easily covered by current IPR legislative standards, he suggests a co-ordinated development of *sui generis* IPR laws which could be drafted to benefit the developing states, rather than those seeking such resources. As he notes, the creation of '*sui generis* regimes has been a strategy employed with great success by the U.S. to protect its own industries' and therefore holds a promise for developing states. Importantly the 'strategy is also perfectly consistent with [the] existing intellectual property convention' of the TRIPs agreement (Drahos 1997: 209–211). In a sense this strategy is an immanent critique allied to the dominant knowledge structural agenda. It requires the developing states to enact their own enclosures before they are imposed from elsewhere. This emergence of a separate but compatible regime would establish a measure of countervailing power to the dominant knowledge-owning corporations in developed states. However, it is also an acceptance of the logic of the agenda set by the knowledge structure. But, as I noted in the previous chapter, even those who are looking for workable alternatives to intellectual property are being forced to incorporate its structures into their resistance strategies. In this sense the knowledge structure continues to contain the debates within certain acceptable alternatives.

Therefore, at this point in time, it seems that by ensuring that a settlement has been concluded which privileges the private over the public, and establishes a mechanism for appropriating more of the public realm through the mechanism of trade-relatedness, some form of new 'enclosures' has been underwritten – whether this is undertaken by the developed or developing states. Those in a position to easily exploit the public/social knowledge available in the developing states, under the TRIPs agreement have seen their interests, their benefit, enhanced at the cost of the continued social availability (or at least potential availability) of such knowledge in the public realm. Thus, currently the global knowledge commons are being circumscribed, not so much by the technology that makes such appropriation possible, but crucially by the legal construction of knowledge as ownable. It is not the material advance of technology that is causing this enclosure (though it is a contributing condition), but rather the construction of a scarcity in intellectual property with the explicit intention of rewarding the legally constituted owners of such property.

Within these debates the justificatory schemata used to construct intellectual property in the first place will be subject to criticism, as not reflecting the real experience of knowledge workers or creators. But it will also be used to defend TRIPs on the basis of the need to conceive of intellectual property in this manner to ensure that individualised rights are protected. If the pundits of the Internet are correct, and at this time the jury is still out, the very notion of intellectual property may be washed away by the torrent of information transfer mediated across the information highways of the future. On the other hand, technological innovations may also produce new ways of supporting and reinforcing those rights which lie at the centre of the TRIPs agreement. In the next two chapters I explore in more detail some of the general points I have made regarding the TRIPs agreement as an international settlement over IPRs. I indicate those aspects of socio-economic relations where intellectual property broadly produces the outcomes it claims and more importantly those where it does not.

4 Sites of resistance

Patenting nature, technology and skills?

Even though the framework within which the political economy of intellectual property rights will be played out has seemingly been settled by the agreement on trade-related aspects of intellectual property rights (TRIPs), sites of resistance remain. Corporations from the developed states have managed to influence the structure of the TRIPs agreement so it broadly reflects their interests but certain aspects of intellectual property are still subject to (occasionally well-publicised) critique. In this chapter I will explore some of the problems which the crucial distinction between the public and private benefits of intellectual property presents in certain areas. This distinction is most often represented in the international dimension as a tension between the interests of the developing states and multi-national corporations. Essentially the 'difference between business interests and developing country positions is that business interests are arguing in individualist terms, while developing countries argue in communal terms' (Steidlmeier and Falbe 1994: 351). Within each justificatory schema there is some space for the recognition of communal or social claims regarding knowledge, but even if it were sufficient, this possibility is seldom allocated any real importance.

Utilising an immanent critique of the dominant justificatory schemata there are some areas where the notion of intellectual property is inappropriate and indeed may be of considerable social disutility. For instance, the questions that surround the patenting of nature and the industries to which this issue is linked – bio-technology and pharmaceuticals – are major sites of contestation which have received wide coverage. Indeed, in terms of public recognition this is the area in which the problems of intellectual property are most well known. But historically, as I noted in the discussion of TRIPs, the question of technology transfer has been the subject of the most bitter disputes concerning the international protection of intellectual property. These debates remain relevant despite their seemingly more arcane or technical nature. A further contemporary difficulty of some interest, with the precedence of the rights of owners rather than knowledge creators under TRIPs together with linked tendencies in employment law, is the struggle over who owns the skills and know-how of a company's employees. The arguments concerning these specific issue areas have a wider resonance and are relevant to many sectors which I do not explicitly discuss. First let me recap and develop the general character of possible critiques of intellectual property.

General and immanent critiques of IPRs

As I have suggested, there are three justificatory schemata which are used with differing weights in various circumstances to support the institution of property and by extension intellectual property: the instrumental; the self-developmental; and the economic schema. The instrumental is concerned to reward the effort that individuals make by allowing them property in the products of their effort: labour and effort earn property. An individual's efforts to 'improve' nature are rewarded by property in that which has been changed or enhanced by effort. Two assumptions underlie this schema: first, that an individual has ownership of his/her efforts, that the individual possesses himself/herself (they are free, owning their own labour); and second, the value added by any particular effort can be recognised. The subsequent transfer of property allows the original creator/labourer/owner to realise an appropriate monetary reward in a market society. By reversing the emphasis, the institution of a property reward encourages the efforts of individuals and is therefore instrumental in encouraging human endeavour. Rewarding productive activities promotes those activities and thus some form of economic development or advance can take place. Therefore it is claimed, no individual would work if there was not a reward linked to property in the results of such effort; without property society would atrophy.

The second stream of justifications is concerned with property as a central element in the construction and definition of self. Here, property is not the reward for effort, rather it establishes the freedom of the individual through its protection of the individual from interference. Property rights are held against the state and other individuals in society, they are the fundamental element of an individual's free existence. The ownership of property is how the individual in society is able to protect and maintain the freedom on which selfhood depends. Property is a fundamental right to which individuals, if they are free, are entitled. In this schema, property rights start with self-possession and include a web of property through which the free self is defended against illegitimate interference. Thus, only by having the right to property can the individual be free. For Marx, under capitalism, it was exactly the individual's lack of property in their creations under wage labour that produced the alienation of the worker from the productive processes. But usually under this schema, property is seen as the rights of the individual to use and dispose of their creations (and possessions) as they see fit. This right is held against forced dispossession and infringement by other members of society or the state. And furthermore the individual is defined through their property; the self is expressed through the ownership of particular property.

The last schema I identified was the more pragmatic and supple justification of property based on the efficient allocation of resources. By allowing transferability of property within a market structure, particular items will pass to those who value the property most highly in economic terms. They value a property most highly because they are able to utilise it more efficiently to produce further economic goods, and they can maximise the return on an investment. The transfer of property supports such economic growth and expansion of social welfare by maximising productivity and efficiency. The competition to secure resources (defined as property) in a market ensures that the most efficient users are able to secure productive resources, because they can afford to pay most. All economic actors are forced to continually enhance their efficiency and productivity to enable them to compete for these scarce and expensive resources. In this model of the economy, only by becoming more efficient can under-performing producers secure more resources to expand their operations in the face of competition. Interestingly, when this schema is deployed for knowledge, the monopoly rights accorded by intellectual property are not compared to the problems that monopolies cause in other markets. The schema assures us that in most cases, the overall effect of the competition for property resources is the enhancement of efficiency in resource use, and therefore growth with the expansion of aggregate socio-economic utility. Rather than suggesting that there is some moral imperative to recognising property rights, the economic justification is based on the consequences of its recognition, the increase in overall social utility through the promotion of efficient and productive activities.

In the realm of intellectual property, these three schemata can be critiqued on the basis of their general claim for a workable analogy between owning things and 'owning' knowledge, or on the basis of their own criteria; that for intellectual property the outcome is not what would be expected from their prescriptions. In this gap between words and deeds there is a space to develop an immanent critique of each schema which avoids the possible counter-criticism of the imposition of irrelevant criteria. However, if not handled carefully, this can lapse into what Robert Cox terms a problem-solving approach. This would limit any engagement with the issue of intellectual property's salience and would only be concerned with amending legislative structures to reflect the chosen schema more clearly. Much of the debate regarding economic justifications of intellectual property revolves around this very issue – how can the law be structured to maximise the efficiency of transfer of IPRs in a particular market? A critical approach requires that the whole analogous treatment of property and intellectual property be questioned. An immanent critique is useful as it reveals the major problems which the knowledge structural settlement around intellectual property has attempted to obscure. A critical approach needs to assess why these problems recur and what plausible alternatives could offer a different settlement for intellectual property.

All three justificatory schemata have problems in dealing with intellectual property if their stipulations are taken seriously, rather than cynically used as a mask for the expansion and reinforcement of the rights of knowledge owners (corporate and otherwise). For the instrumental justification we might ask: is there a just connection between the magnitude of individual effort and the reward that is allocated through the institution of intellectual property? And, does property really act as a stimulus for innovation and creation of knowledge resources, or as an impediment in some circumstances? Given the self-developmental justification's concentration on the protection that (intellectual) property offers to the self, how much protection to the individual does intellectual property offer? Of the three schemata the economic justification is most robust because its claims are based on a much wider and broadly accepted ideology. In this schema, IPRs are subsumed within the familiar language and symbols of liberalism, with all the advantages that familiarity brings (Burch 1995: 229). It also allows for its own modification by recognising cases of market failure to be outside the normal property regime. These few instances enable the schema to rid itself of cases which are easily recognisable as anomalous and by doing so strengthen its ability to support the rest of intellectual property relations. For this schema the central question must be: does intellectual property support the expansion of a *generalised* economic welfare?

One of the main reasons for the rise of intellectual property as an area of political interest has been the widely posited emergence of an information society at both national and global levels. Indeed, the US Congress Office of Technology Assessment (OTA) went as far as to assert that

> intellectual property policy can no longer be separated from other policy concerns. Because information is, in fact, central to most activities, decisions about intellectual property law may be decisions about the distribution of wealth and social status. Furthermore, given the unlimited scope of the new technologies and growing trade in information-based products and services, U.S. intellectual property policy is now inextricably tied to international affairs.
>
> (quoted in Vaver 1990: 116)

As the OTA correctly surmise, in an age that might be characterised as an information society the issues that surround intellectual property law will no longer be an obscure subject of interest only to specialists. More importantly neither is it only of concern in America or the developed states – intellectual property is now a global issue.

Continual innovation has become a crucial element in the maximisation of profit, the speed of competition and effective obsolescence has quickened, the information or knowledge component of economic development is expanding. The important difference between the recent emergence of the 'commodity production of innovation and the commodity production of physical objects . . . [is] in the production of knowledge the main raw material is knowledge itself' (Morris-Suzuki 1988: 79). But where does this knowledge come from? Morris-Suzuki contends that:

> Whereas the knowledge which comes out of this commercial production process is the private property of the corporation, fenced around with monopoly barriers which endow it with market value, the knowledge which goes in as raw material is mostly social knowledge, produced and owned jointly by society as a whole . . . Information capitalism, therefore, not only exploits the labour of those directly employed by corporations, but also depends . . . on the indirect exploitation of the labour of everyone involved in the maintenance, transmission and expansion of social knowledge . . . in the end, everybody.
>
> (ibid.: 80–81)

For the instrumental justification the character of knowledge prior to its use as a resource would have to exist unencumbered by the labour-related property of others. However, social knowledge is not a natural resource existing without any effort or maintenance, it is the product of social reproduction. Though Morris-Suzuki's assertion may be overdrawn, it clearly opens up the problem of knowledge inputs and their relation to the justificatory schemata of IPRs.

The history of human development 'is a history of progressive appropriation, and indeed also of the continuing invention of new things (such as copyrights) that might be appropriated' (Minogue 1980: 12). For IPRs the invention of new things involves the expansion of intellectual property's coverage or legal definition. The line between what can be appropriated and what cannot is one that is continually being repositioned. Therefore what counts as the social reproduction of knowledge is also redefined to reflect the private sector's current interests in knowledge resources and processes. New technologies that enable the appropriation of certain knowledge play a major role in these moves. Social reproduction produces a form of passive knowledge which may have little immediate effect on particular economic transactions. The distinction between basic and applied science for instance can be broadly characterised as the difference between passive and active intellectual property. However, as knowledge is utilised in innovations and commercial inventions, so it crosses the line from being passive to being active and becomes the subject of appropriation strategies.

In Chapter 2 I noted that it is impracticable to try and disaggregate the components of any particular knowledge object to allocate reward on a proportionate basis between its various contributors. Currently intellectual property laws do the exact reverse, they allocate all the reward to the most recent manifestation of the development of an idea. In this they disregard the precursors and the social element of the knowledge object, recognising only the innovative aspect and according the most recent addition full property rights.[1] There is a complete lack of proportionality between effort and reward if immediate labour desert is taken to be the basis on which property is produced. This disproportionality is one way in which the enclosure of knowledge takes place – even if such resources remain in many cases still socially available for other unconnected uses. The claim for labour desert can be modified to allow that intellectual property is accorded to the individual having 'greatest possible interest' rather than exclusive interest. Then other stakeholders might also have rights of access and rights against the actions of the intellectual property owner regarding the property in certain circumstances. This might make the claims of the instrumentalist position easier to defend and highlights the issue of duration of IPRs, the length that social knowledge can be (partially) removed from the pool. Though it may be just that a knowledge creator's rights to benefit should be protected for some time from the date of their invention, long-term protection is unlikely to serve the needs of other stakeholders.

The length of this period of protection then becomes subject to political and ethical arguments. Therefore, as Robert Nozick suggests:

> a known inventor drastically lessens the chances of actual independent invention. For persons who know of an invention usually will not try to reinvent it, and the notion of independent discovery would be murky at best. Yet, we

may assume that in the absence of the original invention, sometime later someone else would have come up with it. This suggests placing a time limit on patents, as a rough rule of thumb to approximate how long it would have taken, in the absence of knowledge of the invention, for independent discovery.

(1974: 182)

Even this compromise requires some judgement about the level of social knowledge in any particular subject of patent. The greater availability of social knowledge, the quicker someone else would come up with the idea, the less time should elapse before the knowledge object ceases to be property. Since the history of technology and science is full of examples of almost simultaneous discovery or invention, this may actually be an argument for shorter protection than might be supposed. When parallel discovery might have taken place, intellectual property impedes the rights of those who would also have made the innovative step, but lagged (for all sorts of reasons) behind the actual innovator. But, while there would be an initial maldistribution of reward, such disproportionately would expire once the duration of the IPR was complete. Social utility would be served by ensuring that new ideas and innovations would be explored and refined, and in any case such knowledge objects would be returned to the social pool at a specified time. The instrumental justification stresses the encouragement of the expansion of new knowledge as a contribution to the expansion of social utility. If intellectual property fails to produce this turn of events, or some other social benefit is preferred, the instrumental justificatory schema would be revealed as a mask for some other interest.

Turning to the self-developmental schema, its central claim is that man can only be free if property is enjoyed in those things that define and support the self. This links with the instrumental justification in that it requires that individuals should be sovereign, owning themselves. Drawing the analogy with sovereign territoriality Aoki suggests that this assertion of sovereignty might be subject to the same problems that have been expressed *vis-à-vis* the state and its sovereignty (Aoki 1996: 1314ff.). In the case of intellectual property this encompasses privacy and its technological invasion (including industrial espionage and trade secrets) as well as the use by others of the knowledge work and products by which the individual expresses self-hood. The moral right of copyright owners (which resonates with this schema) has been compromised in the TRIPs agreement's framework. Indeed, one of the key elements of post-TRIPs intellectual property is its total alienability: to be trade related intellectual property must be tradable, which is to say it must be possible to fully detach these rights from the originator of the knowledge object. While owners have the right to charge rents for use, they must also be able to transfer the property itself to which such a right is attached. Given this requirement, intellectual property may not quite produce the effects on which it is predicated by the self-developmental justificatory schema.

Here the classic objections of Marxist political economy, centred on the issue of wage labour and alienation, play a major role in addressing the question of the schema's efficacy. If the self is to be expressed through the ownership of (intellectual) property, how does this square with the actual mechanisms and outcomes that

IPRs produce in the interactions between individuals under the structures of contemporary economic organisation? If knowledge workers do not retain the rights over the subject matter of their work, does this impact on their freedom and selfhood, is this loss of control an invasion of the self, the very thing that (intellectual) property is supposed to preclude? Unsurprisingly, though sometimes hinted at, the use of the self-development justification has not been as widespread as the others in the discussions and celebrations of the arrival of the knowledge worker and the information society.

Finally, when examining the economic justifications of intellectual property the problems are easily laid out, and are similar to those that beset the instrumental justification. Does the institution of intellectual property promote and further social utility within contemporary market relations? One of the strengths of the economic justification is the allowance that market failure might require non-market solutions – exceptions are dealt with outside the schema. Therefore, when looking at economic justifications it may make more sense to take a more aggregated approach to the issue. Rather than asking in particular cases whether there has been a problem, given the international nature of the TRIPs settlement, I will explore whether social utility on the global scale has been served by IPRs. In this chapter this will be deliberated mainly in the discussion of economic growth and technological transfer.

At its most basic the problem for the economic schema is that 'subjecting new inventions to monopoly control restricts their use and thereby reduces the social benefits' of their advances (Quaedvlieg 1992: 384). This is a problem only to the extent of the duration of the protection allowed to particular innovative products, and therefore the longer the period, the more serious the objection becomes. Monopoly rights may also encourage rent-seeking behaviour by their owners, not further innovations: once the ownership of an intellectual property has been secured, the behaviour of owners may produce distortions in the pattern of economic activity. On the other hand, this can be conceived as a cost-benefit relation, the costs of disruption offset by the general and long-term enhancement of economic activities and development. In copyright economic arguments concerning the furtherment or detriment of social utility and welfare have been indecisive, leaving it to be assessed on the basis of the consequences expected by the other schema. In patents, however, as I will explore below, there are robust arguments that suggest IPRs have had a negative role in technology transfer and the economic development of poorer states. A reinstatement of differential protection regimes based on some assessment of the level of economic development might therefore seem warranted, despite the TRIPs agreement's explicit disavowal of this approach.

All these questions could merely produce a problem-solving strategy: 'yes, there are problems but each set of issues indicates some amendments and adjustments which could be made which would allow the globalised settlement to produce the sorts of outcomes expected'. However, as these problems are explored the implicit foundational problem will emerge – the inappropriate nature of the analogy between property in materially existing objects and knowledge. The rights which are accorded to material property owners need to be so distorted to fit 'owners' of knowledge as to produce severely problematic outcomes. At the root of all other questions in a political economy of intellectual property is the question of whether the products of the intellect can be considered property at all. It is an ideological issue to treat knowledge this way, the role of the knowledge structure is central to ensuring that knowledge can be *conventionally* subjected to the rigour of property relations. If this characterisation of knowledge is not self-evident (or 'natural'), then the knowledge structure plays an important role in the political economy of IPRs. It delimits discussions to the different justificatory regimes and traditions without accepting that there may be a further alternative, which is that there is no *overall* justification for intellectual property *qua* property. This alternative, that property in knowledge cannot be merely analogously treated as property is based on the stark and simple assertion that knowledge does not conform to an understanding of property that is acceptable.

Some problems with intellectual property

In the rest of this chapter I shall look at some serious problems with the use of intellectual property as a characterisation of knowledge. In the main I deal with patent-related problems, but this is not to suggest that copyright suffers no shortcomings. And though in places I will be concerned to note some possible positive effects of the global institutionalisation of intellectual property, for the most part I will leave the advantages of seeing knowledge as property to the next chapter when I consider copyright at some length.

There are two principal issues that need to be examined when intellectual property is used to structure scientific knowledge of nature and its commercial use. Formally, the granting of biotechnological and pharmaceutical patents has been settled by the TRIPs agreement. But, if this knowledge is discovered, which is to say it exists in some form in nature already, it cannot conform to the strictures of patent law (especially newness and non-obviousness), in any real sense. Additionally, what effects do IPRs have on the enlargement of the pool of scientific knowledge? Scientific endeavour during this century has largely taken place through a public realm of knowledge dissemination and transfer. But, within the scientific community there is increasing concern regarding the treatment of innovative scientific results as intellectual property rather than communicable aspects of a general social sphere of scientific knowledge.

Pharmaceuticals

The international pharmaceutical and biotechnology industries are emblematic of the public/private issue in the realm of intellectual property. Demands for the punishment of intellectual 'piracy' by drugs companies have continually come up against 'public goods' arguments in developing states. Some of these states have balked at recognising the intellectual property of transnational drug companies when the cost has been perceived as the health and safety of their citizens

(Chaudhry and Walsh 1995). In many developing states the public interest aspect of the patent's bargain with private rights carries greater weight due to problems of poverty and lack of health care resources. The low cost of 'pirated' generic drugs, while representing a social utility to the developing states, is in the logic of patents a free-rider problem for developed state pharmaceutical companies. States which do not protect drugs' patents are benefiting from the knowledge generated in the developed states while short-circuiting the reward for such innovations. Thus, 'pharmaceutical companies complain that their property is effectively being stolen in developing countries. Yet that "property" is not even recognised as property' in jurisdictions without the requisite legal framework (Henderson 1997: 660). But this isn't necessarily a total denial of the legitimacy of intellectual property, just its use in the field of pharmaceuticals. The over-riding issue for developing states is the cost of access to currently available drugs.

Though the Indian state acted, prior to the TRIPs agreement to enhance IPR protection in the field of computer software, the patenting of pharmaceuticals is an area where there remains some distance between the 'needs' of drug manufacturers and the 'needs' perceived by Indian governments. Drugs 'developed overseas are frequently reverse engineered in India at a fraction of the cost [and] the cost of drugs in India are among the lowest in the world', though there is likely to be a substantial change once TRIPs has been fully implemented (Henderson 1997: 661). For Indian companies to continue to operate in a patent-free market as they have done in the past would open the state up to sanctions under the WTO's dispute settlement mechanism. Side-stepping this problem, when the Indian Defence Institute of Physiology and Allied Sciences developed Neem-based contraceptives which appeal to a wide Indian market, the Institute transferred the process technology to two domestic drug companies at no cost to scale up for sale (Jayaraman 1995). Given the original research that this product is based on, there can be no claims of patent infringement from non-Indian drugs companies. Such a strategy will only be possible where India can develop its own drugs and where they are not regarded as possibilities for export to developed markets. Where such drugs are similar to those available elsewhere it should be recalled that under TRIPs the onus will be on Indian companies to prove they have not breached process patents.

Like China which introduced pharmaceutical patents in 1993, India will likely experience a rise in the cost of drugs. And, if current patterns of distribution, with the majority of patents held by overseas patentees, are mirrored in drug-related applications then it is likely that this price rise will see a transfer of funds out of the India to the developed states. Unless new drugs are more efficient (cost to cure) there will be decline in the health levels of the Indian population. Utilising the instrumental justificatory schema, such protection allows drug companies to recover their costs of discovery and therefore encourages further research. Industry spokesmen routinely dispute the claims regarding price rises under patent protection (citing the price-dampening effects of competition) and note the lack of availability of many useful drugs and treatments in states which lack adequate protection. Additionally, they argue that due to the short period of patent protection, patent drugs are only a small part of the market, without piracy new cures would come down in price once a fair reward had been recovered. However, those states which have introduced intellectual property protection for pharmaceuticals have an average cost of drugs up to ten times as high as states which continue to allow patent infringement by generic drug producers.

Indian intransigence is seen as a major problem by the international pharmaceutical companies and so it was to be expected that the first decision to be brought by a panel of the WTO for the TRIPs agreement involved the Indian failure to provide in its law transitory mechanisms for the recognition of exclusive distribution rights while products (in this case pharmaceuticals) remained unpatentable (Macdonald-Brown and Ferera 1998). Though this mechanism allows protection for IPRs in the interim before full accession, India was unable to successfully argue that these transitory mechanism were also amenable to some transitory delay. The Indian government is required to change domestic law, despite having failed twice to do so prior to the panel ruling. At the time of writing the issue remains unresolved, though it seems likely that in the near future some (though likely minimalist) form of pharmaceutical patent protection will be legislated for.

Significantly, it is not always the case that drugs which come off-patent, allowing the possible entry of generic competitors to the market, are immediately subject to competition and a reduction in price. To some extent, as might be expected, generic competition is concentrated on those drugs which are large revenue-producing products (Bae 1997; Garrett 1997a). But it is also possible to retain market dominance after patent-end through the use of strongly branded products and some physician conservatism regarding the recommendation of new generic drugs. Indeed, in the past, it has not necessarily been the first to market or first to patent that has led to market domination. In the case of Zantac, it was 'a triumph not of research (it arrived five years behind SmithKline Beckman's Tagamet) but of marketing' (*The Economist* 1997a). Thus, despite claims for the centrality of the intellectual property regime to a drug's success and profitability (which supports further developments), there are other factors which may support the company's reward. The key problem remains the higher the cost supported by patents, the less patients in developing states will benefit from any drug. While the social utility function of patents may be served in the developed states, the social utility of denying life-saving drugs to those in poor countries would be a little more difficult to sustain as an argument for IPRs. The crux of the dispute is the rights of pharmaceutical companies, their shareholders, and the societies in which they operate, against the social or public benefit of cheap drugs in the developing world. Which social or public interest is to be allowed more weight – innovation or health?

Currently, under the TRIPs agreement, the social utility of innovative activity is preferred over the social utility of widespread availability, it is more useful to encourage innovations than immediate use in developing states. This distinction is dissolved over time, but remains effective while the patent is valid. Whereas in other areas of patent law the delay of public use or benefit is reflected in the narrower diffusion of one or another productive process, in pharmaceuticals the delay in availability while a labour-desert reward is earned is counted not through a brake on productive activities but through the continuing death and illness of the poor. The rationing inherent in the distributional limit effected by patent does not inhibit further advances but rather limits the possibility of recovery from illness of those unable to access to certain patented drugs. Given the relative poverty levels in developing states, and the prices that would be demanded for drugs under a full patent system, the issue is not so much the reward to labour, but more the entitle-ment to health. Thus though the means to alleviate health problems may exist within the global system, due to the economic structure in which such cures would be delivered, avoidable health problems continue for want of the economic means to address them.[2] Under the previous pragmatic differentiated system this problem was partly alleviated by 'piracy', now under a homogenised global TRIPs settlement there is a lot less room for the developing states to manoeuvre.

Only by conceiving of the public benefit as exclusively the promotion of innovation can pharmaceutical patents appeal to an instrumental justification. To conceive of the public interest as the right to health undermines the arguments the drugs companies put forward. Until the TRIPs agreement there was a *de facto* dual system in operation that recognised different views of the public benefits from patenting pharmaceuticals. Under TRIPs the recognition of this duality is dismantled by Article 8's provision that while there can be provisions for public health within national legislations, these *cannot* be contrary to the stipulations in the rest of the agreement. Effectively, this has taken away the possibility for a dual system, no longer will a blind eye be turned to 'theft'. The discourse has been narrowed from one where the health of developing states' populations might be considered an element in assessing the suitability of intellectual property legislation, to one in which only the morality of 'piracy' and 'theft' is discussed. There is no longer a space in policy discussion for the reasons which underlie such differences in the recognition of drug patents, it is theft and that is it all. But, a discourse of theft is a double-edged sword.

Biotechnology

If biotechnology is the 'use of biological organisms for commercial ends', then the industry is 'almost as old as human civilisation' (Fransman 1994: 42). It is likely that most if not all plants and animals farmed commercially are the result of some form of selective breeding. Though there have been major scientific advances in the industry, most importantly 'genetic engineering', these have been more about process and technique than in the actual logic of combining strains for their particular strengths, or cross-breeding for specific traits: as John Sanders, a patent counsel notes, 'Biotechnology in agriculture does in many cases what plant breeding has done for several thousand years, but does it by a well-thought-out, rather than random, process' (quoted in Thayer 1995). In essence the biotechnology industry takes traditional methods of crop and breed manipulation – animal and plant husbandry – and makes them more efficient, more controllable, and by working at the micro biological level, swifter in execution. It has also established the possibility of genetically linking quite separate species to produce previously unthinkable characteristics in plant varieties. As with other industries that have increased the informational content of their procedures, companies have sought to protect their valuable knowledge resources as intellectual property. While in the past the discussions about pharmaceuticals have been concerned with the issue of the price and distributional effects of IPRs, as biotechnology has sought new resources to use, an additional question has arisen: do the natural resources that are being patented belong to anyone previously, are they being 'enclosed'?

Where DNA-derived products are using DNA strands 'discovered' in developing states' population, this may represent a two-fold enclosure, both of traditional medicines/processes and of actual bio-chemical raw materials (Wilkie 1995). These developments are the result of the increased centralisation of the medical and biotechnological processes of modification. As cross-breeding and manipulation have become more skill and capital-intensive, these processes have become the realm not of individual farmers working through slow and traditional methods of husbandry but rather a scientific intervention at a more molecular level. To substantiate the investment of considerable knowledge and capital resources a return is required in a market-organised sector. However, without the scientific breakthroughs which appeared in the scientific community's pool of socialised knowledge, a biotechnological approach to genetic manipulation could not have been attempted. The contradiction between the attempt to patent, producing a scarcity of knowledge and the free flow of this knowledge through traditional practices has fed into the debate regarding intellectual property in this area.

There are a number of ways that biotechnology is affecting the international political economy. The modification of plants may allow crops previously limited to certain climates to be grown in developed states. This may produce changes in the geographical distribution of cash crops, and their terms of trade, which may result in poorer states' effective climatic comparative advantage being eroded. There is the added possibility of a biotechnology gap opening up, developing states' products may no longer be able to compete with genetically engineered and 'superior' products available in developed states' markets. But equally, other modifications may aid developing states' agricultural sectors by producing new infestation-resistant strains, and 'there is no inherent technological reason why biotechnology should not benefit the poor' (Fransman 1994: 50). However, with the ability to patent discoveries and innovations alongside the need for commercial firms both to recover outlays and maximise profits, access to these new resources may actually be limited through the operation of the market. Though many previous agricultural breakthroughs were made in public institutions, such as universities and national or international research centres, now that these efforts are moving into the private realm, the diffusion of such advances will likely be slowed by both the logic and economics of intellectual property protection.

Central to the intellectual property issues with which I am concerned is the location and capture of natural resources by biotechnology companies, what is sometime referred to as bio-prospecting. As I noted, the discourse of theft might be double-edged for the biotechnology and pharmaceutical industry, given their desire to find new resources in nature. Where bio-prospecting discovers new natural compounds or plant varieties, under the TRIPs agreement these 'newly discovered' bio-resources can be appropriated and removed from the public realm. This removal will also likely be geographic as the biotechnology industry is centralised in the developed states. The UPOV-related provisions within the TRIPs agreement allow biotechnological resources to be patented, and once they are patented in one jurisdiction, it becomes difficult for the patent to be denied elsewhere. This removal, patenting and return-as-product process is regarded by many in the developing states as a theft of their natural resources.

Perhaps the best-known example of the attempt to patent a naturally occurring substance is the case of the Neem tree in India (Shiva and Holla-Bhar 1993; Shiva 1996). At the centre of this dispute is the patenting in the US of various chemical elements essential to 'traditional' processes for exploiting the product of the Neem tree. Traditionally in rural India the Neem tree and its derivatives have been used medicinally, as toiletries, as contraception and various other social roles such as timber, food and as fuel. A number of US (and Japanese) multinationals have taken out patents (though not in India due to the current limitation of pharmaceutical patents mentioned above), on some of these uses and the chemical descriptions of the oil and derivative Neem products. Under TRIPs this protection will be extended to India to ensure that the trade in these products is not disrupted by the 'theft' of the intellectual property embodied within them. W.R. Grace & Co. has gone as far as establishing processing plants in India and is seeking to expand its market share based on Neem-derived products and derivatives despite the current lack of patent protection (which itself undermines their position regarding the need for patents). The question on which resistance to this particular instance, and more widely against the incorporation of IPRs into the WTO rests, is whether the company has actually innovated in any way or has merely westernised traditional methods.

Resistance has been widely evident among traditional users and local manufacturers who recognise a threat to their traditional knowledge base in such patent protection. Resistance is not limited to Indian farmers, however. A coalition of over 200 aid groups have been lobbying the US Patents and Trademarks Office to withdraw Neem tree derivative patents. In preparation for the limitation of the market for Neem products it expects with patenting, 'Grace [is] prepared to pay up to $300 per tonne of Neem seeds' to control its raw material. Thus 'what used to be a free resource has now become a highly priced one', causing Indian farmers considerable problems and pushing them towards a eventual reliance on Grace's 're-engineered' Neem seed (Dickson and Jayaraman 1995). This and other connected issues have not been resolved but what is of interest is even the possibility that pharmaceutical companies can seek to establish intellectual property in knowledge and natural resources which have a widespread social currency. This has led to the Convention on Biodiversity Conservation supporting a position where traditional or farmers' seeds, which 'also embody a significant intellectual contribution by third world farmers' over years of cross-fertilisation, might be recognised as a form of intellectual property. This proposes that the 'seeds sold by transnational corporations can no longer be regarded as the only ones embodying an intellectual contribution' (Shiva 1996: 1622). The difficulty here is that under intellectual property law IPRs are accorded to legally constituted individuals or bodies not social groups.

Social groups, on the other hand, are exactly the types of owners who might be identified for naturally occurring resources and thus the raw materials required by the biotechnology industry. Shiva sums up the issue by noting that

> [after] centuries of the gene-rich south having contributed biological resources freely to the north, third world governments are no longer willing to have biological wealth taken for free and sold back at exorbitant prices to the third world as 'improved' seeds and packaged drugs. From the third world viewpoint, it is considered highly unjust that the South's Bio-diversity be treated as the 'common heritage of mankind' and the return flow of biological commodities be patented as the private property of northern corporations.
>
> (1996: 1623)

Under the instrumental justificatory schema, if there has been an improvement, then the reward for labour is in the property produced by these improvements. The notion of a communal ownership of resources dropped out of property law in the seventeenth century and as a result does not appear in the analogous con-struction of intellectual property. It is this absence of communal ownership that both allows bio-prospecting related 'theft' and sparks the critics' resistance. The current intellectual property regime recognises the rights of individuals (those who fulfil the authorial function) but does not recognise the intellectual contribution made by communities over time. Thus, resistance to the notion of plant patents has revolved round the issue of farmers' rights (Shiva 1996: 1631). While the WTO recognises that farmers have certain privileges regarding the self-seeding and natural reproduction of seeds, these are not rights that allow resale or alienation of such products where they run parallel to products that are protected as intellectual property. Given that over 70 per cent of seed supply in India comes from farmers' sale of their reproduced seeds, the imposition of property rights in varieties would change the nature of the market significantly.

One possible resistance strategy is to widen property rights to include the raw materials of the biotechnology sector. If this approach was followed, rather than try to alleviate the social costs of intellectual property in biotechnological resources, social groups would claim rents within the broad system which is in place. However, this contradicts the United Nations Food and Agriculture Organisation's traditional position that these resources are the 'common heritage of mankind' and should be available without restriction. As Shiva has pointed out, this is all very well, but not when such a freedom is then removed once the resources become trade related. The approach of widening the coverage of property rights would hope to ensure that biotechnology companies pay a rent for their natural inputs. Within current intellectual property practice (and its justifications) a legally constituted owner would need to be recognised but this could proceed in a similar way to the development of tradable pollution rights. However, this then requires the law to make a distinction between traditional users who should still be able to conduct seed sales or other activities, and users who wish to develop or innovate on the basis of these resources. This would also be difficult given that bio-prospecting itself can sometime be undertaken by developing states' nationals (*Pacific News Bulletin* 1995). Equally, provisions to control bio-prospecting would need to exclude indigenous population traditional harvesting and husbandry activities. Thus, the indigenous knowledge encapsulated in bio-diversity would need to be separated from bio-diversity itself. The problem for these sorts of approaches is that intellectual property necessarily constructs a scarcity in knowledge, whereas bio-diversity supporting rights would require them to be non-exclusive, and thus not intellectual property as currently understood.

Where patent drugs are concerned, the pharmaceutical companies see the lack of patents as encouraging theft but when it comes to the need to secure the resources of nature that are needed by their biotechnological arms, the absence of patents in nature works to their advantage. This disjuncture suggests that the TRIPs mechanism is drafted in such a way that the developed states' companies rights are given priority over the social (or even human) rights of those who live in the areas where 90 per cent of biotechnological related resources are located. Accusations of colonialism and imperialism are common currency in the criticisms of bio-prospecting and biotechnology, and the demands to secure a price for these resources has taken on a radical political hue. Concerns regarding biotechnology have not been limited to developing states' populations and governments, however. In 1998 Monsanto undertook a major advertising campaign (including web-site addresses for Friends of the Earth, Greenpeace and Food for our Future, perhaps seen as 'acceptable' critics) which while recognising that there 'are many views of biotechnology', centred on the ability of genetically modified crops to reduce the need for chemical fertilisers and herbicides. However, the view that these resources might be stolen was not one of the concerns the campaign sought to address, the issue is kept off Monsanto's agenda entirely. One of the reasons that biotechnology attorney Douglas Olson gives for the continuing support offered by venture capitalists to the sector is that patent protection 'prevents big companies from coming and taking the fruits of research without paying for it' (Thayer 1995). But, on the other hand the patent regime *does* allow these companies to 'take the fruits' of traditional husbandry 'without paying' for them.

Nevertheless, the major drug and biotechnology companies claim that without intellectual property protection, they will be unable to profit from their expensively researched innovations and will be unable to continue to develop the new drugs the world needs (Mossinghoff and Bombelles 1996). This is a straightforward labour-desert argument involving a claim that over 60 per cent of new drugs would not be developed or introduced without adequate patent protection in the US. This is partly compromised by the 'tax dollars spent on biomedical research funded by the national Institutes of Health' resulting in the awarding to 'private pharma-ceutical firms exclusive rights to commercialise what amounts to hundreds of millions of dollars of free research' (Chaudhry and Walsh 1995: 89). For instance, in the third of all US patents that cite scientific papers in 1996, 75 per cent of such papers were produced through public-funded research, and only 25 per cent from industrial scientists (Hinde 1998). While companies filing these patents could justify some reward for their labour (or more accurately their employee's labour) in developing the commodity form of such knowledge, the underlying scientific knowledge itself has often been produced socially (or at least through the mediated form of the state's use of tax receipts).

The crux of this matter is the distinction contrasting private rights of exploitation and benefit, with social or public rights of availability and access. Even if the original scientific papers are still available it is unlikely that a share of the reward for their exploitation flows to the original researchers. This is complicated in biotechnology by the undoubted novelty of the emerging products, which are derived from 'free' resources. Within an instrumental justification nature has been modified and a reward has been earned, and under the economic schema, allowing intellectual property in the results has spurred on innovation and efficient use of resources. Once again, as with pharmaceuticals the problem lies with the definition of public or social interest. If the public interest is conceptualised as prioritising the incidence of innovation in developed states, then biotechnology 'with high research costs, enormous regulatory costs, and low imitation costs, offers a classic and nearly unique example of a sector in which the patent system' is of enormous benefit (Barton 1995: 611). If, on the other hand, the swift availability of such innovations, or the recognition of the rights of states to benefit from their bio-resources became part of the public interest, then the assessment of benefit offered by patents is directly compromised.

Somewhat ironically biotechnology is dependent on a broad patent awarded in 1980 to Stanley Cohen (Stanford University) and Herbert Boyer (University of California, San Francisco) which 'gave rights over any and all uses of recombinant DNA technology'. Stanford University 'which oversees the patent, has provided inexpensive, non-exclusive licenses to nearly all researchers, companies and other groups involved in biotechnology' (Thayer 1995). Despite this example, industry practitioners continue to argue that the exploitation, and thus wide availability of biotechnological innovation require exclusivity.

Scientific knowledge

The biotechnology industry wants to characterise its products as property, and therefore one of the key concerns is whether the results of manipulation are actually new and non-obvious (as patenting requires). Furthermore as genetic engineering isolated specific genes and DNA, and as these informational items (such as genes for specific aspects of development) potentially have become extremely valuable, there has been a move to secure patents. Unfortunately, the political and legal debate around this issue has been conducted in a remarkably limited manner. So for instance, in a landmark decision of the Californian Supreme Court regarding a leukaemia patient's rights to receive some of the profits from a biotechnological advance made with cells from their body the only complaint that was upheld was the breach of duty on behalf of the medical staff concerned for not telling the patient the possible uses to which removed cells might be put. The subsequent

> legal literature has devoted considerable time and space to the discussion of whether, and if then to what extent, a person who places valuable bodily substances at the disposal of medical R&D work, should participate in resulting commercial gains.
>
> (Moufang 1994: 512)

Whether such materials were actually patentable was largely ignored. Elsewhere, when the patenting of genes has been criticised this has been on the basis of the rights the individual has to their own body. In this sense the self-developmental schema is utilised to draw a limit to that which might be conceived of as intellectual property. But again as the legal debate insists, ownership implies alienability – to own something is to be able to profit from its transfer. Where such materials have been taken without a fully informed acquiescence, the problem lies not with the actual transfer but with the bio-prospectors' lack of openness. The problematic nature of patenting this material has largely become a non-question.

These resources (especially where such resources are knowledge-rich) are no longer to be held in common, as previous scientific breakthroughs this century have been. Rather, genes and other biotechnological materials are becoming property because the biotechnology industry asserts that it requires property rights in its innovations to ensure reward is allocated effectively and innovation encouraged. Thus while Dr Angus Clarke of the Institute of Medical Genetics, Cardiff argues that patenting 'is a breach of the implicit trust that this work will be for the general good of human welfare, and not for the enrichment of commercial companies' (quoted in Wilkie 1995), for the instrumental justification these two ends are not conflictual. Only by assuring profit (enrichment) of companies will the general human welfare be maximised through the support of further research. These strictures were not important while the possibilities for both reproduction and marketing of genetically based products were limited. But once technical advance had produced the means for profitable exploitation of science in the area of genetic manipulation, then the legal formulations which pervade the information economy, need also to be applied to this scientific knowledge, which swiftly became trade-related (Etzkowtiz and Webster 1995: 482–484). The knowledge structure ensures that as science is commercialised, property-based mechanisms are introduced because they are 'common sense' in market transactions.

The claim that scientific knowledge fills the criterion of patentability is, however, less than robust. In general terms a discovery of something that already exists in the realm of nature can hardly be said to have produced something that is 'new'. The discovery already existed, it was merely the case that no one had found it. Patenting discoveries rather than inventions is difficult to resolve with the normal criterion of patent. But many biotechnological patents actually cover manipulations of naturally occurring elements in ways that are not evident in their natural habitat. Thus, where natural elements are combined using scientific processes, the product of the procedure may indeed be 'new', but this then raises the question of whether the discovery is non-obvious. If any other competent practitioner using known processes could also have produced a similar product then the second criteria has not been fulfilled.

Nevertheless, patents are routinely allocated to pharmaceutical and bio-technological products that have been produced in laboratories using known methods whereby another practitioner could produce the same result. Indeed, the ability of others to duplicate the result is one of the key scientific tests of any discovery. These issues prompt a further question regarding the continued transfer of scientific knowledge around the international community of scientists.

In the scientific community there has been a move away from the free dissemination of knowledge based on the publication of findings in peer-reviewed journals. During a discussion of hierarchy and its construction among scientists, Robert Merton argues that the process (the 'Matthew effect') whereby advances, and the reputation for making them, adhere to those more well known in the field, has been enhanced by the intervention of a formalised (though extra-legal) intellectual property mechanism based on citation and referencing (Merton 1988). Essentially, this ensures that those who have already established a reputation, and are part of a team (or less formalised group) of less renown who make a further breakthrough, receive a disproportionate increase in their reputation relative to their centrality to the advance. Where Merton's argument is of interest is in his discussion of the shift in the understanding of the intellectual property which is established in these breakthroughs.

First, Merton distinguishes various coinage of reputation in science, ranging from the pinnacle of an era named after an individual (Newtonian, Freudian . . .) through prizes (Nobel, society medals) down to citation. This is built on the foundation of the open system of publication and free use and communication of scientific ideas. And as he then points out, within the 'commons of science it is structurally the case that the give and the take both work to enlarge the common resource of accessible knowledge' (Merton 1988: 620). This period of relative free circulation of scientific knowledge may only date from the early part of the twentieth century, however: from the seventeenth century to around ninety years ago, discoveries were most often made by scientists funded by companies who patented new processes for their own use and control (Silverstein 1991). With the slower pace of innovation, the delay through patent had little effect on the growth of scientific knowledge. For the individual scientist in the twentieth century the principal mechanism for the retention of intellectual property was the clear citation of others' work and the damage to reputation that can be exacted in light of the discovery of plagiarism. Thus a symbolic system is (re)produced which recognises that advances in scientific knowledge are the result of standing on the shoulders of the giants that went before.[3] Thus, for Merton the 'sole property right of scientists in their discoveries has long resided in peer recognition of it and in derivative collegial esteem'. This is an intellectual property valuing system that is *not* based on a set of marketised property relations. However, he also recognises that the encroachment of 'entrepreneurial science' will undermine this historical intellectual property settlement (Merton 1988: 623).

This encroachment stands at the centre of intellectual property disputes within the scientific community. The market organisation of knowledge distribution (and valorisation) is intended to ensure that knowledge flows to those who would value it most economically and thus ensure that society derives the maximum benefit. This argument from the economic schema is usually deployed against the notion of a centralised distribution point for knowledge (such as the state), rather than against the social organisation of science (O'Neill 1990: 602–603). Though it is important to remember that while there was no legal link between discovery and reward (mediated by intellectual property), reputation and 'theft' were closely associated. Plagiarism and the distortion of results led to a decline in reputation and this could easily impact on wealth through employability. Equally, a much cited and important breakthrough could lead to its initiator benefiting considerably through new posts, fees for further research and other rewards. Neither of these dynamics are dependent on a formalised intellectual property regime, but existed alongside an acceptance of the commonalty of scientific knowledge. And despite the argument that commons are subject to 'free-riding' and degradation from over-use, in the paradigmic case of the pre-enclosure commons there were institutions which quite efficiently governed resource allocation and usage (Frow 1996: 100). However, the knowledge structure's intervention though the logic of the economic schema removes non-property arrangements as a 'plausible' alternative in such circumstances.

There is a widespread belief that the introduction of intellectual property markets (patents, copyrights and trade secrets) into the scientific community undermines 'good practice' and the open communication on which scientific discovery is based (Macilwain 1996). The market is an inappropriate mechanism for dealing with scientific knowledge as,

> the market encourages egoism not primarily because it encourages an individual to be self-interested – it would be unrealistic not to expect individuals to act for the greater part in a self-interested manner – but rather because it defines an individual's interests in a particularly narrow fashion, most notably in terms of certain material goods.

(O'Neill 1990: 615)

The over-riding self-interest of scientist and those interested in scientific discovery might be the free flow of the knowledge that is the raw material of further work, rather than control and profit from specific knowledge items. But part of the argument for the market is the unworkability of the centralised allocation and direction of scientific endeavour and knowledge production. This presents only two possibilities, either market or command; the third organisational logic of the professions is ruled out despite its actual historical achievements, and obscured as a possible contemporary solution by the knowledge structure.

Interestingly Silverstein argues that there should be a distinction between commercial processes based on scientific discoveries and the discoveries themselves. This should be established because the patenting of discoveries has slowed innovations in the developed states which has had a considerable effect on technological competitiveness (Silverstein 1991: 302ff.). The public or social benefit of knowledge has been compromised by the awarding of patents. However, it is precisely this limitation that the bargain underpinning patents institutionalises. The encouragement of private innovation is bought at the cost of a delay in public dissemination. Thus, if the delay is too long, and this is 'unnecessarily' stifling economic development, then the period of protection should be shortened, or certain scientific knowledge should be outside the patent regime. However, this argument accepts that only the market failure in innovation justifies this limitation of intellectual property, which again reveals the subtlety of the economic justification and its ability to compromise with critics while retaining its logic.

Despite such arguments, 'science and property, formally independent and even opposed concepts . . . have been made contingent upon each other', and this has not always been against the individual interest of scientists (Etzkowtiz and Webster 1995: 481–482). Indeed, many have become more entrepreneurial in their activities, forming joint-ventures to exploit breakthroughs (Garrett 1997a) and research centres to capture resources through organisational efficiency. Though still interested in acquiring prestige among their peers, many scientists' reputations

> that previously would have been recognised only eponymously – as in 'Boyle's law' or 'Einstein's theory of relativity' – are recognised as belonging to a certain scientist, or team of scientists, because of the patent they hold on it – such as the Cohen-Boyer patent on DNA cloning techniques.
>
> (Etzkowtiz and Webster 1995: 487)

To gain prestige it is increasingly important to have generated economically exploitable knowledge of one sort or another. One of the key problems for science (and economic development in the longer term) is how does a patent system support science for which there is no current application, or which produces 'answers to un-posed questions' (Polanyi 1969)? If it is broadly true that scientists have moved towards a prestige system based on the ownership of property in innovations, then the generation of basic scientific advance may become problematic.

The characterisation of scientific knowledge as intellectual property, while establishing and recognising individualised effort in the advancement of science, may also skew such advances towards the economically useful. These advances are not only the ones it might be easier to patent, but also the ones in which holding a patent might be profitable. The private/public bargain in the scientific patent undervalues the role of basic science in the production (somewhere down the line) of economically valuable innovation. Despite the common utilisation of market failure arguments to justify continued basic science funding outside the patent regime, the failure to recognise the social or public side of the issue in this formulation presents greater problems than this widespread practical 'fix' acknowledges. The increasing concentration on industrial utility by many governments in a period of retrenchment of public spending has led to technology foresight studies setting the parameters (or agendas) of publicly funded research (Cook 1997: 147). But, while there is some public benefit in the wealth impact of innovation supported in this manner, if this is seen as the defining role for public research then the continuance of basic science and the answering of un-posed questions may be compromised in the competition for limited resources.

Paradoxically, the continued funding for state-supported basic science has become partly dependent on its success at showing relevance to market activities. In the long term, the public benefit of non-market-oriented research will be compromised *because of* the over-emphasis of the private (economic) benefits that are instituted in the patent system. Thus, while at any particular juncture the balance between public and private represented by scientific patents may seem broadly acceptable, in time, the prioritising of private benefits will disable the ability of society to produce new and ultimately vital scientific breakthroughs. The patent system in this area would seem to be likely to fail by its justification of enhancing the social benefit in the long run. As O'Neill points out, the 'market provides the wrong kind of public test for knowledge': not only does it fail to cost the likely benefits of any breakthrough (due to the short time horizon of expected returns), it also fails to ensure the right level of assessment. Economic agents are not always (or even often) best qualified to evaluate scientific knowledge, only assessing it on the basis if immediate or near immediate application (O'Neill 1990: 612–613). Where the furtherance of particular aspects of science may have no clear economic 'pay-off', a market mechanism will not value their continuance, quite possibly leading to a narrowing of the horizons of scientific endeavour. But it is not only patents which can place limits on the flow and development of scientific knowledge.

Utilising the wider and longer protection that is accorded to copyright, there have been cases of funders (to whom copyright of published results may well be assigned) refusing to publish results that did not accord with their interests. These cases are often only rumoured as the limitation on publication of results and confidentiality clauses reduce the profile of the findings and the ability of researchers to make public the constriction. As with most contractual relations (discussed in the last section of this chapter) the intellectual property that results from the contract is the property not of the knowledge workers themselves but of the funder. For instance, Boots funded research comparing its drug Synthroid with cheaper alternatives claiming to provide the same benefit to patients. When a team at the University of California, Santa Barbara found that the drug used by around 8 million patients a day in the US worked no better than three cheaper alternatives, Boots 'threatened legal action to enforce its contractual right to prevent publication' of the results. Boots then co-ordinated a campaign to discredit the research leading to a 16-page refutation of the findings in the *American Journal of Therapeutics* by their medical services director, despite the fact that Boots had already ensured through legal action that the original study was not widely available (Reed and McKie 1996). While this case became somewhat of a *cause célèbre* in the academic science community, other cases, while difficult to track down, are recognised as a growing trend.

The private interests of intellectual property owners are not often compatible with the social interest in the disclosure of scientific knowledge. A bargain struck within the instrumental justificatory schema of patents – that property rewards innovation and the price of delayed dissemination is acceptable given the eventual return to the social pool of knowledge – is compromised in science. The social interest extends beyond the continuing support for innovation, and especially in the realm of scientific knowledge, may sharply contradict the interests of the owners of the relevant IPRs. While the economic schema allows a space for market failure to limit the coverage of intellectual property, the only market failure this recognises (again) is that of innovation. Other characterisations of the public interest regarding scientific knowledge are downplayed, even when in the case of genes these accord well with the self-developmental schema sometime used to justify IPRs more generally. These problems, while having historical precedents, have come to the fore through the commercialisation and industrialisation of biological science.

The transfer of technology

Historically, technology transfer has been one of the major elements of political debates regarding intellectual property. The transfer of technology to developing states has often been limited by the costs of licensing within a patent system. One of the key demands of the negotiations towards a New International Economic Order during the 1970s and early 1980s was to enhance the transfer of technology while at the same time reducing its cost to developing states (Helleiner 1977: 299, 313; Sell 1998: 81ff.). This led, as I noted in the previous chapter, to demands for the slackening of intellectual property protection demanded of developing states. But, those companies (and others) who control process and industrial patents in the developed states have always argued that any transfer of technological expertise should take place within a system that allows a fair reward to be earned by the innovator, and this was subsequently reflected in the move towards the agenda of the TRIPs agreement. For late-developing states it is easier (and more effective) to adopt already existing technologies rather than 'reinvent the wheel', and therefore the dynamics of technology transfer remains a subject of considerable political concern.

Technological innovation is usually seen as mainly exogenous to developing states and therefore to support economic development new technologies must be secured from developed states' corporations. Technological advance promotes both internal industrial development and competitive advantage in the global economy. In some recent cases of development (most notably Brazil, Argentina and Columbia) a form of agriculturally founded development has been followed. Growth in agricultural exports has supported the expansion of technology in that sector leading to growth in productivity and the increased incidence of new technologies in other sectors. Agriculture (essentially niche cash crops for a global market) has been the lead sector (*The Economist* 1997d). However, there is still a general belief that economic development is predicated on the acquisition of higher level manufacturing technologies, and given the account of biotechnology above, the agricultural sector may have its own intellectual property problems for developing states. There are of course wide-ranging and unsettled debates about pathways of development, but here I will only discuss development as it is related to the issue of intellectual property.

It is difficult to assess the level of technology transfer as technology itself is differentiated and diverse. This sometimes leads research on the issue to take levels of foreign direct investment (FDI) as an indication of the extent of transfer. But despite the centrality of the link between IPRs and technology transfer in political arguments it is 'difficult to establish strong theoretical and empirical linkages between IPRs and FDI and technology trade' (Maskus 1997: 689) On the other hand there is at least 'broad evidence that differences in technology, rather than differences in resources, are the most important determinant of the pattern of comparative advantage' (Krugman 1995: 349). The problem then becomes the capture and development of technological advance. The instrumental schema asserts that to support innovation and therefore technological advance the innovator should be rewarded through property rights in the technological advance. Economic justifications of intellectual property accord with this logic, suggesting that by allowing property in these advances the economic actors able to make best and most efficient use of these advances will secure them. In both perspectives the social utility and growth effect of the innovation will be maximised, and thus economic development itself will be furthered.

However, technological advances are often external to a state's legal jurisdiction and the product cycle is still a useful way of thinking about these cross-border technology flows. In a domestic arena the product cycle starts with the development of a technology which is then launched through its commercialisation, demand for its associated products grows until the market is saturated, leading to a decline into obsolescence. Though simplistic and one-dimensional this helps explain the rise and decline both of firms and whole industries (Krugman 1995: 349–355). Extended to the international dimension the model suggests that as a particular technology reaches maturity in its original market, its owners or exploiters will seek new areas where the particular cycle might be less developed (Vernon 1971). Thus, the move to operate in lesser developed states is encouraged by their relative lack of technological development. A second or even third linked product cycle could spring from the same technology as it diffuses through the international system. If this suggests a certain compartmentalisation of the international economy it may be less empirically valid than it once was. However, where the compartments are reinforced by the operation of legal structures based on national territories, the notion of a technology cascade may still broadly hold.

If there is extensive international trade then a technology may be known outside the area in which the original product cycle took place. A move to operate in lesser developed areas may then prove less advantageous due to the copying of the technology by indigenous manufacturers. But on the other hand, one way of supporting the competitiveness of a particular product, once it has matured technologically, is to shift production to states with a significant wage advantage. Thus, older products may enhance their life in developed markets through production in developing states and price competition. In general the product cycle illuminates the technology gap between developed and developing states revealing the interest that companies may have in introducing technologies to developing states: they can export back to the original market to compete on price rather than innovative value; and they can compete in the developing state on the basis of continuing technological advantage. The technology gap is reproduced through the workings of the international economy and multinational companies and is enforced by the use of intellectual property to define and describe specific technologies.

One of the effects of a stronger patent protection, which under the TRIPs agreement includes a *weakening* of the legal constraints regarding the working of patents in jurisdictions where they are granted, may actually be to lessen the transfer of technology. Where market access can be gained through trade with lower tariff barriers, and patent protection can halt generic technological competition, it may make more sense to centralise production for regions than to produce in each market. Thus though the goods may be available, the technology to produce them will only be available to some developing states – mainly the largest regional economies.

The wide (and widening) technological gap itself between the developed and developing states means that the technologies that could be transferred in any case 'are less suitable to [developed states'] resource endowments and more difficult to master' (Adelman 1991: 503). The large technological gap between the developed states and those who lag behind might suggest that the problem of IPRs impeding technological transfer is negligible. The technologies that are useful for the resources and workforce in these developing states are likely to no longer be subject to patent protection. Furthermore, the capital intensity of newer technologies makes their adoption difficult for cash-strapped economies already labouring under large institutional and commercial foreign debts, except as part of the internal organisation of multinational corporations. One explanation why these basic technologies (which Matsui refers to as 'peti' inventions) may not be transferred to developing states is exactly because they are outside patent protection and thus introducing such an advance would immediately produce further competitors (Matsui 1977: 620–623). Only by securing a reward for the providers will these older technologies be transferred.

In the logic of the developed states' corporations, the extension of the patent system rather than its weakening might serve to support developing states' technological advance. An expansion akin to this suggestion has been incorporated into the TRIPs agreement through the inclusion of trade secrets. Under Article 39 (Protection of Undisclosed Information), information that

> is secret in the sense that it is not, as a body or in the precise configuration and assembly of its components, generally known among or readily accessible to persons within the circles that normally deal with the kind of information in question

must be protected (GATT 1994, A1C: 18). The unauthorised revelation of know-how is coded as 'unfair competition' and aims to stem the unofficial flow of tacit technical information through the casual transfer of know-how. This inclusion of know-how within the intellectual property regime recognises its importance and aims to ensure a full price is paid to secure it. Thus know-how that is not part of formal technology is also protected and an avenue of informal technology transfer is inhibited. But with no requirement to work the patent under the TRIPs agreement, there may be no transfer of technology as demand will be filled by trade rather than domestic production.

If increasing the protection afforded intellectual property through the TRIPs agreement results in little or no gain in the technology transferred, then there will be a net increase in payments by customers in the developing states to the owners of the IPRs – the multinational companies and other holders of patents in the developed states. If under better legal protection there *was* an increase in the level of technology transfer then though there would be an initial increase in payments relative to the GDP, as the national economy grew (through the use of these new technologies) there would quite possibly be a net social benefit despite the payment to innovators outside the state. Local innovation might be captured by foreign MNCs and produce further royalty outflows, but the overall social benefit again could plausibly nullify the impact of these transfers. However, this supposes the reason that technology transfer fails is entirely (or at least largely) due to the lack of patent protection in developing states. With the TRIPs agreement's legal agenda in place, if other factors inhibit the transfer of technology then while there will be a possible increase in the remittances from developing state licence holders, there will not necessarily be an increased flow of technology in the opposite direction.

This question of causality of technological transfer is both important and difficult to resolve. The increasing use of flexible production practices to produce short-run, specialised components with increasingly sophisticated inventory control has promoted just-in-time supply chains with enhanced value on proximity. Thus, for many production processes moving production to developing states no longer holds the same attraction. At the same time advances in communications have enabled firms to disperse other production activities while retaining centralised control. But the vast majority of research and development (R&D), and therefore technological innovation, takes place in a multinational's home country – these activities are seldom diffused through its complex organisational linkages. Thus, for multi-nationals while high technology (and flexible) aspects of the production process can be retained in developed states, high labour content commodity component manufacture can be moved to lesser developed states (Wade 1996: 82–84). The technology gap is also reinforced by shortages of skilled labour in the developing states. Developed states largely retain their comparative advantage in the supply of skilled labour, though this is eroding in some industries – the software industry in India, for instance. And as skilled workers are less scarce than in developing states they command less of a price premium relative to unskilled workers. Developing states also lack a residual common socialised technical skills base shared by a large part of the workforce.

If more stringent protection under the TRIPs agreement does not enhance technology transfer then these states will enjoy a net loss of income. But if they refuse to sign up they cannot remain as members of the WTO and therefore lose the possibility of exporting to developed states' markets, generating foreign income to reduce or service their current foreign debt. Since it is unlikely that many states' governments will attempt to retreat from the global trading system, the issue of whether technology transfer will be supported by strengthened patent protection becomes a crucial issue for policy-makers. The standard technology sector view, which is supported by some research studies, is that only by protecting intellectual property will domestic innovation be supported, technology transfer take place and economic growth accelerate. Thus, Gould and Gruben

> utilise cross-country data on overall levels of patent protection, trade regime and country-specific characteristics and find that intellectual property protection (as measured by the degree of patent protection) is an important determinant of economic growth.
>
> (1996: 324)

Their study established that states with higher rates of economic growth have more stringent patent protection, and this correlates to some extent with their degree of openness to the international economy. But as the authors point out, the 'positive relationship between growth, intellectual property rights and openness may be sensitive to other factors correlated with [the] trade regime and intellectual property rights' (ibid.: 341–342). Though there is a correlation of growth and IPR protection, the research is unable to establish a robust causal relationship, leaving it quite possible that both relate to a further state-level variable.

Summarising their own findings that IPR protection may affect growth by 'stimulating the accumulation of factor inputs' such as physical capital and R&D related capital, Park and Ginarte also note that the 'institution of IPRs does not have any *direct* role in explaining international variations in growth. That is, the existence of intellectual property laws does not appear to affect directly the technical efficiency of production' (1997: 51, emphasis added). The major implication as regards the subject of developing states' patent protection laws is that 'countries not conducting innovative research or conducting a limited amount would enjoy few, if any, of the benefits of intellectual property protection because an innovation sector through which IPRs affect economic growth is absent' (ibid.). The authors conclude that rather than innovation and R&D being prompted by the protection of intellectual property, it is more likely that the incidence of domestic innovation and research produces political pressure for a patent regime of some description. Where technological development is essentially imitative of innovations else-where, there will be little interest in building such an institution. However, when the TRIPs agreement forces states without indigenous innovation sectors to protect intellectual property not only will they halt imitative technological activities, unless a national innovation sector is swiftly developed the technology gap will be strengthened.

The likelihood of being the site for multinational corporation research and development activities in actuality does not seem to be linked to the strength of intellectual property protection. High technology research activities are usually centralised in the developed state homes of multinationals. The location of other R&D activities is linked to the markets at which their efforts are aimed. Thus, research to adapt already extant technologies to a local market usually takes place in the vicinity whether or not there is strong IPR protection. The location of R&D is the result of the other activities being undertaken by the multinational, and the ability of the host state to offer support in the form of local technological resources and capabilities, not the IPR regime. Thus, market size is a considerably more important issue than patent laws (Kumar 1996). This is unwelcome news for developing states which are currently not the site of any R&D activity either by their own nationals or foreign corporations. Now that compulsory licences have been severely curtailed, where a patent is not being worked (and demand is satisfied through importation), there is little recourse to law to force technology transfer even if this might be in the public interest of a particular economy. Given the reasonably strong correlation between patent protection levels and import pene-tration, this might suggest that 'exporting firms discriminate in their sales decisions . . . taking account of local patent laws' (Maskus and Penubarti 1995: 244). Once their market position is protected from generic and reverse-engineering driven competition, these companies have no need to transfer technology to gain access to a particular market. Under the TRIPs agreement this protection against localised generic competition has become more robust, re-emphasising the current distribution pattern of innovation sectors between the developed and developing states, as well as between developing states themselves.

On balance, by concentrating on the social utility of innovation within a unitary global economic system, the TRIPs agreement actually produces a severe disutility for those developing states that do not have innovation sectors of one sort or another already in place. Even within the OECD research and development is reasonably centralised with the member states relying for over half the growth effects from innovation on advances patented in the US, Germany and Japan. Alongside these three, only France and Great Britain garner over 10 per cent of growth effect from domestic research and innovation (Eaton and Kortum 1996). For countries outside the OECD the promotion of growth through innovation is likely to be even lower. Though the social good of supporting innovation, which is one of the key facets of patents' justification, will be furthered in a general sense, looking at individual jurisdictions the result is not as clear. Perhaps more importantly, most successful recent industrialisation strategies have been ruled off the agenda of possible alternatives under the TRIPs agreement. South Korea, Indonesia, Singapore and other states have utilised an initially imitative strategy to accelerate their economic development before moving to a more balanced R&D path. Under the TRIPs agreement this is no longer an option, except through formal licence agreements. Thus, the new structure of intellectual property protection in the global system will solidify the technology gap that exists currently, and while fulfilling the needs of the developed states, will compromise the developmental paths of poorer states. The links that can be established between IPR protection and growth are negative rather than positive and indicate that in all likelihood the protection of IPRs will stifle indigenous innovation while rewarding those innovators already embedded in well-established innovation systems.

Therefore as with the issue of pharmaceutical patents, the underlying issue is the definition of the public interest or social benefit. While it is in the interest of developing states to have patents worked and technologically advanced production transferred to their national markets, allowing for transfer both of physical capabilities and of appropriate skills, it is not always in the interest of the owners of such technology. Their private interests, justified through the instrumental schema is to maximise their reward for innovating in the first place. This may or may not require them to transfer technology but it does not depend on the likely benefit to the prospective host state and its economic development. These rights of the owner are given precedence in the TRIPs agreement, and the notion that such rights might also include some global level social responsibility is not even considered (Khan 1990). While in the past developing states could try and remake this bargain through a different balance in their national patent legislation (different durations and coverage), this possibility is now unacceptable except in very specific cases. Under the knowledge structure the concentration on the innovators' rights to a reward have become the prime consideration in reforming the patent law regarding technology transfer. However, it is not clear that the ability to patent inventions is a significant driving force behind innovation outside the pharmaceutical sector.

Edward Mansfield has suggested, based on a sampling of American industries in the mid-1980s that

> it appears that patent protection was judged to be essential for the development of introduction of 30 percent or more of the inventions in only two industries – pharmaceuticals and chemicals. In another three industries (petroleum, machinery and fabricated metal products) patent protection was estimated to be essential for the development and introduction of about 10–20 percent of their inventions. In the remaining seven industries (electrical equipment, office equipment, motor vehicles, instruments, primary metals, rubber and textiles) patent protection was estimated to be of much more limited importance in this regard. Indeed, in office equipment, motor vehicles, rubber and textiles, the firms were unanimous in reporting patent protection was not essential for the development or introduction of any of their inventions.
>
> (1988: 13)

But, this should not be taken to indicate that therefore patents were not taken out, in fact patents were applied for in around two-thirds of all cases. Thus, while the justificatory schema suggest that innovation would not take place without the reward allocated through IPRs, such a reward may actually be a bonus rather than the driving force behind innovative behaviour. If this is the case, then the social bargain of patent has been compromised, even in the developed states. For technology-receiving states the patent system allows knowledge owners to secure a reward without the necessity of the mandated social benefits of technology transfer or support for innovation. This disjuncture is conveniently obscured by the knowledge structure's promotion of the instrumental and economic schemata, centred as they are on the behaviour and encouragement of the idealised individual innovator.

Finally, it is as well to note that much of the debate in the US over intellectual property takes place within a discourse of competitiveness. The US government, during the TRIPs agreement negotiations and in its more public exortions, for instance those by Assistant Secretary of Commerce Bruce Lehman, stressed the need for the US to ensure that it 'creates, owns, preserves and protects its intellectual property' to retain its competitive advantage in the global system (Lehman 1996: 6). This explicitly does not involve the transfer of up-to-date technology, competitiveness is about maintaining the gap to ensure national advantage. This gap can be legitimised through intellectual property as the protection, not of advantage, but of the rights of the individual knowledge innovators. Reporting on a recent OECD study of R&D, *The Economist* (1997b) argued that

> [if] firms that develop new technologies wield monopoly power, they can charge higher prices and so capture most of the benefits of innovations for themselves. The high price will slow the adoption of the new technology elsewhere in the economy, retarding the productivity gains, that the new technology could bring.

They go on to suggest that competition is the way to ensure such unbalanced benefits are reduced. Though *The Economist*'s report was only concerned with OECD economies, taking this argument to cover the global economy, the TRIPs agreement, supported by *The Economist* and OECD governments produces these self-same results. It supports the monopoly power of developed states' firms, it retards the productivity gains in developing states and ensures that competition in the knowledge-intensive sectors is constrained. But the knowledge structure obscures this as well by ensuring in this arena it is not productivity, or social benefit that drives the justification of policy but the stimulation of individualised innovation. This leads me to consider in the final section of this chapter, intellectual property as it relates to these innovators themselves rather than the corporate owners of knowledge objects.

The ownership of tacit knowledge and skills

Up until now the innovator or individual knowledge creator has appeared as an idealised agent whose interests are protected by the legal construction of intellectual property. Otherwise he or she has been largely absent. And as I have stressed above, the benefits that flow from the institution of intellectual property are concerned with rewarding the owner, whether or not they are the actual creator. Moving away from an idealised notion of the creative and innovative individual there are two aspects of real intellectual property relations that are important in this regard: employment contracts and the treatment of putative trade secrets which I briefly mentioned in Chapter 2; and the problems encountered by individual knowledge workers/innovators in securing (or retaining) the benefits of their intellectual activity. These issues will act as a bridge to the more positive aspects of intellectual property I explore in the next chapter.

The legal theory of 'inevitable disclosure' is broadly representative of intellectual property issues in the workplace and is exemplified by the dispute over Jose Ignacio Lopez's move from General Motors to Volkswagen. While Head of Global Purchasing at GM Mr Lopez developed (or borrowed from Toyota) a systematic approach to component cost reduction. This required component suppliers to cut their costs of production through more efficient manufacture and less waste. Lopez realised that while it was possible to increase the productivity of the plants owned by GM when assembly represented only 7 per cent of the total cost of the car, the real site of likely productivity gains were the component supplier's factories. So looking not only for speedier manufacture but also less remedial work, Lopez turned his attention to GM's suppliers. In reality this approach is not dissimilar to the famous Toyota system, though in Lopez's hands the trust aspect of relationship contracting was ignored and replaced by more adversarial links between GM and its suppliers (*The Economist* 1993a, 1993b, 1993c). When Mr Lopez took a job with Volkswagen in March 1993 an interesting dispute was set in motion. Volkswagen were keen for him to introduce similar cost saving and efficiency gains to their production processes, and employed seven of his erstwhile colleagues from GM to help produce this advance in their operations. However, GM went to the German courts on the basis that Lopez and his colleagues had stolen GM's industrial secrets which they were putting to work at Volkswagen.

This accusation is what makes the dispute interesting from an intellectual property point of view. While Lopez and his new employers argued that it was his skill at cost-cutting that was being used, GM insisted that the approach which Lopez had developed (along with its supporting manuals and processes) was their intellectual property. It was alleged that Lopez and his team took with them from GM '4,000 pages of computer print-out listing the 60,000 separate motor parts . . . suppliers, prices, terms and delivery schedules' (Tyler 1997). Though these claims were never tested in court, the case between the car makers was finally settled in 1997 with a payment of $100m damages to GM and the departure of Lopez from VW. While the removing materials from GM, if proved, would clearly have been theft, the case really revolved around who owned the 'system' which Lopez had devised while working for GM. Who 'owned' the processes and system which enabled GM and VW to reduce costs while Lopez was in their employ? At the heart of GM's claim was the perception that what an employee developed during their employment was not theirs but was owned by the employer, and indeed many employment contracts explicitly spell this out. However, when the innovation is not so much a set of measurable and definable knowledge objects, but rather an approach to a problem, a set of questions that need to be asked of suppliers, this approaches something that might be better termed the skill of the employee, or know-how. This was VW's case, they had employed an expert with valuable skills, and these skills were owned by Lopez not his previous employer. His know-how was not a trade secret of GM nor their intellectual property.

In this case Lopez's contract was cut short as part of the out-of-court settlement and he received a large severance payment four years after having gone to work for VW. When the criminal case of theft was finally dropped by the German courts in July 1998 Lopez was ordered to pay DM400,000 to charity. However, though of somewhat theatrical proportions this case highlights the problem of the ownership of employee know-how. The doctrine of 'inevitable disclosure' has been elaborated under the US Uniform Trade Secrets Act (UTSA), which was designed to codify the basic principles of common law protection for trade secrets. And while the act itself does not mention 'inevitable disclosure', it does 'permit an injunction against threatened or actual misappropriation of trade secrets'. But the theory of inevitable disclosure does not focus on the intent (or interests) of the employee who is moving jobs, rather it considers three factors:

1. the level of competition between the former employer and the new employer;
2. whether the employee's position with the new employer is comparable to the position held with the former employer; and
3. the actions the new employer has taken to prevent the employee from using or disclosing trade secrets to the former employer.

(Di Fronzo 1996)

Thus, an employee is only able to avoid the charge if they move to a non-competitor, or to a non-comparable position (both which would likely involve a reduction in remuneration if they have specialised skills), or to an employer who ensures that they will not use any knowledge that might be construed to be the trade secrets of their previous employer. Given that most of us move from one job to another based on the skills and knowledge we have developed while working, there would seem likely to be some impediment for career development outside the confines of a single employer. One might even argue that this was a constriction of an individual's right to benefit from their own labour on which the instrumental justificatory schema for intellectual property is founded.

When William Redmond Jnr left PepsiCo to join Snapple, PepsiCo applied for an injunction to prevent him taking the post on the grounds that this new job 'would inevitably lead him to use PepsiCo trade secrets'. Redmond's intimate knowledge of PepsiCo's pricing, marketing and distribution plans would be revealed to Snapple because he would not be able to feed into similar planning at Snapple without using this knowledge. The Seventh Circuit US Court of Appeals entered a permanent injunction against Redmond and Snapple, ruling that

> threatened misappropriation can occur when an employee who knows of his employer's trade secrets is hired by a competitor to perform a job with similar duties. In such circumstances, the inevitable disclosure or use of trade secrets by the employee in his new job constitutes misappropriation or threatened misappropriation under the Uniform Trade Secrets Act.

(quoted in Di Fronzo 1996)

The magnitude of this move in intellectual property related law towards the interests of the employer (or knowledge owner) is revealed by the opposite turn of events in an earlier case in 1991 when IBM sued a former employee and his new employer Seagate Technology. In this case US District Court of Minnesota concluded that the 'absence of a covenant not to compete or a finding of actual or an intent to disclose trade secrets, employees may pursue their chosen field of endeavour in direct competition with their prior employer' (quoted in Di Fronzo 1996). In this case the employee was able to carry on working for his new employer. As hinted in this judgment, one way that employers have always resolved this problem to their advantage is to write strict intellectual property clauses into employment contracts. Where this fails, the courts may now also argue that inevitable disclosure is a infringement of the rights of the corporate knowledge owner.

There is some resistance, not least among employees, to this move. On one level the doctrine of inevitable disclosure is built on a paradox: unless the employer has fully formed the intellectual development of the employee, their initial reserves of skill and knowledge must have belonged to a prior employer. Only those intellectual items explicitly identified as the company's intellectual property should be the subject of such disputes. Thus 'unless the employee misappropriated propriety materials or there is some specific and novel device design or process involved, the court should leave employer and employee where it finds them' (Spanner 1996). But while this might be logically so, the general thrust of intellectual property law has been to reward the most recent owner, not the pattern of previous inputs to the knowledge object, in this case the collection of employee skills and knowledge. And in knowledge-based companies this repository needs to be secured. Though some of this knowledge may appear in patents and other accepted legal forms, much is located in employee know-how and ingrained institutional practices. Companies who rely on such resources for their competitive advantage will want to ensure they do not pass to their competitors. One way of achieving this end is to expand the characterisation of intellectual property to include such knowledge. The use of a doctrine of 'inevitable disclosure' is likely to continue to expand, 'despite the reluctance of most courts to transform, in effect, an employee's agreement not to disclose trade secrets into a covenant not to compete', because it is an excellent way of trying to use their skills for a competitor (Berger *et al.* 1997). Where there was once transferable skills there may now increasingly be firm-specific intellectual property assets.

To some extent, the non-competition aspect of this sort of clause is open to the claim that it is a restriction on trade for the individual. Though some courts in the US find non-competition employment contract clauses 'reasonable', it is by no means certain that such clauses will always be upheld. The most satisfactory method for employers to secure knowledge objects is to ensure that the employment contract explicitly assigns the intellectual property in any innovations the employee or contractor produces to the company for whom they are working. For copyright, under the doctrine of a 'work made for hire', the copyright of knowledge objects produced by an employee within the terms of their contracted employment belongs to the company (Little and Trepanier 1997: 54). Though this has long been accepted by employees, for contracting parties Little and Trepanier recommend the transfer of copyright is made an explicit part of the agreement to ensure that the contractor does not retain any interest in the knowledge object produced during the contract. With patents a similar approach, under the 'hired to invent' doctrine, ensures that employees' innovations are captured by the employer and cannot be taken with them to a new job. An employee might refuse to sign these sort of contracts, but on the other hand may need the job. The power relations between employer and employee are therefore essentially unchanged by the incidence of knowledge work (May 1998).

Just to emphasise that this is a widespread problem for employees and not limited to the cut and thrust of the high technology sector, another illustration of this tendency is drawn from the US education sector (Noble 1998). In the rush to commercialisation, universities throughout the world have emphasised research and the generation of intellectual property. This has engendered a crisis in teaching delivery as resources have been reassigned to commercial research projects and centres. The strategy adopted to alleviate this problem at UCLA has been to transform teaching materials into software. This is not only supposed to reduce the direct labour content of teaching, but also to provide the university with a marketable output in the form of distance learning resources. From the perspective of intellectual property, the most important aspect of this development is the transfer of skills and knowledge from the labour force (lecturers) to the employer (the University) who owns the software used. During a similar programme at York University

> at least one part-time faculty member was required to put her courses on video, CD-ROM or the Internet or lose her job. She was then hired to teach her now-automated course at a fraction of her former compensation.
>
> (Noble 1998: 48)

This deskilling, or capture of knowledge resources, is defended through intellectual property laws, the new educational resource is a product owned by the university. Like other sectors university employment is gradually becoming more reliant on contract employment, with a decline in permanent posts. Contract workers can be pressured into producing knowledge outputs that will outlast their contracts and will ultimately make them at least partly redundant as labouring resources.

Now knowledge is seen as a valuable resource companies wish to capture it for exclusive use, and to reduce their costs once it has been captured. As John Kay points out in his advice to managers seeking the 'Foundations of Corporate Success',

> if the company is to add value, it needs to create organisational knowledge from the skills of its members. This is achieved when the combined skills of two experts increases the value of each. The problems the organisation faces are, first, those of securing the exchange of knowledge and, secondly, those of

preventing that knowledge, and the rewards associated with it, being captured by one or both of the individuals concerned.

(Kay 1993: 73 emphasis added)

This exploitation of the production of knowledge and the prevention of capture by the employee is exactly the operation that an intellectual property system predicated not on real individuals but on legally constituted individuals aims to provide. The justificatory schema within the knowledge structure elides the slippage between these two categories of 'person', aiming to justify IPRs on the basis of acceptable individual rights, while allowing companies to actually enjoy such rights. Conversely, Nonaka and Takeuchi's extensive discussion of the knowledge-creating company does not even consider this ownership problem, tacitly assuming that any knowledge created within the company by its knowledge workers must belong to the company. The notion that this might even be an issue of concern has apparently dropped off the agenda leaving only the mechanisms by which the company can induce innovation within its workforce (Nonaka and Takeuchi 1995). After all, under the agenda set in the knowledge structure, who else would own such knowledge except for the company?

When real individuals try and capture the rights on which the instrumental schema is built they often find that their way is hampered by obstacles. In the realm of patents one of the most problematic is the registration fee and subsequent renewal fees to keep the patent current. These may be different from state to state and to keep a patent live in a number of jurisdictions may be extremely expensive. The whole system of patent may be of little use to the individual with limited resources. In the assessment of Roger Ashby of the University of Southampton's technology transfer company: 'if you have not got the appetite to spend £100,000–£150,000 to do it properly, there is little point spending the £6,000 in the first stages of the process' (quoted in Patel 1998). James Dyson for instance was forced to abandon one of the elements of his complex of vacuum cleaner patents because he was unable to afford a renewal fee when he was still trying to start production – it is now being used by his competitors. Though lawyers suggest that this is to ensure that the patent is being worked while it is protected, for large companies the fees remain trifling, only onerous to individuals trying to protect their invention to market it (Halstead 1997). But even if the inventing individual takes out a patent, the struggle is not finished. Unless they are able to form their own company to take advantage of the invention, they need to interest a backer or manufacturer. Dyson Vacuums which remains independent and Workbench (now owned by Black and Decker) are exceptions where inventors set up their own successful companies. But in neither case was this the preferred strategy, but rather one taken in the face of corporate disinterest. More often a desperate inventor at the end of their funds accepts an unfavourable licensing agreement from a manufacturer and loses much of the eventual benefit from the invention.

Intellectual property – but not for me?

In reality the intellectual property system (typified above by patents) is often used not to reward the innovator, nor protect the benefits of their intellectual work, but to separate them from their knowledge creations. And though this is undertaken using the rubric of the social interest, it serves only a very particular social interest. The ability to identify what *is* intellectual property and what is not is crucial to the operation of power in intellectual property relations. Companies claiming that certain knowledge *is* in the public realm, even if its 'owners' differ, as in the natural resources 'stolen' by biotechnology and bio-prospecting, have their claims reinforced by the knowledge structure's agenda for property in knowledge resources. The ability to deny certain 'knowledge' is intellectual property until it is recognised as being 'trade related' is vital to allow the necessary initial enclosure of knowledge commons. In this chapter I have been concerned to establish some areas where there seem to be some disparity between the justificatory schema which has been utilised in the TRIPs agreement and the outcomes from the institution of intellectual property. The key issues which have emerged have been the different interpretation put upon the question of social or public benefit, the efficacy of the instrumental schema's claims to stimulate innovation, and the possible differences between the interests of real individuals and their legally constituted counterparts.

The social benefit which is emphasised by the knowledge structure in the field of intellectual property, and most stridently in the field of patent, is the encouragement of innovation. From this particular public good all other social benefits flow. By supporting and rewarding innovation the overall social and economic well-being of the economy will be served and enhanced. The linked social good of technological diffusion is given a second place, it is regarded as dependent on the incidence of innovation. However, as I have stressed above, it is by no means clear, especially at the level of the global system, whether this is a reasonable depiction of the character of technological advance. While at a local level there may be some encouragement of innovation by the patent system, the problems of the technology gap between the developed and developing states looms much larger to the non-innovating states. Once a different aspect of social utility is emphasised, public health in poor states, the need to acquire new technologies for economic development, or the rights of states with bio-resources to receive benefit from their exploitation, then the explicit public/private bargain of patent seems misapplied and dysfunctional.

The partial and unsatisfactory depiction of the public interest embedded within the TRIPs agreement is not the only problem: the rights actually enjoyed by knowledge creators are less than satisfactory. As I have already suggested, the law has increasingly taken the rights of the owner of intellectual property to be paramount. The law also acts to separate the creator of intellectual property from their creation and to place the ownership of such resources in the hand of companies. These legally constituted individuals then receive the benefits that are justified on the basis that they encourage the innovative behaviour of real people. Thus, in the intellectual property settlement enshrined in the TRIPs agreement there is both a limitation of the social benefit that is recognised as well as a preference for a particular type of owner of intellectual property. Finally, there is the possibility that an exclusive or monopoly right, in the form of IPRs, is always going to produce problems that in many circumstances outweigh any realistic social benefit from intellectual property. It is possible that the analogy between material property and property in knowledge is unworkable. But before considering this argument, in the next chapter I examine some avenues in which the problems I have identified here seem less endemic. The next stage of my critical project is to see what can be salvaged from the current settlement.

5 Sites of consolidation

Legitimate authorship?

At the close of the previous chapter the individual knowledge producer began to emerge from the position of an idealised subject within the instrumental and self-developmental justificatory schemata, to be considered in terms of real social relations. Having explored a number of issues that problematise the justification and current settlement of intellectual property (mainly regarding patents), the emphasis now changes to a more positive side of the issue (for the creator at least), in the main centred on copyright issues. There is an intuitive distinction between innovations which might be considered tools or processes which have social use beyond the individual innovator (and as such are subject to patent), and the sort of knowledge object which might be described as the expression of an individual's own creativity. To some extent this follows the idea/expression dichotomy within the history of intellectual property. Though the distinction is often blurred and problematic, in general, intellectual property that is rooted in creative acts is widely seen as more legitimate than intellectual property that constricts the social use of productive ideas.

There is a popularly held perception of ideas which can be traced back at least to Herodutus and other early Greek writers. This recognises the claim that someone has 'stolen' an idea as the depiction of an actual social event, even if it is difficult to pin down in empirical terms. This formulation is used widely in everyday discussion and recognises that each of us 'owns' what we think – our thoughts are ours in some manner. While this notion allows a space in which the legal construction of intellectual property can flourish, this perception and its legal representation are by no means the same thing. Indeed, a major problem for the instrumental and self-developmental schema is that not only are the general public confused about what the law over intellectual property actually involves, so are many practitioners (Litman 1991). Failure to understand the workings of patents by those who actually produce innovations is widespread and can easily lead to the rights to innovations not being covered by successful patent applications (Garrett 1997b; Patel 1998). Authors and other expressive creators' general understanding of copyright is little better. If those whose behaviour should be shaped by intellectual property law do not necessarily understand its operation, then it seems unlikely the justificatory schemata can be an accurate depiction of their motivation. And if not, the justification of intellectual property is thrown back more firmly on the role of social benefits which are problematic as noted in the last chapter.

Patents are often unflatteringly compared with copyrights which are both free and not subject to renewal or exhaustion during the lifetime of the knowledge creator. However, individuals seldom have the resources to reproduce their creations to provide substantial returns. Like the individual patent holder they usually need to seek a backer or company that will produce the commercialised version of their knowledge object – a publisher, a record company, a software house. However, as these companies want the exclusive rights to the property they exploit, the intellectual property needs to be assigned to the company for the artists and/or creators to receive the benefit. Within copyright at least, and in accordance with the self-developmental schema, there is currently some ability to ensure that the use of the copyrighted knowledge object accords with the intent of the creator. But though the moral rights of authors and artists have traditionally been recognised in European law, and since 1988 can be asserted in Britain, this particular aspect of protection for intellectual property seems endangered under the TRIPs agreement. For patents, even this possible extension of the individual knowledge creator's rights is not available; once an innovation is licensed, the inventor loses any right over the use put to their invention.

Though the knowledge structure has managed to support a legitimised intellectual property settlement at the level of international and multilateral diplomacy, on the ground there is considerable resistance. Difficulties lie in the difference between actual outcomes in intellectual property law and those that might be expected under the justificatory schemata (the site of an immanent critique). Additionally, in everyday life the confused manner in which individuals actually understand ideas or knowledge objects as property presents some difficulties for the justification of intellectual property. But these shortcomings are in some ways less pronounced for copyright than for patents. And there is also a more general problem of 'piracy' to which I shall return at the end of the chapter.

Key knowledge industries

The publishing, software, and entertainments industries have often been nominated as typical industries of the future. They are presented as the paradigmic knowledge industries which will be mimicked by other sectors as they switch to a higher knowledge content for their own products. In the 1970s Marc Porat made the distinction between primary and secondary knowledge sectors. The primary encompassed those industries that utilised and reproduced knowledge as the central logic of their organisation. The secondary included those industries (essentially the rest of the economy) which utilised knowledge elements within the production of material goods – the knowledge element, while significant, did not define the character of the product. But more recently the knowledge content of material goods (the brand, design, marketing or innovative aspects) has grown and the secondary information sector has approached the primary both in logic and character. Some of this shift has been caused by the fragmentation of the technical division of labour, with many knowledge-related tasks now being carried out by contractors rather than in-house. This has enlarged the primary knowledge sector as service companies have concentrated on this sector's knowledge-intensive tasks through a more developed social division of labour (May 1998). In these knowledge-intensive sectors there is sometimes more ground to accept the justificatory schemata's depiction of intellectual property.

Publishing

The publishing industry is the oldest knowledge industry of all. With Guttenburg and the invention of movable type, printing engendered the first modern information revolution. The development of cheap reproduction transformed the diffusion of knowledge in a very short time. In the fifty years after the invention of the printing press in the 1450s, it seems likely that more books were available than had been produced in the entire previous history of mankind (Eisenstein 1980: 45). The mechanisation of reproduction produced a knowledge-based industry. For the first time books and other written work (songs, broadsheets) were reproduced as exact copies rather than left to the vagaries of individual scholars' copying (with all the possibility for variation and error which that entailed). These were uniform of text and presentation for each copy; they became commodities. And, with the possibility of large-scale reproduction for sale pressure began to build up to prevent unauthorised copies from being sold alongside or in competition with authorised versions. It is to such pressures that copyright traces its origins. The legal formalisation of copyright in the Act of Anne in 1710 was preceded by forms of proto-copyrights in Venice (Bettig 1992: 133–139; Feather 1994). But, the first reported 'copyright' dispute may be even earlier, with the case of

> Saint Columbia, who in the year 567 surreptitiously copied a psalm book belonging to his teacher, Finnian of Moville. When Finnian objected, the dispute went before King Diarmed. The king concluded that both the original and the copy belonged to Finnian saying, 'To every cow her calf, and accordingly to every book its copy'. Diarmed saw the book as Finnian's property, the ownership of which entitled Finnian to its product, the copy.
>
> (Stearns 1992: 535)

Today problems within publishing remain centred on unauthorised reproduction. In a strange echo of the pre-printing age's serial copying, it is the individual copies (re)produced through photocopying that are now the main intellectual property problem identified by the sector.

Before discussing the issue of individual copying, it is worth noting the issue of plagiarism as it resonates through many intellectual property issues. It is a difficult subject, because if knowledge creators are social individuals, located within the prior history of their field then they must draw on what has gone before. Only the unsocialised author or innovator (the feral author) could distinguish themselves from their predecessors. On the other hand, in theory at least, an innovator should be able to identify where all the elements of a knowledge creation find their roots and the actual spark of invention or addition they themselves added. While this might be possible in theory, given the complexity of any particular idea and its elements ranging from the language in which is expressed to the 'common sense' which it encompasses, finding the correct proportions is unlikely to be feasible. As I previously noted, the outcome has been to award the most recent innovator the full economic rent from the innovation. In the real world of creative processes, the knowledge creator stands somewhere between these two positions. Unable to separate themselves from their predecessors, they are also unlikely to remember or have much interest in tracing the roots of all the elements of their work or creation (a job usually left to the much maligned critic). As such, plagiarism is not so much a definite level of unsignified commonalty with another work, but rather the attempt to knowingly pass it off as one's own.

Stearns argues that people are generally scornful of the plagiarist, not because such acts produce necessarily inferior work, 'but because it is a form of cheating that allows the plagiarist an unearned benefit'. More subtly, and more importantly for my argument there is also generally a clear distinction drawn between this behaviour and the copying of copyrighted works: 'Individuals who do not hesitate to photocopy copyrighted books or videotape copyrighted broadcasts would never dream of representing themselves as the authors of the books or tapes' (Stearns 1992: 519). It is not the result of intellectual activity which is questioned but rather the process by which a result was reached. The three main areas of difference between what is generally recognised as plagiarism and what actually constitutes copyright infringement are therefore copying, attribution and intent. Plagiarism is broader than legal infringement, in that it may involve the copying of ideas, use of words or expression, none of which would necessarily infringe a particular copyright. However, copyright is wider in another respect, as unlike plagiarism the defence of ignorance or lack of intent does not suffice (ibid.: 524). But under 'fair use' or 'fair dealing' doctrines within copyright codes, it is usual to exempt a certain level of explicit copying, regarded as necessary for criticism and other legitimate uses, from the law of infringement.

Like Merton's conception of the reputation system for scientists, the plagiarist if unmasked may find his or her professional stature devalued. Conversely, the attributed use of another's work in a text is one of the ways that scholarly arguments are conventionally constructed and the use of ideas acknowledged. Indeed there is frequently some link between the general level of citation and the reputation of the author or knowledge creator. Though, citation indexes are not the only method for gauging the level of a particular academic or other knowledge producer's reputation, they certainly play a role. If there is some truth to Barthes' famous statement that the 'text is a tissue of quotations drawn from innumerable centres of culture . . . [with the author's] only power to mix writings, to counter ones with the others, in such a way as never to rest on any one of them' (Barthes 1977: 146), then plagiarism is the over reliance on one or other text. Thus in a recent case Graham Swift's 1996 Booker Prize winning novel was subsequently charged with reproducing the main theme and a number of literary devices from William Faulkner's *As I Lay Dying*. Swift admitted that while he knew the book, his borrowings were incidental, but his critics suggested that nevertheless some statement of attribution should have been made.

In another case, Ben Okri accused a French author, who had won an award from the French Academy for her book, of plagiarising *The Famished Road*. Her defence of the similarity between her and Okri's text was simply that 'we live in the same world and come from the same background' and therefore were likely to produce similar fictions (quoted in Julius 1996). This problem is not limited to books of course: Stephen Spielberg's Amblin Productions was subject to a failed copyright claim from Barbara Chase-Riboud. She alleged that Spielberg's production company despite having decided in the late 1980s not to adapt her book *Echo of Lions*, made a substantially similar story (sharing both names and incidents) into the film *Amistad*. The problem for Chase-Riboud lay in the history that both her book and the film drew on. Amblin claimed that the story was drawn from Debbie Allen's research into a particular incident which was not included in Chase-Riboud's best-selling book on the subject. Though both works draw on an actual incident (which was difficult to reconstruct), the author claimed that the film 'contains themes, dialogue, character, relationships, plots and scenes that were originally created for *Echo of Lions* and have no basis in historical fact' (quoted in Goodwin 1997). Nevertheless, Amblin's defence that the author could not claim copyright in actual events succeeded, despite the similarities with the earlier work and the claim that fictional elements had been carried across. The distinction between plagiarism and copyright infringement is seldom clear or uncontested. This brings the problem back to the issue of the social milieu in which intellectual activity takes place – what is copying and what is coincident thought?

The process which copyright aims to protect owners against is the unauthorised copying of specific intellectual property and the sale of subsequent reproductions. Where two individuals have independently arrived at the same intellectual object, under copyright each enjoys the rights according to their own creation – it is merely enough to show independent development. Under the TRIPs agreement this co-development defence has been compromised for process patents as I have already discussed. Such a legal innovation has yet to be introduced for copyright, though such an extension of particular owners' rights would be of major importance. In the history of copyright the key problem for publishers was pirate editions of particular works, especially in states whose copyright laws were not stringently observed, or where such laws only protected the worked of nationals. Voltaire, for instance, secretly distributed manuscripts of *Candide* to his publishers in various European cities for simultaneous publication to try and avoid this cross-border problem. Even in the nineteenth century British and US statutes did not protect foreign copyright holders, allowing the Anglo-Saxon publishing industries to be built partly on the basis of what would now be considered pirate editions. Under WIPO this problem was slowly alleviated through the gradual widening of the Berne Convention. And while there are still pirate editions of books in some parts of the world this is no longer the difficulty which the industry focuses its attention on. Now, it is the individual empowered though new and not so new technologies to gain access to copies of material the publishers control without requisite payment, who is the locus of concern.

Before moving to the technology that has sparked the most intense recent anxiety about intellectual property, it is worth noting that for a couple of decades the photocopier has been the copyright infringer's technology of choice. Though, WIPO's main efforts have been against the prospect of pirated editions, with increasing harmonisation of copyright and the increasingly global nature of publishing these publishing infringements have become a small scale and none too bothersome an activity. However, localised individual copyright infringement is almost routine and not even recognised as possibly illegal within the education sector and many business organisations. In education this happens at two levels – individual students copying chapters (or even whole books) and academics providing handouts of articles or chapters to cohorts. This is allowed up to certain limits in most jurisdictions, for instance in Britain currently 5 per cent or one chapter of a book, one article or story or poem from a journal is deemed acceptable. For individual students, the allowance of 'fair dealing' is usually limited to an extract for private study and research that is not 'substantial'. These terms are open to interpretation, but many textbook and other education publishers believe that the levels of 'theft' on campuses are much too high (Kingston 1996). In the non-education sector there is no allowance for fair dealing, yet throughout the world office staff distribute copies of articles or chapters of books around companies. But whereas access to education facilities to assess levels of copyright infringement is reasonably easy, encouraging large (or small) companies to police copyright is neither easy nor practical.

Why do seemingly responsible people regard photocopying a publication as a legitimate and legal activity? The simple answer is that this appears to be a 'victimless crime'. For this to be plausible the notion of the copyrighted artefact must have been partially detached from the individual who wrote it, as indeed it has in most cases (alienation and reproduction by the knowledge industry). But often the act of photocopying is one not so much of theft but the first stage in assimilation and 'fair dealing' recognises this. Thus, the author is recognised as worthy of photocopying – the ideas expressed are valued – and it is the ability to refer to those views through the use of the photocopy at a later date that the process ensures. Going back to the distinction I made for plagiarism, what seems to obtain here is a distinction between process and idea. Photocopies are very seldom directly passed off as the work of the photocopying individual, though aspects of the ideas may turn up in other works. But unless the exact words were reproduced at some length then there would have been no copyright infringement. It is a short step to multiple copying, for colleagues or students and the difference under law may not always be apparent to the individual. The requirements of speed, competition for resources and also the ability through the technology of photocopying produce a temptation just to photocopy the requisite article for reference or discussion purposes without the perception of an illegal act. Around education institutions next to every photocopier there are copyright infringement warning notices setting out the legal limits though at least anecdotally these seem to have no effect on behaviour.

The photocopying of articles and extracts may actually be less of a problem than initially supposed. The books or articles have been bought by a library ensuring at least some return and it is far from clear that those copying extracts would have purchased the whole book or journal in the absence of the photocopier's availability. Thus, the copyright holder, while benefiting from one sale may not have lost subsequent sales because the 'infringer' would not have purchased the text at full market price. Inasmuch as photocopied sections widen the reputation of a specific text there may also be an argument that this serves the interests of the writer (at least) in advancing their social profile, which in some cases may feed into larger fees or payments in the future (I will return to this logic when I discuss computer software). And, where in the past course and module leaders used to provide copied handouts, this practice has been largely constrained in Britain at least, by the Copyright Licensing Agency's activities which have heightened the perception of the 'problem' for universities and in some well-publicised cases have secured for copyright holders significant damages (Kingston 1996). However, if the photocopying problem has been brought under some sort of control by the publishing industry, the Internet and advances in computer technology have opened up a much larger area of possible copyright 'theft'.

The issue of text digitalisation and the availability of such resources on the Internet has led publishers to worry about the future of their ability to make a return on content provision. In much the same way that the advent of printing completely changed the distribution and dissemination of text-based knowledge and information, it is frequently claimed the Internet will do the same. William Martin, writing for the Association for Information Management suggests that

> [the] traditional arrangements between authors, publishers and libraries are no longer appropriate for an electronic environment in which users can access and download information at will . . . with the growth not just of international but global networks, copyright and intellectual property have become subject to the ultimate uncertainty and extraterritoriality of cyberspace.
>
> (1995: 116)

And certainly this is not an uncommon observation. However, there is a need to moderate this claim by differentiating between books and other sorts of publishing (most specifically academic papers, newspapers and other current affairs providers). Books will continue to have advantages over information technology for some time, after all a book is more portable, less power reliant, has easy random access and is less fragile than most current computing technologies. For some uses (especially fiction and leisure reading) the book may have a lot of life left in it. This is not the part of the publishing sector that currently finds the Internet and communications technologies a major challenge: general book sales are presently expanding in developed markets, not declining.

The digitalisation and the electronic availability of time-sensitive information, the stuff of the daily, weekly and monthly print media are much more likely to be revolutionised in the way Martin suggests. In many ways it already is. Once information or knowledge is available on the Internet for retrieval by anyone who has the appropriate technology, and provided access to the particular location is not limited, then the monopoly rights that were enjoyed by any provider of information which were limited to their authorised distribution method (or carrier) no longer exist. For the instrumental justification-based model of knowledge production this is a major problem. As *The Economist* (1996b) succinctly put it: 'Wipe out the monopoly profits of producers of copyrighted material, and you wipe out much of their incentive to produce.' Given the unlikelihood of being able to push back technological advance, this sector of the publishing industry has been forced to rethink their use and relation to copyright. In the education sector, the digitalisation of material and its use in libraries are starting to be subject to negotiation between the parties involved and frameworks for agreement on a reworking of some form of licensing arrangement are being mapped out (Durham 1998). However, elsewhere the race to encompass the new technology has led to two distinct strategies for the publishing sector.

Either the problem is resolved by giving away the information/knowledge product (making it freely available on a website) with a return made in a manner which is articulated to the knowledge object. Or, availability on the Internet can be regarded as another version of pay-per-view with entry to the site guarded by gate keeping, membership and password charges. Publishing has used both methods. Journals from academic quarterlies to the weekly *Economist* have linked access to an Internet site to their subscription system. Developing a secure method for transferring credit card charges in a form of recognisable Internet account settlement to pay for such services has become a key part of e-commerce. From the point of view of copyright, a service which enables the amount of visits and material transferred to be policed and recorded should allow some form of royalty agreement to be arranged, though this might involve an amendment to current copyright. In the case of free access with articulated services, often name and details are captured for subsequent more traditional marketing activities, the role of copyright is to some extent marginalised. Though predicated on the worth of information and knowledge, this is more akin to broadcast media, and thus copyright might in these instances become something like an appearance fee, but also might be non-exclusive. Thus, a particular article might appear on many sites, all carrying various other mixes of material, with adverts that paid for the site, and the author would receive a small syndication fee based on downloaded numbers.

Historically copyright has rewarded the author (or authorial functionary) for the length of lifetime and beyond without having to register a claim (though moral rights in Britain need to be positively asserted). From the point of view of the individual knowledge creator this has considerable advantages over patent. In addition, the two main forms of intellectual property can be distinguished on the basis of the importance accorded to social use. Patents protect ideas that may have wide social utility and are often linked to the expansion of economic welfare, private benefits are balanced by a recognition of social need. For expressions, which are conventionally the subject matter of copyright, little social disutility is presumed to flow from a restriction of distribution. In this area of intellectual property law the self-developmental justification comes into its own. Even if ideas are in the main the result of socialisation, each individual has a complex psycho-social history that will lead them to express these ideas in a infinite multitude of ways. Each is the representation of the self and property in these expressions provides the self with some protection from interference in the creative act. An economic justification grounds the need to allow transfer of these rights to ensure that the return is maximised, but few would suggest that writers or artists only create to enjoy the rewards – this is only a small element in our conception of the creative individual.

The key point is that the authorial function in copyright is not something that is seen as social. Rather, since the emergence of the 'author' in the eighteenth century

> inspiration [has come] to be regarded as emanating not from outside or above, but from within the writer himself. 'Inspiration' [has come] to be explicated in terms of *original genius*, with the consequence that the inspired work was made peculiarly and distinctively the product – and the property – of the writer.
>
> (Woodmansee 1984: 427)

Thus, the author's rights are more important than the free availability of their work. Free availability would be a theft of an individual's expression of themselves, selves that are firmly distinguished from their social context. Again this underlines why the plagiarist is contemptible, they try and pass off another's expression as their own, they steal an idea, even if this 'theft' might be outside the parameters of copyright. The author, be they writer, columnist, reporter or other producer of text has been quite well served by copyright. This has ensured that in the main, with some exceptions such as those within employment contracts, they have managed to retain the ability to profit from their labour. That said, currently for instance, 'Condé Naste . . . gives freelance magazine writers exclusive rights to sell their work for just 90 days, after which either the author *or the company* can reuse the work in any form' (Bettig 1997: 148 emphasis in original). This requires writers to forego their exclusive rights in the interests of getting published by Condé Naste's prestigious magazines, the pay-off being in reputation or kudos. In effect, instead of enjoying copyright in their work for their lifetime plus fifty years, their copyright lasts three months after which the publisher can resell the work without their knowledge or necessary reward. Nevertheless it is the general (if relative) success in securing rewards for knowledge work that makes copyright the model to which a number of reformulations of intellectual property aspire.

Unlike patent which was subject to considerable diplomatic debate in the negotiations towards the TRIPs agreement, copyright did not attract nearly such strident criticism, and in the main the romantic author is largely accepted as the expressive actor. Rewarding individuals for expressive work on first examination produces much less constriction in the social pool of knowledge and is therefore less of a concern to international negotiators. Within the international political economy of intellectual property the only area of contestation has been the expansion of copyright – the move to include more knowledge objects and most importantly computer software. However, in the realm of publishing the expansion of copyright has not been as successful as might be presumed from the expansion of owner's rights in other areas. Copyright is the most durable form of intellectual property, it has a low level of proof, it is cheap and, perhaps most importantly, copyright infringement in many jurisdictions is seen as a criminal offence not a civil one (like patent infringement). While this makes the standard of proof higher for many infringements, it also makes the recourse to law that much more effective. Given these advantages of copyright it is an attractive possibility to those who wish to protect intellectual property.

For publishing, the authorial function has historically included the work of editing and compilation, in certain cases recognising a 'sweat of the brow' argument for labour inputs for these knowledge objects. This notion that the effort that collecting already existing facts into compilations of useful data should be rewarded fits in with the instrumental schema as well as the self-developmental. The intellectual work that goes into the selection and ordering of already existing information may therefore enable copyright to be claimed. However, in the case of Feist Publications vs. Rural Telephone Service, the US Supreme Court in 1991 refused to allow copyright protection to a compiler of telephone directories. Even though fictitious entries included by the compiler to show copying turned up in the directory which was allegedly infringing the copyright, the court ruled that there was insufficient originality in the original collection for it to claim protection. In the US this landmark case reduced the coverage of copyright rather than expanded it and for the compilers of data had two contradictory implications: their information could not be protected through copyright from the reproduction by other providers; but compilers could use other data collections to produce new arrangements of data more cheaply than expending direct research effort (Samuelson 1992).

Nevertheless, directories continue to assert their copyright status, trusting that courts will still recognise the effort-derived rights over the data, as they have done in the past. Indeed, the Court allowed that despite its judgment in the Feist case, the 'vast majority of compilations should qualify as original works of authorship' while protection should only be denied to 'a narrow category of works in which the creative spark is utterly lacking or so trivial to be virtually non-existent' (quoted in Sterk 1996: 1222). Thus the implications of this case may actually be limited despite the expansive language of some of the commentaries upon it. On the other hand, database copyright rules have been the subject of considerable negotiation at WIPO and the TRIPs agreement includes them under Article 10:

> Compilations of data or other material, whether in machine readable or other form, which by reason of the selection or arrangement of their contents constitute intellectual creations shall be protected as such. Such protection, which shall not extend to the data or material itself, shall be without prejudice to any copyright subsisting in the data or material itself.
>
> (GATT 1994, A1C: 2)

Thus, information that might be in the public realm, when collected into a resource that would enable its programmatic use, will attract copyright. This has already led to considerable unease in the scientific community among 'astronomers, climatologists, oceanographers and others who rely on free access to large observational databases [and who] would have to seek permission and perhaps pay' to use such data in their research (Macilwain 1996). In recognising the labour of those who compile databases, the dissemination of information in the public realm is marketised. While, such information may continue to be available in fragmented form, its use value is considerably enhanced when collected together. This compromises the social utility of such data and proposes a question about copyright's ability to recognise social utility in factual expressions rather than artistic ones.

In the main, however, copyright has enabled the individual knowledge producer to obtain at least some benefit from their work. The question of social disutility from non-dissemination of knowledge has been side-tracked as an argument, though as factual works are becoming more heavily protected, this exclusion will become increasingly difficult to maintain. The current repudiation of social utility has been achieved by the utilisation of the idea/expression dichotomy – no ideas are protected, just their particular expression, using fiction as the paradigmic activity. However, copyright covers journals and other 'factual' information sources as well. For specialised journals (most importantly in science and medicine) valuable information is often limited in its distribution through the costs of subscriptions or sale, which base their scarcity price on the limitations mandated through copyright. Returning to social utility issues the dissemination to poor and developing states of valuable information may well be limited by virtue of the protection accorded to the contents of these publications (Altbach 1995). The social benefit of this information is reduced by virtue of its cost, though the advent of the Internet is already changing the dynamic of information dissemination in science and medicine. It is possible that alongside the limitations on technology transfer, the transfer of up-to-date knowledge in science and medicine has previously also been limited by the copyright enjoyed by writers (and by extension by their publishers). However, this protection is somewhat eroded by the widespread activities of copy shops and individual knowledge users in developing states who distribute knowledge often in pirated form. These secondary users are unlikely to be able to afford copyright maintained prices and thus publishers have usually accepted that publications that find their way to developing states will be pirated in this manner.

This problem was hardly raised in the negotiations towards the TRIPs agreement and certainly there has been little political pressure to reform copyrights from the developing states. This is partly due to the need for work to be translated, reducing its utility in its copyrighted form, and also the discourse of copyright being conducted mainly on the basis of novels and fiction. Additionally, in an echo of the transfer of know-how problem, because the individual pirated article depends on considerable reserves of other knowledge, the transfer is limited by the overall cultural limitations of education and knowledge attainment. For the authors the problems of the publishing sector relate not so much to the protection or otherwise accorded to copyright (fair use enables considerable cross-use), rather, it is the competition among authors for limited publication opportunities. For authors generally there is an excess of supply relative to the demand of the global publishing industry for raw materials, and most authors find getting published the problem, not piracy or the theft of their expressions. However, for another knowledge industry the 'problem' of piracy is of a completely different magnitude. If publishing was the first knowledge industry, then the music industry has been one of the major knowledge sectors (at least as far as rhetoric is concerned) in the emerging 'information age'.

The music industry

If it is true that there is no industry more reliant on intellectual property than the music industry (Lash and Urry 1994: 135), then it is unsurprising that much of the rhetoric of piracy and theft should be related to the copying and reproduction of music. Though the problem of photocopying has been an irritant to the publishing industry, home taping and the advent of the recordable compact disc have led the music industry to worry incessantly and loudly about the abuse of their copyrights by individuals and organised crime. The music industry relies more than most industries on the knowledge content of the product to produce the value added. Though estimates differ (not least between those inside and those outside the industry) CDs cost around 50p or less than 5 per cent of the retail price to physically manufacture. Though the return needs to cover fixed costs of the industry, research and development activities (finding new artists, recording their albums) and the subsidy of those acts which fail to break even, the music industry is constantly beset by criticisms over price. Once again, individual consumers have separated out their understanding of the property involved in music recordings. While unlikely to pass off such recording as their own, the re-recording of tracks onto cassette (or now, CD) compilations, or the recording of whole CDs for friends does not appear to the general public as an illegal activity. Once purchased most buyers believe they have the right to re-record the contents of the CD, though few would necessarily extend this to reproduction for sale. Fair use doctrines, despite the best efforts of the music industry, have led courts to hold that individual re-recording does not contravene copyright.

The reproduction of intellectual property at home by individuals has been a problem which has been exacerbated by new technologies in most knowledge industries. Avenell and Thompson go as far as to suggest that the sector of capital that develops and manufacturers the technologies enabling such actions are 'parasitic capitalists', surviving in direct tension with intellectual property producing capital (Avernell and Thompson 1994). Thus, the manufactures of recordable CD technologies, and before them the developers of audio cassette recording systems, can only profit due to the wanton disregard of the intellectual property of another sector by purchasers of copying-capable products. The 'parasitic' product violates the commodity relationship established in the first instance by the intellectual property producer; it allows a dilution of the constructed scarcity through the act of copying. The introduction of re-recording technologies as consumer commodities has in each case (audio cassettes, digital recording or DAT technologies and most recently recordable CDs) produced demands from the music industry to limit their abilities. A similar problem beset the TV and film industries with the advent of the cheap video recorder (Frow 1994). Demands for the limitation of the technical properties of such devices have continually been side-stepped by the hardware manufacturers.

Intellectual property law aims to maintain the economic rewards that flow to the knowledge entrepreneurs of the pirated sector while allowing the manufacturers of the offending technologies to continue production. It does this by recognising that the purchase of a knowledge product must allow some fair use of the knowledge it encapsulates. The key threshold the individual cannot cross is to enter in a further market relation with those receiving copies. Thus, while the music industry would in an ideal world forbid copying altogether, copyright law has settled on copying for sale being illegal, but copying for private use being legitimate. This is consistent as the rights of owners still carry considerable weight, even if these owners are not the copyright holders. This is the main disadvantage for knowledge producers in relying on a form of property regime. By allowing that the product can be sold, and thus owned, the owner becomes a rights holder (even if these rights are secondary and circumscribed in relation to the intellectual property's reproduction) and has legally legitimate rights regarding the use of such property to their private ends (where those ends may include their relations, outside the market, with other social individuals). But, from the music industry's perspective 'home taping is killing music', as a large-scale but seemingly ineffective campaign told all record buyers in the 1980s.

This claim is couched in legal terms that rely on the legitimacy of intellectual property. Property-ness is asserted, allowing the product to be alienated from the producer and thus sold, while limitations on the property's subsequent use are also asserted, and thus the lack of final alienability from the producer. Within this paradox lies the problem for the music industry, it is seen as separate from and exploitative of both artists and consumers. The high price of the product and the variability of the artistic standards have contributed to consumers' attempt to lower prices they pay to the companies. Thus, the ability of pirates to provide (nowadays) excellent copies of the products at low prices allows consumers to think they have found a bargain. One music industry source has suggested that 'three times as much music is privately copied as is legally sold', though recipients of copies would not necessarily pay the full price of the contents of their 'bootlegged' recording (*The Economist* 1996a). Also, at least some private copying may act as a word-of-mouth marketing channel to increase sales. Despite these possibilities the representation of piracy as theft is an attempt to establish a particular reading of intellectual property. The industry has so far failed to conclusively substantiate a position where individuals even feel guilty about home recording. This is partly because the technology that enables these practices is clearly legally available and assessed (and marketed) on its ability to produce satisfactory results from copying.

But it is not always only individuals whose 'theft' is actually legal. Prior to the TRIPs agreement the arbitrary duration of copyright under national regimes provided another problem for the industry. Japanese copyright protection, which was considerably shorter than that of America (though this will now change), led to material returning to the public domain for unlicensed exploitation, when its non-Japanese copyright owners would expect continued protection if Japanese law had had the same length of protection accorded in their national jurisdictions. Unsurprisingly this led to accusations of theft. While this 'problem' remained unresolved many major copyrighted works by artists such as the Beatles, Frank Sinatra, or the Rolling Stones as well as jazz and classical music recordings from the 1960s, were available outside copyright in the Japanese market (Bates and Rafferty 1996). Certainly this sort of problem pales into insignificance when compared to the incidence of piracy, but on the other hand led to problems of parallel imports.[1] Though formally illegal as they contravened copyright in the destination market, when sold through third parties there was nothing that US recording companies could do to halt the manufacture of these products. In Japan they were perfectly legal, and only the international trade was subject to the then more vague international restrictions of copyright. However, as I have noted, these sort of problems will be dissolved by the harmonisation of legislation under the TRIPs agreement.

One area of piracy which may be less of a problem is the bootleg live recordings of artists who are under exclusive contract to record companies. The companies sometimes make the claim that these infringements of their contract with the artist compromise the quality of the output for the 'fans' as they are often badly recorded and packaged. However, it is usually the case that these recordings only sell to fans who have already brought most if not all of the 'legitimate' output of the particular artist and for whom the sound quality of these recordings relative to CDs is not an important issue. Though the copyright of these recordings does not lie with performers under strict contracts, it is not unusual for the artists themselves to connive or at least turn a blind eye to such activities. Famously in the case of the Grateful Dead, the band let it be known that they were not only happy for fans to record their concerts for distribution and sale among 'Deadheads' but they would co-operate in this activity by allowing audio feeds from the mixing desk. The logic was partly ideological or libertarian, and partly economic in that such recordings would convince more people to see the Grateful Dead live and as such enhance both their reputation and ticket sales. As part of a strategy that saw the band become one of the most profitable live concert draws during the 1970s and 1980s, this must be considered a reasonable success. Subsequently their lyricist John Perry Barlow has adopted a well known anti-intellectual property stance as part of the 'information wants to be free' strand of Internet debate regarding IPRs (Barlow 1993).

In much the same way that intellectual property has generally served authors well in publishing, so copyright in the music industry has provided considerable benefits to creators or artists. Where their copyright has been recognised, considerable rewards have been captured on their behalf and in most cases has finally benefited them. This benefit has been shared with the record companies, but in most cases the extent of benefit from self-distribution is considerably exceeded by that which can be secured from the activities of the major record companies. That said, the early history of the industry exhibited rather less benign tendencies, with artists being paid on the basis of session time, their copyrights being bought out (without their full understanding of what was being sold) and their future earnings accruing to the owners of these copyrights rather than the artists themselves. This was most often accomplished within the law by assigning the authorship of the song not to the writer but the producer. And even if the song writer was correctly identified, the publishing rights organisations who collect royalty payments frequently had (and continue to have) different names registered to collect the royalties, as the rights have been sold.[2] Copyright by being alienable can be transferred and pressure was often brought to bear to ensure that copyright was transferred, or sometimes an artist's ignorance of the law served a producer well (Chapple and Garofalo 1977: 240). In recent years many artists of 'race' records and early blues recording have sought through the courts to gain the royalties which they lost in this process. This has been a slow if ultimately reasonably successful process.

One of the most celebrated cases was that of Muddy Waters which enabled the writer to obtain considerable royalties form the sales of an (unattributed) cover version of his song 'You Need Love', recorded by Led Zeppelin as 'A Whole Lotta Love' in the 1970s. In another, George Harrison was found to have infringed the copyright of the Chifons' 'He's So Fine' with his 1971 hit 'My Sweet Lord' (Sweeting 1998). Many blues artists have managed to secure some recompense from British rhythm and blues related bands of the 1960s and 1970s, who used the earlier blues and R'n'B records as a profitable source for their compositions. As these groups became better known, they switched to writing their own lyrics and melodies. And thus the Rolling Stones who had covered many blues songs themselves successfully sued to obtain the royalties to 'Bittersweet Symphony' by the Verve which used an unauthorised (sampled) segment of the Andrew Oldham Orchestra's orchestral version of 'The Last Time'. The rights owners, Allen Klein, Mick Jagger and Keith Richards obtained all writing royalties from sales of the recording.

Samplers, another technological advance with profound consequences for copyright, have enabled artists to take a small segment of a particular recording and manipulate it to produce a 'new' effect. The use of very small segments (though often easily recognisable) has complicated the fair use doctrine somewhat, and as a legal issue remains unresolved though much discussed if not litigated. This method of producing audio soundscapes has been most successfully utilised in rap music in America. However, the sampling of other records to produce new ones has not led to a vast number of copyright cases, litigation is mostly settled before it comes to court, so precedents have been slow to emerge. As Rose points out, before

> rap music began grossing millions of dollars, the use of these musical passages went un-noticed by publishing administrators and copyright holders. Sampling clearance was a relatively minor legal issue. Limited visibility, relatively small profits and legal costs to pursue illegal uses of sampled materials made policing such theft undesirable for record executives. Furthermore, these samples

encouraged the sale of new records. For a recording label to win a law suit in order to take a share of another label's profit raised the possibility that similar profits would have to be paid (in full) in another case. Because all major record companies distribute sampled material, law suits would be traded rather heavily.

(Rose 1994: 90)

For instance when Geffen records recently considered suing RT Mark who had produced a CD made up of one of their artist's recordings cut up and put back together in seemingly random sequence, on a CD suitably called 'Deconstructing Beck', they were advised to drop the case. Given Beck's own use of samples (by no means all legally cleared) 'the Advisory on Law Practice in Art . . . plainly described the trouble Geffen would have if it tried to prosecute' (Elkin 1998).

Another aspect of this issue is typified by the case of James Brown who had been sampled heavily and whose career was rescued from terminal decline in the 1980s by the interest in his back catalogue this created. In the middle of the James Brown sampling boom, he was a guest of honour at a DJ convention in the Albert Hall in London, and by all accounts was completely bemused at a standing ovation that lasted over five minutes. Another artist who revived her career if only temporarily was Loretta Holloway. Having heard her own voice as the central part of the Black Box record 'Right on Time', she received an out-of-court settlement and was able to profit from the re-release of some of her output from Salsoul records.[3] While historically there has been some sharp practice within the music industry, copyright laws *do* enable artists to seek remuneration after the event, and appealing to a self-developmental justification, as well as labour-desert arguments regarding the rewards earned from disputed copyrights, these cases have often been successful.

In the early history of the industry copyrights were held by the companies (often illegally or at least in direct contravention of the spirit of the law), more recently artists have realised the value which copyrights can capture for them and the control they may be able to wield through the law. The (remaining) Beatles managed to stop the use of their song 'Revolution' which their American record label had licensed to Nike for television advertising. The case revolved around who owned the mechanical rights to particular performances of Beatles songs which were recorded under contract to their record label. Though a complicated case regarding the actual rights which accrue to the mechanical (which is to say specific performance) rights holder, in the end Capitol/EMI settled out of court and Nike had to stop using the song. Though Nike had acted with good faith, the record label conceded in the end that the rights were not their to license (Eliot 1989: 206–209). Though few bands have the resources to challenge a multinational record company in court, nevertheless the possibility of copyright protecting the original artist or writer is clearly significant. Part of the reason that these sorts of cases are increasingly coming to court is that as intellectual property becomes more valuable (and artists realise where their worth lies), the veil of artist ignorance has lifted. The 'myth' of the romantic author is becoming further established in the music industry: in groups, those who write the songs are accorded status and rewards well in excess of merely performing members. It is sometimes possible to seek further rewards, not least of all by suing for part of the song writing royalties on the basis of unrecognised contributions to the writing process. Mike Joyce and Andy Rourke (drummer and bassist respectively of The Smiths) for instance sued the song-writing partnership of Morrissey and Marr who wrote the material the band performed on the basis that their contribution to the group's success had not been sufficiently rewarded (Gilbert 1997). But normally performing members who do not write material do not share the industry's potentially massive rewards.

Even as artists are recognising their rights within the music industry and are doing more to assert them, new challenges to the scarcity constructed through copyright have emerged to challenge the returns made by artists and record companies. Though the problems of piracy continue for the industry (not least of all due to the high quality of illegal CD copies), the Internet may represent the 'most serious threat ever to its revenues'. The new MP3 technology for the distribution of music 'wave files' over the Internet, free through newsgroups where 'pirates' put files for downloading, has created panic in the industry. The ability to continue to support the necessary scarcity that is required for the notion of copyright over recording to make any sense is being fast eroded by technological and network developments. As audio compression software becomes widely available and as more pirates set up song warehouses, so computer owners can record their own selection of songs onto recordable CDs and it is likely that the record companies will find it hard to maintain the sales of legitimate CDs. While the Performing Rights Society is trying to enforce copyright payments, the available sanctions are not extensive nor easy to apply (Wylie 1996). The advent of the Internet may therefore change the whole way music is delivered. Alan McGee (owner of Oasis' record label Creation Records) has argued that

> There will be no record companies in five or 10 years' time. It will be sexier for bands to sell their records on the Internet – cut out the record company and deliver straight to the fans . . . If you are an Indie band and you sell 5,000 records through a record label, that will make you nothing in England. But if you sell them through the Internet at £10 a time, it will cost you a pound to cut the CD and you've made £45,000 in one fell swoop.
>
> (quoted in Wroe 1998)

But, many see McGee's scenario as alarmist and overstated. Nevertheless the Internet will fundamentally change the industry.

Record companies play more than a distributional role, they spend considerable time and resources marketing and promoting groups across the global music market. Small independent groups would still lack the resources to drive up their profile. Even on the Internet, if no-one has heard of your band they will not be prepared to buy a CD or even download a new piece of music to be put on their writeable CD. Additionally, much of the industry's turnover is represented by back catalogue. While the copyright for these performances is held by the record companies, and importantly while they can continue to defend such copyrights, a significant part of the industry will continue to be controlled by the major global record companies. Thus, the challenge from new ways for bands distributing their music may be a medium- to long-term issue. Of more immediate concern for the industry is the current copyright infringements that are happening on the Internet as well as more traditional methods of piracy. The major companies are looking for ways of defending their copyrights through their own use of the Internet as an avenue of distribution. But even more immediately the quality of digital copies on pirate CDs is now so good that they are all but indistinguishable from the 'real' article. Thus, piracy remains a severe problem for the industry whatever the technological problems of the Internet may bring. And given that whatever its problems, for most musical artists, the key to major rewards is working through the industry, this may produce severe problems for them. Though the industry is being challenged by the Internet and digital copying, the ability of artists to secure rewards for their creations is also under threat. New methods may emerge, either within or outside the regimes of copyright, but at present what they might be is less than clear. However, this is not to suggest that copyrights hold no problems for the emerging technologies themselves.

The computer industries

For intellectual property to behave as property, its supply must be limited. However, the digital revolution undercuts this construction of scarcity. Without the ability to restrict the distribution of the knowledge object which is copyrighted, the copyright itself becomes nearly worthless and, in a sense, no longer property. This leads to a problem for the individual knowledge creator. The bargains (some of which are better than others) which knowledge workers/creators strike within knowledge industries exchange the rights in their work for a proportion of the return that is generated through economic exploitation. The company retains a proportion to support the continuation of their activities (allowing a 'reasonable' profit), the originator receives a larger reward than their limited resources would enable them to secure distributing the work themselves. Under the logic of the instrumental schema these bargains will no longer be made if the company is unable to produce a scarcity and thus a return by distributing this information. As a technological sector, the Internet and the computer software industry are the site of the most interesting and important contemporary challenge to previous intellectual property practices. Indeed, in the above discussions of the publishing and music industries it was impossible to discuss the current situation without also alluding to the impact of the Internet. (The Internet is still growing and expanding and, therefore, these issues are likely to be more expansive in the future, rather than less.)

As providers move away from the model of information distribution reliant on materialised carriers (magazines, journals, CDs), so the organisation of these industries will change (and indeed is changing). Utilising the Internet or the 'information super highway' effectively means that holders of IPRs will be unable to control further reproduction of works they distribute. Obviously it is possible to charge for entry to sites and many subscriber-based organisations' or service providers' sites only allow full access on the basis of a code word or membership number. While this enables the site-maintaining company to capture revenue from users, the problems lie in the subsequent reproduction of digitally transferred information once it has left the site. This is a similar problem to home taping. Once a legitimate and paying user has downloaded whatever information or knowledge object is offered by the site, what is to stop further copies being distributed by the purchaser? It is already clear that the multiplication of materials on the Internet proceeds at a considerable pace. Unlike home taping where the links between the original and the copy still include the physical transfer and material scarcity of the copied item, this is not the case for Internet users. Not only does the copy remain on their machine in digital form which can be continually recopied to other users, many of those who maintain their own personal Internet sites make available all sorts of material that was originally copyrighted. While commercial sites are eager to extract rent from site usage, most personal sites are constructed as part of the self-expression of individuals. As such, attempts to limit what might be exhibited on such sites come up against a form of the self-developmental schema – by not charging for access these sites are in effect saying 'here is something interesting' not trying to make a profit from reproduction. And in a digital age, such an assertion is part of a legitimate expression of an individual's will.

In intellectual property law there has been a move to try and reintegrate computer-related or computer-carried knowledge and information into a workable property regime. The central question which the Internet poses is whether Bettig's assertion of the ability of intellectual property law to deal with new technologies will be borne out once again.

> The initial period following the introduction of a new communications medium often involves a temporary loss of control by copyright owners over the use of their property. However, the logic of copyright generally favours the economic rights of the owners. The protection of economic rights has [historically] prevailed over a logic based on social utility.
>
> (Bettig 1997: 140)

The defining issue for copyright holders is keeping track of the digitised copies which can be now be made. Given the need to allow reproduction to earn a return, the copyright holder needs to be able to effectively halt or punish non-authorised duplication or copying. If this is impossible, then copyright law in its current form will not be able to function. Previous technologies involved a generational deterioration – a copy of a copy was never as good, and thus as things were recopied serially so the quality deteriorated. Digital technologies have neatly side-stepped this problem by reducing all the required information to the pattern of 1s and 0s of digitised data. There is now no generational degradation and thus copies are as good as originals. But, on the other hand, the technology itself may hold the answer.

One of the methods that seems to hold some promise for copyright holders is the digital watermarking of materials distributed across the Internet (*The Economist* 1998a). Provided these watermarks were corrupted by even slight tampering which would include second generation copying, then illegal copies could be easily recognised, even if they could not actually be stopped. This would enable copyright (in a similar form to current legal practice) to be enforceable; once a copy had been located a price (and damages) could be settled through court action. In theory at least as cases were successfully prosecuted, so the deterrence value of copyright would be re-established. Alternatively, if encryption of some sort became widely used, the need to purchase yet more equipment in the form of decoders would imply higher costs for accessing the Internet. This has social utility implications that seem not to have been factored into the industry's calculations (Tang 1997: 205). Copyright would then be structured around the legitimate access to sites and the payment for entry codes. In the first generation, a legal scarcity would be reimposed but the issue of second generation copying would remain. Another, perhaps rather extreme conclusion would be a self-destruct on copy function hidden within the digital codes of particular objects. This is already happening with upgrade software. Microsoft and others have developed upgrade programs which when loaded onto stand-alone computers check that there is legal version of the program, one that is registered to the same owner and not copied from elsewhere, to upgrade. If not, the upgrade fails, maintaining the manufacturers' copyright and leaving the user out of pocket. However, for every technological fix there is an 'answer'. All encryption must be decodable or it would be pointless, and therefore there will always be (successful) attempts to break the code.

As Emery Simon of the Alliance to Promote Software Innovation points out, while the 'method of purchase is radically different, the end result is no different than with traditional film, book or sound-recording distribution. The end result is a digital copy within the end user's physical control' (1996: 33). But the problem for Internet copyright lies in the preview. In a bookshop one can browse through books without purchasing them or infringing copyright. However, computer technology requires that to view a document over the Internet, it is transferred (temporarily) to the machine of the user. How can transfer for subsequent storage (or even further reproduction) be differentiated from merely browsing or viewing? Copyright requires that such a distinction is made because it is in the very nature of informational goods that one would want to assess the product before purchase. However, once a file has been transferred, it is currently impossible to know what has become of it – has the document been stored, reproduced in quantity or destroyed? Though some Internet sites only allow partial previews prior to membership of the site, once access is gained, the multiple copying of downloaded materials remains uncontrollable and undetectable. The copyright holder is essentially unable to control the distribution of their work – any available rights are swiftly exhausted by subsequent and unknown recopying.

As limitation on reproduction is the chief way in which scarcity has been imposed in the past, Simon's assertion would seem difficult to sustain – the end product is different due to its potential to act as a further 'original'. Rather optimistically

Simon argues that encryption techniques and other technological fixes will enable dissemination to be controlled *provided* these technical process are protected themselves against 'hacking' by further new technologies. Indeed, he goes as far as to argue that

> it would be best to prohibit the use of such devices as well as the act of neutralising technical protections. Once copy-breaking devices are in the hands of users and are being used to unlock copyrighted works without authorisation, it may do little good to only have a legal claim against the device manufacturer or importer.
>
> (Simon 1996: 37)

This argument is remarkably familiar, bearing a close resemblance to those which were raised against cassette recorders, video recorders and recordable CDs. Given the pace of technological change, this attempt to hold back further developments is unlikely to be a successful strategy. And without a global jurisdiction, banning such products in one state would merely produce a competitive advantage in another state that allowed their manufacture and international sale.

However, not all those involved in the software industry necessarily see the need to operate a copyright system as it has traditionally been practised. At the very least there is likely to be some form of fragmentation of copyright; the rights which are held by 'owners', say, to produce CDs may not extend without formal agreement to the Internet. In much the same way there were once broadcast rights, that then divided into terrestrial, cable, video and satellite, so a new Internet right may be established in the future. However, with digitalisation the ability to maintain such distinctions will be difficult due to the heightened ability of digitalised data to be transferred from one sector to another with ease (Higham 1993). It has become clear to some practitioners and legal scholars that while other areas of technological advance can be effectively included within current intellectual property regimes (such as biotechnology, despite other criticisms which I have outlined), for the computer sector what is required is a *sui generis* regime (Barton 1993). The problems lie in trying to translate pervious precedents and case law to make them relevant to the realm of computer technology. This has proved difficult with no clear framework emerging though there has been some work on hybrid regimes that draw from patent and copyright.

One way that software houses have tried to deal with copying is to distribute free or at greatly reduced prices versions of their software for evaluation. Shareware is distributed on the basis that users who continue to the use the product after the nominal evaluation period register with the software company to receive manuals for full use of the version they have and often more up-to-date or fuller versions of the program. Thus, while allowing copying for evaluation, the companies are appealing to the goodwill of users to pay for improved versions. Thus, though casual and low end users may effectively 'steal' the software, those with high end needs can evaluate the software outside a property regime, but enter an intellectual property relation once a full or recent version is requested. Rather than dispensing with intellectual property altogether, this works to establish value with the user, and also encourages distribution of trial versions more widely than if their 'true' price was charged. Thus IPRs are only claimed against serious users, and low end users are allowed to 'break' copyright in the interests of promotion and goodwill. Individual programmers have built reputations based on the distribution of such software, and there is an echo of the Mertonian notion of benefits from knowledge work outside an intellectual property system. The rewards to be garnered from reputation for good programming (and programming innovations) are considerable, at least in the geographical locations where software writers have clustered, most especially 'Silicon Valley' in California.

Though less widespread among the larger software companies this practice continues. Larger companies tend to distribute much more truncated versions than their predecessors, and these often come with automatic 30-day shut-down. But essentially even large companies accept a certain amount of loss as part of the hugely expanded distribution base that can be accessed through Internet software downloading (*The Economist* 1996b). By offering help desk support, free upgrades and other services to authenticated purchasers the attraction of copies may be eroded. Companies may also switch to a strategy that owes more to broadcasting than the distribution of scarce goods. As anyone using the Internet has noticed, increasingly search engines and other gateways have the equivalent of billboards advertising all sorts of services with links that require only a click of the mouse. Like commercial television, the broadcaster (or site manager) is delivering the user to the advertiser, not the information or knowledge products to the user. While this may allow small-scale sites to fund their activities on the Internet, the competition for marketing and advertising spending may make such income even more volatile than in print publishing. And, there is always the question of the compromises that content providers may need to make to attract (or retain) advertisers – a problem with a long history.

Though the structure of copyright is rendered problematic at the interface between industry and Internet user, within the computer software industry things are no better. Formally, software is written in a form of language and exists in a (written) digitised from. Unlike patents which *describe* in language a material process or product, the process which software performs is undertaken through written instructions to the computer concerned. Thus, in the past software has been deemed intellectual property under copyright. Though programs are tools or processes, they are protected as if they were merely expressions of an idea. However, many software elements are actually common to numerous programs. And when under the pressure of a deadline to solve a particular processing problem there is a temptation to utilise a solution from another (competitor's) program. The code may be amended or hidden within the new program but the idea remains the same. Thus, the problem within software is two-fold. First, though copyright protects the written program, it does not protect the idea of a solution to a problem. Therefore, by changing the coding other programmers can 'steal' the idea with some hope of impunity. On the other hand, given that programs are tools, and given the speed of technological change of only limited durability, copyright protection of writer's lifetime-plus seems unaccountably long. In one way this is the technology gap problem discussed in the last chapter, revisited.

American intellectual property lawyers 'insist that while theft of intellectual property is rife in Silicon Valley usually it is swept under the carpet' (*Sunday Business* 1996). In much the same way that sampling cases are unlikely to come to court because of the danger of being countersued, few software companies are likely to find that their products do not include elements which might conceivably be the intellectual property of another company. This is partly because the industry has quite volatile employment patterns which see programmers moving from firm to firm before often setting up on their own. And while the employment contract solution which I have already mentioned is frequently used, it is particularly difficult to police in this sector as their is little agreement about where the common language of computing ends and the intellectual property of specific owners begins. And given the complex nature of programs, short of wholesale duplication of entire program segments, 'theft' may be difficult to locate and prove. Leaving the practical problems aside, the industry has always maintained that intellectual property protection is vital to its continued health and expansion (e.g. Bale 1988; *The Economist* 1996a; Simon 1996). Appealing to the instrumental schema, those speaking on behalf of the industry conclude that without protection of their IPRs there would be no reason to continue to innovate. But if IPRs are not enforced then they are essentially worthless – or non-existent as property. The industry as a whole wishes to operate a system that is enforceable and in the main appeals to some form of copyright as that system. However, industry practices mitigate against this possibility, at least between software companies themselves.

Computer programs have considerably more obvious social utility than other expressive works and thus the logic of copyright may not be particularly appropriate to them in any case. But process patent-type protection remains largely unworkable due to the difficulty of isolating the 'idea(s)' within a particular piece of software – the language in which they are expressed is not separable from the process they perform. In most cases, if there were no difficulty in fitting programmes into intellectual property categories, given their use and economic character, they would be considered 'industrial property' and thus patentable. But, as Reichman has argued:

> A line that appears unclear or poorly defended will tempt entrepreneurs to circumnavigate the strict prerequisites of patent law, with its basic require-ments of novelty, utility and non-obviousness, in order to shelter industrial creations within the more receptive and generous embrace of copyright law.
>
> (1992: 327)

A process which has been evident throughout the history of intellectual property in the computer industry. And thus the main danger is that 'manufacturers of electronic information tools stand to obtain patent-like protection on soft conditions for a very long period of time, even though innovation in information science occurs through "sequential and cumulative improvements"'. (ibid.: 345)

Thus, rather than encouraging innovation, such protection actually represents a restriction on the ability of others to carry on their trade in the industry within the (claimed) legal constrictions. That this seems the case is evidenced by the assertion above that though infringement is widespread, little is done about it as everyone who is developing or innovating programs is drawing from the same pool. But by retaining a patina of protection infringement remains costly, it needs to be hidden, it cannot be too obvious and thus at least some of the value of the instrumental schema is retained. Nevertheless, the honouring of intellectual property in the breach is hardly satisfactory for those seeking protection within the industry.

As computers have become ever more ubiquitous, intellectual property laws with different assessments of social utility, private rights and economic efficiencies have been brought together. Unfortunately both jurists and practitioners find themselves in a new environment, a new nexus of law technology and social processes. This makes the application of previous models of IPR protection difficult if not impossible, and while *ad hoc* arrangements persist there is a need to rethink what intellectual property means, and how it might be justified in this new environment (Barton 1993). But by developing methods for dealing with 'piracy' that have used intellectual property-related strategies but also value-added and built-in obso-lescence approaches, the software industry has to some extent undercut its own argument for the continuing relevance of intellectual property. The speed of innovation and advance in software continues, despite the practical and legal difficulties of instigating a workable intellectual property protection structure. The computer industry as a whole seems to be currently the agent of its own problems, by its technological advances it is undermining the very property system it wished in general to appeal to. And despite instrumental schema based claims the IPR problems do not seem to have significantly slowed innovation or reduced the rewards earned by software companies.

Piracy, piracy everywhere

In the sectors I have discussed above, as well as many others 'piracy' is presented as a damaging and dangerous attack on the well-being of legitimate market actors. Despite this chorus, consumers of these industries and others developing knowledge-reliant products seldom see the (re)production of copies as theft, but rather as the fair use of a commodity which they now *own*. The conception of property which is promoted by these industries is not an unqualified benefit. The disadvantage is rooted in the construction of intellectual property as *both* alienable property and rights-based inalienable property. The continued rhetoric of theft is concerned to reinforce the legitimacy of intellectual property and combat organised rather than individual piracy. It is not unusual for the piracy of products to be characterised as 'epidemic', producing a 'swelling tide' of counterfeit goods (for instance, Harvey 1993; Millar 1997). One reason for this discourse of alarm is to underline and further reinforce the notion of intellectual property *qua* property. Something can only be stolen if it is already owned – for there to be theft there must be property. Two levels of activities are lumped together under the rubric of piracy: organised criminal activities – systematic counterfeit for sale; and individual copying of legitimately purchased goods. But, there is a third level of intra-sectoral piracy that is less discussed though it is evident in all knowledge industries.

The rhetoric of theft also stretches to cases where legally speaking no such 'theft' has taken place, as in the Japanese copyright example noted above, or in the retention of skills by employees discussed in the last chapter. This suggests the notion of theft is not necessarily a technical term but a rhetorical device deployed within the knowledge structure. The use of theft and piracy-based arguments rather than social utility or access in the negotiations towards the TRIPs agreement, stressed the rights of the individual owner – theft is the illegitimate wresting of property from a legally constituted individual. However, as I noted in the discussion of biotechnology something that looks like theft from the developing states' perspective, is not theft under TRIPs if what is stolen is *not yet* seen as property. One of the key mechanisms for turning what was not property into intellectual property is the recognition of its emergent trade-related-ness. Thus, some observers and developing states' negotiators came to perceive the TRIPs agreement's harmonisation of intellectual property protection not merely as a co-ordination of legal instruments, but a strategy by the 'information-rich' to enclose the intellectual commons currently available to the 'information-poor'. By defining the debates in terms of theft and piracy, the rights of owners were stressed and advantaged over and above other (social) rights. The argument that theft needs to be combated, by appealing once again to the analogy with material property and the widespread notion of ownership, aims to reinforce the 'common sense' of a property approach to knowledge.

The ideology of the author as paradigmic knowledge producer and owner of their ideas ties together these arguments. Though the author is legally constituted (and as such can be a company) the domination of the individualised charac-terisation of knowledge production is overwhelming. This depiction of the author, as I have argued, is one that is strangely atemporal – the author is conceived as producing knowledge outside the history and development of previous knowledge in which the creative process *must* be embedded. The author does not (at least in the legal characterisation of the process) depend on previous knowledge(s) but rather produces a particular intellectual property outside the social development of knowledge. Intellectual property rights, unlike real or material property, are delineated by time. If time is becoming faster (Giddens 1990; Harvey 1989), one way to reintroduce a slower temporality (as a barrier to competitors) is for the company to establish intellectual property as a major element of the marketable product or service. Intellectual property rights are an increasingly important defence against the time based erosion of a company's competitive advantage. By establishing intellectual property in a product competition can be held off allowing the monopoly rents accruing to the copyright or patent to be exploited. Piracy eats into these rents by producing the very competition that IPRs were deployed to halt. Piracy undermines the constructed monopoly or scarcity and thus both reduces the rents which can be captured as well as reversing the deceleration of time that IPRs achieve.

Figures on piracy are unreliable at best and almost certainly inflated by industries concerned to bring pressure to bear on policy-makers, not least of all in the TRIPs agreement negotiations (Sell 1998). For instance the International Federation of the Phonographic Industry (IFPI) produced figures which 'showed' that in 1995 $944 million worth of pirated CDs were sold in Europe, a further $434m in Asia, $303m in North America, $298m in Latin America and over $40m worth elsewhere (Millar 1997). Thus in Europe, whose recorded music market was worth around $22.5 billion, even on these figures pirated discs only accounted for around 4.5 per cent of sales. Nevertheless the industry claims it is being 'swamped'. The heightened rhetoric still relies on the normal instrumental justifications: Rupert Perry of EMI Europe has claimed 'People don't realise that by saving a few pounds buying a CD by their favourite artist they are jeopardising the future of the artist because there will be no money for reinvestment. This is theft, albeit on a massive scale' (quoted in Millar 1997). However, despite this 'massive theft' in the period 1988–1995 the 'big five' recording companies Bertelsmann, Polygram, Sony, Thorn EMI and Time Warner, all remained remarkably profitable, with some variations due to special circumstances such as the purchase of smaller record labels. Both Polygram and Thorn EMI managed to produce world-wide profits in excess of 10 per cent of total sales in 1995, a level which they had maintained for some years (Sadler 1997: 1927). But the industry's sales pattern are notoriously volatile, and its assets are unreliable. One anonymous industry source suggested that it was 'a business where your strongest assets might literally dissolve overnight. Oasis can have a fight and break up and you can write off any projections for future record sales' (quoted in Bell 1998). Given these vagaries, the pirates serve a useful purpose – they are an identifiable drain on income whose effect can be exaggerated to deal with forecasting problems. Perhaps more importantly, the recording industry relies on a small minority of globally successful stars to generate the income that allows the high rate of failure of aspiring new artists. Though there is a high rate of attrition and loss, the industry requires only a few major selling acts to produce its customary profits – but these are the very artists that pirates habitually target.

The identification of piracy as a problem is not limited to the recording industry. Perfumery and clothing are both sectors where the information element of the product is high, in this case the brand. Calvin Klein, Giorgio and other perfume brands have frequently been pirated as have the clothes of Ralph Lauren, Fred Perry, Chanel and others with high profile labels. Raids have uncovered hoards of 'swing tickets' (for numerous designers) and garment labels waiting to be attached to 'knock-offs' which are then sold in small batches (Rowe 1997). Throughout developed states' goods masquerading as designer labelled items are being sold cheaply on street corners, in discount stores and in tourist markets. Whether anybody is actually fooled is another question and it is unlikely in most cases whether those purchasing pirated copies would buy the full-priced versions. But, where brand value is concerned, it is not lost customers that is the real problem for the manufacturer, rather it is the exclusivity of the brand which is threatened. When the value is in the brand, as it becomes more common, its scarcity value declines and the brand is diluted. The customer who has paid for an original will find it possibly confused with the 'knock off' and will move on to a more exclusive (and less pirated) brand. But branding is increasingly entering all sorts of sectors such as arms (*The Economist* 1997c) and drugs. By some estimates around 5 per cent of world trade is accounted for by counterfeit goods, though as always such figures are little more than guesses whose accuracy is less important than their political utility.

Quite apart from the intellectual property issues I discussed in the last chapter, the pharmaceuticals industry also has a rather dangerous brand piracy problem. For instance, a counterfeit branded meningitis vaccine led to several hundred dying from the disease or suffering permanent brain damage. Though branded, the drugs were in effect placebos. The World Health Organisation has found such fake pharmaceuticals in twenty-eight countries, and has established that they directly led to at least 500 deaths in 1996 in Nigeria, Bangladesh, India, Argentina and Haiti. In another case, 'a fake branded cough medicine, which contained an industrial solvent . . . caused 3,000 deaths in Africa (Finch 1997). This is a completely different issue from the sale and distribution of generic copies by developing states' pharmaceutical companies. Many of those companies while violating the intellectual property of the particular drug, are at least offering a similar (and effective) product. However, piracy of branded medicines where the brand is pirated to sell useless or actively dangerous products is often lumped together with the generic producers as different aspects of the same crime of piracy. This rhetoric aims to obscure the health issue of drug scarcity by concentrating on the damage done by pirates utilising brands. Piracy and theft are useful ways of simplifying the complex issues of intellectual property and the distribution of rights or benefits that flow from knowledge.

The simple accusation of theft helps substantiate the description of a 'tidal wave' of counterfeit goods 'swamping' legitimate businesses. Though I certainly do not want to dismiss the extent or seriousness of these issues, there is further aspect of piracy which the knowledge industries seldom introduce into popular discussions of the piracy epidemic. Piracy is not only a problem between particular industries and 'thieves' but is also a problem within many sectors themselves. Indeed as one computer industry commentator summed it up: 'It is ironic that an industry which often rails against the way its customers copy its products should itself be riddled with corruption' (*Sunday Business* 1996). The software industry has replicated the public use versus private benefit problems which have always been played out in the legal construction of intellectual property. One programmer's piracy of a particular way of instructing the computer is another's best practice, common knowledge or self-evident solution. But this realisation that intellectual property between companies is difficult to distinguish or protect, turns attention to those outside the industry whose 'piracy' is much easier to identify.

Though sometimes the instrumental and self-developmental schema is utilised to make arguments within the industry about the 'theft' of particular software elements, only when entire or nearly whole programs have been lifted have court cases been successfully prosecuted. Otherwise, large software houses (Microsoft, Oracle, and others) have preferred to buy small innovative companies outright to secure their products. In this sense the protection of intellectual property in the sector utilises the economic schema internally, on the basis that those companies best placed to utilise innovations have purchased the IPRs (embedded within small companies) and maximised the return. In the main the industry has accepted some level of internal 'piracy', though there have been efforts to stop programmers taking their knowledge with them it has proved difficult to enforce. The industry continues to focus on external pirates – those reproducing branded programs illegally, rather than trying to (with some exceptions) to litigate against other software companies. Thus, the main problem recognised in the industry is the rate of software piracy in Asia (and especially Hong Kong and China) where pirated software represents nearly the entire market. Even in the US it has reached 25 per cent, with 35 per cent approximately pirated in Great Britain. These represent a slightly different phenomena in developed states, pirated copies are often extra copies run off in institutions who either have no multiple licences or an insufficient coverage. In Asia especially the pirated copies are produced for sale and their production is controlled by elements of organised crime. This is the sort of piracy that the knowledge industries would like policy-makers to focus on, not the problems nearer to home, between themselves.

I have already discussed sampling, but the music industry is beset by another form of intra-sectoral piracy, the copying of styles and arrangements. This is almost impossible to police as cover versions pay royalties to the writer. But if the performance has also been partly or even totally reproduced in the second recording this is seen not as an intellectual property issue. A cover version can become almost a duplicated version of the original song (Sweeting 1998). In a complex artistic product it is not merely the formal writing that might embody intellectual effort and innovation but also its performance and other elements of its final realisation. But unless the actual performance is used, the reproduction of a performance style is treated by the law as a new expression and therefore unprotectable. In other industries these reworkings of others ideas are endemic – in the clothing industry this form of 'theft' almost *is* the industry. Design details are notoriously unreliable as intellectual property. Again, like software there is the issue of a common language – there are only so many combinations of design elements that can make a piece of clothing distinctive. Thus the 'borrowing' of details is common but seldom the subject of legal action. Even where there have been notable victories by designers against large high street companies that have stolen their ideas, it is an area that is difficult for courts to produce satisfactory judgements. Many high street and mass market retailers regularly utilise the distinctive new-season's details which designers have included in their collections. This is seldom seen as piracy, not least of all because the ideas seldom turn up in exactly the same form. However when ideas are copied too closely there can be a case to answer.

In the mid-1990s Antoni and Alison produced a black tee-shirt with the slogan 'I feel amazing fantastic incredible brilliant fabulous great' in a white sans serif font. Within a few months Armani Jeans from Giorgio Armani had started selling a black tee-shirt with the slogan 'I feel outrageous amazing brilliant terrific great' in a white sans serif font. Though finally settled out of court the original designers had a strong case by virtue of the simplicity of the design, the similarity of the wording and the layout of the slogan, all of which had been copied (Rawlinson 1995). The main difficulty in these cases is that the larger company usually has financial resources to conduct a robust defence whereas the designer is often a smaller operator with limited resources. In Britain at least, where a designer is not a limited company (and Antoni and Alison were not) they can obtain legal aid to fight the case (Tuck 1994). As legal recourse may be expensive and fruitless, many designers are reluctant to fund their own court actions, given the risk of having to pay the costs of the expensive lawyers that may be used by the other side. Designers may 'know' that a design has been copied, the public may be buying it because it is a cheaper high street version of a design they have seen on the fashion pages, but providing legal proof which will stand up to legal argument is frequently impossible. Thus, while fashion pages continue to suggest how the catwalk look can be recreated through high street stores (and thus in a sense the ideas of the designer copied without buying their designs), the industry as a whole has sought recourse in a swing to branding and language-based motifs. It is considerably easier to show piracy of trademarks and, as the Antoni and Alison case suggest, of slogans, than it is of design details.

The reliance on trademarks and brands re-orientates the conception of theft from one that is concerned with the creative process, to one that is concerned with the organised reproduction of unauthorised copies. It moves protection from copyright law to trademark legislation and introduces the crime of 'passing off' goods as something they are not. The notion that intellectual property is about protecting the creative process which a key part of the justificatory schemata, is thus subsumed beneath the general rhetoric of the theft of the property of the owner of the design, the trademark, the software or whatever knowledge element is being reproduced. That within the knowledge industries such piracy of their own creative processes is taking place is de-emphasised and the rights of commercial owners, rather than individual knowledge creators are emphasised. This represents a shift back to the self-developmental schema – trademarks are linked to the expression of a particular company, and passing off infringes the rights of the (legal) individual to be seen as an individual.

Unsurprisingly, piracy affects those products that are successful much more than those which have limited global coverage, and therefore the victims of piracy are often large companies. These large firms may not always receive much sympathy from consumers and the general public and thus the discourse of theft and piracy serves a useful purpose of making the issue appear to be one that could effect everyone. As *The Economist* (1996b) puts it (as ever supporting the discourse of property):

> Pirating music or software . . . is not like stealing a car: it leaves the owner still with the original property. Some copyrighted material – textbooks and software, say – benefits developing countries more than the loss of incline hurts producers. Surely as with drugs patents, this often overrides private property

rights? . . . [But] it is no more righteous to steal from the rich than the poor. Because you cannot afford a car, there is no excuse for stealing mine.

But, this picture of piracy is incomplete – intellectual property is generally only recognised as subject to piracy outside the sector in which it is developed. Moreover, the identification of intellectual property as 'trade-related' sets some parameters to its recognition that favours those who own IPRs and trade in them, over the knowledge producers themselves. One last example of how 'piracy' might actually include some common industrial practices comes from the redesign of the British Airways aeroplane fleet.

In the early 1990s Cg'ose Ntcox'o, an artist from the Kalahari desert exhibited some work in a London gallery through the Kuru Development Trust (KDT). British Airways, having purchased one of her works decided to utilise it as one of the designs that would grace their new 'world' tail fins in 1996. A representative from British Airways flew to Africa to see the artist and in her words gave her 'a piece of paper and told [her] to make a cross', after all as a representative of the KDT pointed out 'the artist is illiterate . . . she has no need for money'. Mrs Ntcox'o received half of the approximately £3,800 fee British Airways paid for the painting, the other half went to the trust who had arranged the sale. However, when she discovered the use to which her work had been put the artist was enraged and sought further recompense for the use of her art. British Airways claimed she had got a 'fair deal', the contract she had signed had been a legal transfer of copyright. And thus, despite her illiteracy she was deemed to have legally transferred her rights, even though she claims not to have been advised what would happen to the work (Harding 1998). Though there is nothing necessarily illegal about this transaction, it is hard to see how the artist's interests have been respected by the working of the law. And while this case may be an extreme example, this is far from uncommon practice. In most cases the only protection from this sort of theft is one's own fame or reputation.

The relationship between piracy and intellectual property production is related to the level of recognition of the individual (or their work) *vis-à-vis* the copier. Thus, lesser (or unknown) individuals can be subject to piracy within a knowledge industrial sector – for them piracy is essentially a problem of major economic actors pirating their ideas, or at the very least undervaluing them. However, once some sort of reputation is built up, inside the sector intellectual property becomes more robust. Conversely, once particular intellectual work is known and its profile is heightened by legitimate reproduction, the piracy of knowledge objects becomes more profitable and thus the axis of piracy swings to an external relation. In the general coverage of piracy however it is only this external axis that is discussed, the internalised piracy is just seen as 'paying your dues', or part of the cross-fertilisation process of the sectors public resources or language. Piracy is therefore an incomplete discourse maintained through the knowledge structure; one that is limited to certain relations between knowledge-object and unauthorised reproduction, favouring the owners not the producers of intellectual property. Certainly, for well-known artists, designers, authors and other knowledge producers the system of intellectual property ownership works well but there are many others whose work is not well protected against the more powerful in their chosen area of creativity. This is not the only area of intellectual property law's protection that depends on the sort of individual you are, however.

And real individuals?

While some civilisations think the camera captures the soul and thus the self, under intellectual property law a similar logic can be used to enhance privacy and the control of some individuals' own image. In the above discussions I have only recognised the individual as one who wished to sell their creations to earn a return. However, intellectual property law also purports to reinforce the property the individual has in themselves. The self-developmental schema has been utilised in intellectual property to protect privacy and also to ensure that one's image remains one's own to do with as one sees fit. The image itself may be a repository of possible economic value even if the individual does not seek to always exploit this value, of which a recent apposite example might be Princess Diana. One of the most instructive (and successful) cases of establishing the image as profitable resource were the actions of the Elvis Presley estate during the 1980s and into the 1990s.

The 'policing' of this property through the US courts has in the main ensured that the commercial rewards for the public reproduction of the image of Elvis have been (re)captured by his estate. During the legal disputes which followed the 'King's' untimely demise the estate came near to the loss of control of his image (*qua* property). Intellectual property law was utilised to bring it back from the public realm (which it had entered prior to death, through 'bad management'). The reinvention of Elvis as a copyrighted image aimed to make its protection more robust to ensure the estate maximised the possible returns or rents from its use (Wall 1996: 132–137). This was achieved through a number of different legal instruments including the law of 'passing off'. Once an image of Elvis had been defined as an intellectual property of the estate, competing images could be (re)defined as products trying to 'pass themselves off' as the legitimate intellectual property. What is of interest here is the ability of those wishing to trade and profit from the post-mortem Elvis (his estate) to (re)establish legal provenance. They were able to rescue his image from the public realm, reconstructing it as tradable (based on its scarcity) at the monopoly price which could be secured for licences to use the image, and thus its trade-relatedness was re-established.

Uncommon and particular material conditions underlay the (re)enclosure of Presley as intellectual property. Presley's career coincided with the massive expansion of the music industry: his sales eventually topped one billion units, which puts him among the biggest selling artists of all time, if not *the* biggest seller (Elliott 1989: 64). This expansion was predicated on the availability in the 1950s of a cheap technology of mass reproduction allied with the post-war American social conditions of a newly (economically) enfranchised youth culture looking for its own 'identity'. Against these developments the underlying economic worth of the image of Elvis becomes clearer. But this suggests the uphill struggle this could have been, the image had in a sense become common property. As a signifier well beyond its meaning merely as Elvis, it had become an icon of a particular generation and the emergence of youth culture. None the less, through various court actions against users of the image, the estate was able to bring its control to bear on Elvis (the image) when used as a tradable product. This particular property strategy within popular culture and its artefacts has been unusual but not unparalleled; for instance, the 'branding' of Michael Jackson or Madonna and others more recently. Furthermore, the proliferation of 'authorised' merchandise may be symptomatic of a move in this direction with performers (and their management) attempting to establish the value of their intellectual property (in their image or logo) whenever possible.

As the avenues for the exploitation of a particular individual's activities in the knowledge industries have expanded, so have demands to ensure that the rights which repose in the image should be codified and controlled. Elvis is atypical in the number of judgments which make up the case law surrounding the use of his image – in the period 1980–1994 there were 82 legal actions which were Elvis related (Wall 1996: 132). But these judgments have been important in establishing the right for the artist to control the reproduction of their image for sale. Though photographic images for media use remain in the public domain, the use of the image on reproduced consumer goods has become more tightly controlled. But, controlling one's image does not necessarily require the actual image of the individual to be used. In 1983 a Christian Dior advertisement appearing in the *New Yorker* magazine depicted a wedding where one of the characters in the background was a Jackie Onassis look-alike. Dior and the advertising agency were taken to court by Mrs Onassis and damages awarded. The image of her face was her property even if it was expressed in this instance by a look-alike rather than by herself (Gaines 1992: 84–104). Thus, Jackie Onassis was able to maintain control not only of the use of representations of herself (this protection would not have stretched to use, say, of her image on the gossip page), but also allowed her to control the use of her image even if it was an impression of her rather than the real her.[4] The key issue in cases such as these under US law is that to seek such protection through intellectual property law, one's image needs to be recognisable. Where an image is not one that has a currency, and is therefore not 'valuable', it also cannot be owned as property. Paradoxically, only when the image is well known (in effect widely distributed) can its distribution be curtailed by legal actions.

But whereas Jackie Onassis relied on a *post-hoc* valuing of her image, nowadays well-known figures are more likely to pre-empt marketers (or other image traders) by registering aspects of their appearance as well as their names as trade marks. This enables them to ensure the rights to profit from their image, through merchandising or other uses are owned by themselves. Thus, a spokesman for Formula One driver Damon Hill explained that Hill wanted to stop his fans 'being ripped off by people selling poor quality [merchandise] . . . and he felt it was unfair that his fans should suffer from inferior goods' (quoted in Roper 1996). While such attention to the welfare of his fans is admirable, he also benefits financially by establishing the monopoly rights over his image, enabling him to control the flow of products using his name or image and maintaining a suitable scarcity. But, unfortunately there is nothing to stop one person from trademarking another's name or image. Thus, the fleetingly famous British environmental activist 'Swampy' discovered that an enterprising pub landlord had applied for and received a trademark to market merchandise under his name. Swampy stood to gain nothing and while the trademark was maintained will be unable to use his nickname for any trade-related activity (Penman 1997). If Swampy wants to market T-shirts with his nickname and image on he can't, and he does not even benefit from those which are marketed by Mr Bramley, the landlord. Once again the owner (in this case of the trademark) was able to establish rights against an individual who would have seemed to have been the legitimate owner of a particular IPR.

Though anyone could trademark their name, few not trading under it would bother. Equally, an individual's image is not valuable except as part of a piece of work which is an expression of another authorial functionary, say, a photographer. Thus, the occasional cases that are brought against photographers by their chance subjects when the photos have been used as posters are never upheld. Despite a number of cases the French photographer Robert Doisneau for instance has not had to recompense the young couple who feature in his widely reproduced photo of Paris from the door of a café. Indeed, the issue of privacy has largely been removed from intellectual property law where unknown individuals are concerned. Rights of privacy for the non-famous are tempered by public interest and the needs of the state. Thus the politics of privacy and intrusion, the politics of surveillance,[5] are not intellectual property issues because the individual in these cases is recognised as having a different sort of status from the famous individual whose image is trade-related. Indeed, in one sense their image is not property as it cannot be traded outside the context of its revelation in the public interest. It is here that the nature of intellectual property law becomes visible. The individual as a knowledge creator or owner is only a knowledge creator or owner if such knowledge objects, in Minogue's term, are active. Intellectual property rights can only be enjoyed as economic rights, like property they convey rights to profit in a market from their utilisation and the right to hold an interest in them.

Two of the justificatory schemata of intellectual property – instrumental and self-developmental – rely for their salience on the recognition of legitimate rights for individuals. From this basis is built a justification that can then be used by legally constituted individuals as well. The economic justification relies on no such contention, it is only concerned with the efficiency of resource use which it links to the informational use of price and the beneficial effect of competition for resources, which it claims requires the institution of property. Leaving this third schema to one side, the other two common methods of justifying intellectual property are at least formally linked to some notion of individual rights. However, it is by no means clear that the mere existence of an individual as a knowledge-creator necessitates protection by the actual law of intellectual property in its many forms. Only certain groups of legally constituted individuals can effectively utilise the law to protect their interests in knowledge objects. Additionally, not all knowledge objects are the same, which is not to draw a distinction between copyright, patent, trademarks, trade secrets or other forms, but to suggest another difference. The difference between those knowledge objects that are trade-related and those which are not, is crucial. As I have suggested previously, the notion of trade-related-ness is the chief manner in which knowledge is brought across Minogue's line between passive and active property.

If the issue of trade-related-ness is crucial, then the most important attribute that a putative IPR owner must enjoy is the ability to trade in the particular knowledge object. Without the ability to trade, the knowledge object remains only potential intellectual property (or passive property). While they may be held as passive property, they have no legal reality as intellectual property – only when held by a (legal) individual who can trade them in some manner are they activated. Thus, real individuals often need legal individuals to establish their intellectual property as these legal individuals (companies) have the resources to trade profitably in intellectual property. Only by transferring IPRs to knowledge sector companies are individuals able to activate intellectual property and earn a return on its exploitation. While this transfer can sit well within the economic justification, for the instrumental and self-developmental schemata this extra step disrupts their reliance for justification on individual rights. It appears that these rights are contingent on certain attributes and are therefore not individual rights at all but qualified rights.

Therefore, while in many of the cases above the producer of knowledge objects (the authorial functionary) has been well served by intellectual property, it has become clear that the possible rewards (and their protection) are related to ability to trade in the knowledge objects themselves which favours companies. The system of protecting intellectual property is weighted towards those whose reputation is well known and regarded, and towards organised capital. Adamant that their intellectual property must be protected when it is traded in established markets, these industries look differently on intellectual property within their own confines. Thus, the social utility doctrine is largely followed (implicitly rather than explicitly) within their relations with their legitimate competitors, whereas it is discounted in their external relations. This leads me to suggest that within these industries there is a recognition of the complex nature of the knowledge object, its reliance on socialised knowledge and the difficulty of delimiting where one knowledge object stops and another starts. However, outside the industries their products are presented as clear cases of unproblematic intellectual property. The knowledge structure both furthers this characterisation of the issue and hides behaviour which contradicts such claims within the industry's own relations. A more stringent application of the law of intellectual property, both under the TRIPs agreement and as the result of more heated sectoral competition, will expose this tension between external and internal intellectual property relations.

Technology has also had a major impact on intellectual property. In the first instance it has changed the field of active intellectual property and the character of knowledge object that can be brought across the line from passive property. But, while technological developments have expanded the possibilities for trading intellectual property, for producing IPRs from passive knowledge objects, it has also allowed for greater unauthorised reproduction. As I noted above, the piracy 'epidemic' is driven by the ability to produce almost indistinguishable copies of intellectual property. While older forms of piracy remain (the use of inferior or non-active ingredients in medicines for instance), for the knowledge industries the proliferation of indistinguishable copies if of greater long-term concern. The further development of the Internet as a major knowledge conduit will continue to produce problems for the knowledge industries. These technological issues have already led to some attempts to modify intellectual property law, as well as the TRIPs agreement's attempt to universalise the justificatory schemata. However, contra-dictions remain between the schemata and the outcomes which they produce when used to legitimise intellectual property practice. The attempts to ensure the trade-related-ness of intellectual property may in the final analysis have been the move which has revealed the flaws in the current settlement – by removing the previous loopholes and compromises, the TRIPs agreement has also removed the possibility of hiding the disjuncture between the legal settlement and its justifications.

6 Between commons and individuals

Intellectual property is one of the key elements of contemporary political economic relations; like material property, it renders socio-economic relations of power as 'free' contractual relations. In the preceding chapters I have explored the interaction between the rhetoric of the justificatory schemata supporting intellectual property rights (IPRs) and the actual relations they mediate. This has led me to the conclusion that the justificatory schemata used to legitimise intellectual property's current settlement do not sit well with real and existing intellectual property relations. There is not an easy fit between the rhetoric of property and the character of knowledge but despite this, the schemata are widely promulgated. Crucially, the schemata were utilised (explicitly and implicitly) throughout the negotiations which produced the agreement on trade-related intellectual property rights (TRIPs) during the Uruguay Round. And, they continue to be deployed by developed states' representatives at the World Trade Organisation as intellectual property conflicts are raised in the dispute resolution mechanism. However the disjuncture between the justificatory schemata and the effects of IPRs is not merely an issue of rhetoric within international negotiation. Given the proposed emergence of a global information society, this is an ideal juncture to be thinking through how the current settlement of intellectual property might be amended before, like property, it essential tenets are set in stone.

Changes in the economic organisation of productive endeavour within contemporary capitalism underlie the current debates about intellectual property. There has been a move in the social sciences, and perhaps more importantly in policy circles to discuss this under the rubric of 'information society'. Though claims concerning the social transformational effects of this new organisational logic have been exaggerated (May 1998), there remains a consensus that the development of powerful information and communication technologies have allowed the increasing commodification of knowledge and information. Thus, whatever its effects, intellectual property is likely to be a subject of widening political and economic importance in the coming years. The ability to trade in the various products of intellect is an important component in economic development at all levels (state, firm and individual). In the past, trade was defined mainly in terms of the physical transfer of material goods; now, trade between economic actors based on the exchange of non-material information based services and rights to use knowledge is expanding relative to the trade in material products. Thus, as the economic justification would have it, if there is to be trade in intellectual resources, those resources need to be treated as property. And, in these circumstances, those with the technological and ideational resources to capitalise on recent developments are favoured by the legal construction of knowledge as property.

The move to value information and knowledge more highly in economic relations has involved an increasingly constricted view of the social worth of knowledge. In the justificatory schemata there is an important elision made possible through the operation of the knowledge structure. When the justification of IPRs are discussed, generally the notion of a wide social utility is mobilised to show why there is a need to limit the duration of protection. This asserts that even if intellectual property rights are monopoly privileges rather than contingent rights, their duration is limited by social considerations. However, for patents the actual social utility that is accorded priority is the need to encourage innovation. This is predicated on innovation's link with economic development and mobilised through the need to reward the knowledge worker or creator with property in their product. Conventionally, this interest outweighs arguments for the swift social diffusion of knowledge, as I discussed in regard to the problems of technological transfer to developing states. Though delays of twenty years may have seen acceptable in the pre-information society global system, nowadays such delays are not merely entrenching the technological gap but progressively widening it.

For copyrights a similar narrow view of social utility is evident; the encouragement of expressive 'authorship' is promoted above all other possible social uses. Where copyright material embodies socially valuable or developmentally useful knowledge and information, again it is the encouragement of the individual 'author' that is prioritised. And given copyright's paradigmatic characterisation of expression as fictional (or creative) expression, protection for owners is considerably longer than patents without the same recognition of the social costs of such constriction. While there was a reasonably robust distinction between idea and expression this was hardly a serious political issue. But with the evident collapse of this distinction in some areas (such as computer software) the curtailment of social utility represented by limits to the diffusion of important knowledge is a serious problem. Thus, the central ideological issue that effects the political economy of intellectual property is the contradiction between strong individualised rights and the possibility of wide social (or even global) utility.

Additionally, while the justificatory schemata suggest knowledge-creating individuals are the prime beneficiaries of IPRs, in actuality the beneficiaries are more often companies. They are recognised as legally constituted individuals by states' laws which enable them to obscure their socio-economic position *vis-à-vis* real individuals. Though some individuals may still be able to build considerable power based on their work or individuality, in most circumstances it remains the knowledge using and reproducing companies who benefit most from the commodification of knowledge. The contrast between the individual whose supposed interest are the foundations on which the labour-desert and self-developmental schemata are constructed and a company, which enjoys these benefits through their legal characterisation as an 'individual', is the second major contradiction in the current settlement. These companies are able to maximise their gains relative to real individuals, but companies' ability to produce large returns also encourages real individuals to transfer their rights to legal 'individuals'. Knowledge-creating individuals can usually garner a greater reward through such a relation then their own efforts would produce. One of the effects of the current legal settlement has been to maintain the imbalance between real individuals and legally constituted individuals while allowing the latter to claim the benefits which are justified through the 'rights' of the former.

A critical theory of intellectual property can be developed from these contradictions. The justificatory schemata mobilised in the political economic relations of the global information society are contradicted by the actuality of those relations. The knowledge structure is mobilised to obscure this contradiction, but such structural power cannot fully achieve this end. The knowledge structure itself is reliant on both ideational and material elements, revealing a tension that could (and should) produce political economic action for change. Thus, my critique does not suggest that the knowledge structure is a chimera, rather it reveals the necessarily incomplete (and thus continuing) project of obfuscation practised by (and on behalf of) those who benefit from the current intellectual property settlement. The revelation of these contradictions leads me to argue that the current settlement is not necessarily robust and can be the subject of political reformulation. This reformulation can take two paths: first, it needs to reformulate the global public realm, expanding its legal and effective character to meet the needs of the whole global system, not merely the commercial interest of certain states' companies; second, throughout the system, political action is required to produce a intellectual property settlement that reflects the interests of real knowledge creators, not their idealised phantom nor the legally constituted individuals (which is to say, companies) who have largely displaced them as the beneficiaries of intellectual property laws.

The global information society

The emergence of the global information society, even if such a transformation is far from complete, is taking place in a global system largely patterned by neo-Liberalism. There are many facets to this patterning, but the important issue here is the support neo-Liberalism gives to the institution of property rights. During the early 1980s there was a major move among policy-makers and their advisors back to neo-classical models of thinking about the relations between state and economy (Biersteker 1992). This return to classical economics promoted among other things a re-emphasis on private economic activity and relations mediated though contract. The economic schema (which directly flows from such neo-Liberal assumptions) is predicated on the recognition of property rights if resources are to be efficiently allocated. Knowledge is a resource that is increasingly useful, and therefore it must be integrated into the global economic system. This is accomplished through the institution of intellectual property which has been strengthened by the TRIPs agreement's provisions to harmonise international laws, and expanded into new areas such as bio-resources and computer software. The 'triumph' of neo-classical economics in policy-making and the economy as a whole suggested the use of property rights – privatisation of nationalised utilities' industries or tradable pollution permits, for instance – could promote or enhance the efficiency of economic and political relations.[1]

This revival of market and property as the favoured solutions to distributional and allocation issues coincided with the accelerating expansion of information and communication technologies. Driven by technology on one side and the re-emphasis on property rights on the other, intellectual property fits well with the triumphal discourse of neo-Liberalism. As the information age was accelerating the dominant discourse in economics supported the expansion of the sorts of knowledge which could be defined as property. Technology allowed an increasingly viable trade in digitised knowledge, alongside an increase in the speed (and value) of innovation. Economic policy supported the expansion of contractual relations and intellectual property became a key issue for international trade negotiators trying to formalise and globalise the governance mechanisms of world trade. Economic policy-makers drew sustenance from the historical 'success' of the General Agreement on Tariffs and Trade to argue that a similar international agreement would benefit the emerging economic organisation of knowledge and information flows. Thus, a global information society started to emerge alongside a neo-classical economic policy dynamic, producing a particular settlement around IPRs. Not only did technological development enable the capture of more knowledge and its recoding as 'trade-related', but the logic of economic policy supported the recognition of this 'new' knowledge as property. And, this further encouraged technical innovation in this area.

This policy dynamic, reinforced and furthered through the knowledge structure's reduction of options on any negotiating agenda, produced a particular intellectual property settlement; enhancing the rights of owners rather than users of intellectual property. It is proposed that individual rights through a property regime support economic efficiency. This was not necessarily a new departure but represented an expansion of the pervious uneven and only partly enforced regime at the international level. Those able to trade in knowledge objects by virtue of having the means to own them found their position bolstered through their increased rights under the TRIPs agreement. The information society as policy discourse (especially in the realm of intellectual property rights) has furthered the commercial interests of certain elements of capital. The information society has supported the enclosure by these companies of public knowledge making it their 'tradable' property, expanding the character of intellectual property, to include more knowledge resources as they can be rendered digitally. While this is a technological issue, it also impacts on the boundaries between private and public knowledge. Though there is still knowledge that is not regarded as intellectual property it can be brought over the demarcation line by the assertion of its 'trade-related-ness', by its commodification. This steady encroachment of the public sphere of knowledge if taken to its logical conclusion will remove the notion of public knowledge resources from many areas of social life.

However, unlike material property which by its physical nature can only exist in one place at one time, knowledge is not finally amenable to such limits. Scarcity of knowledge has to be constantly policed and shored up; without continued attention to its constriction knowledge quickly enters the public realm. The knowledge structure does its best to obscure this contradiction by mobilising the justificatory schemata to maintain the fiction that the manufactured scarcity of intellectual property is self-evidently socially valuable. Despite the rhetoric of competition within neo-Liberalism, the monopoly rights which are accorded to IPRs constrict the 'free' flow of knowledge. But, despite the market foundations of the policy networks of the global information society, this shortcoming is not the subject of any extensive attention by economic commentators, business groups or policy-makers. Rather, the reward of private actors (legally constituted individuals) to support the furtherance of innovation and economic advance is continually stressed and prioritised. For instance, Antoon Quaedvlieg, 'a lawyer . . . philosophising about justice', was led to the conclusion that

> one should be very cautious when abolishing or restricting intellectual property rights which by non-specialists – including judges – are considered a just reward . . . [But] to a certain extent the justification of property rights forms at the same time their limitation. The reasons which justify property rights do not justify monopolies, particularly since monopolies may damage other men's [sic] property in a broad sense. This leads to the conclusion that monopolistic effects resulting from intellectual property regulations . . . will be acceptable *only if they are supported by a clear economic rationale.*
>
> (1992: 393, emphasis added)

The knowledge structure of the information society does its utmost to prioritise innovation and individualised rights as supportive of economic growth and asserts that this outweighs any danger of monopoly. In this sense IPRs *are* 'supported by a clear economic rationale'; the problem lies in how that rationale relates to the character of knowledge objects.

Intellectual property is not scarce until it is made so through legal intervention. The current international policy debate has led to a set of policy prescriptions that seek to establish that states must prioritise incentives rather than the free flow of information, their laws must prioritise ownership over and above the need to guard against monopoly. This economic rationale, elaborated through the economic schema and reinforced by the instrumental schema, establishes certain outcomes as valuable and others as insignificant. Private rights of innovators are therefore deemed more economically useful than social benefits of wide and swift knowledge diffusion. The TRIPs agreement offers developing states the carrot of inclusion in the information society of the future while at the same time ensuring that the 'rules of the game' are those which have already advantaged the developed states. Though information and knowledge are the key resources, it is necessary to limit their diffusion to ensure innovation continues. Paradoxically, under these circumstances the information society does not produce a massive leap in knowledge use or distribution; instead it enforces and expands the benefits accruing to those with the wherewithal to trade in IPRs. Whatever its potential, the global information society utilises the institutions of intellectual property to reproduce the uneven access to, and benefits from, the resources needed for economic development.

Nevertheless, the information society has introduced a potential change in the relations of power in the global system. Whereas the material property needed for economic development is by definition scarce, in an information society, the key resource can be scarce through its legal construction as intellectual property but it is not necessarily so. This emerging shift in the potential for the distribution of productive resources has led to the mobilisation of power in the knowledge structure to reinforce the scarcity of knowledge. But the possibility of an opening for the recognition of contradictions between the dominant characterisation of knowledge as property and the potentially (and in many cases) existing ways that know-ledge can flow through the global system has created a space for political action. Thus on one side, changes in material social relations mediated through previous advances in technology have heightened the value of information, and the knowledge structure has responded by including more knowledge resources into the neo-Liberal regime of governance through property rights. But on the other, the rise in importance of information and knowledge has engendered a dawning realisation of the contradiction between absolute property rights in knowledge and the plausible distributional dynamic of knowledge. The knowledge structure tries to obscure such a contradiction but this important site of resistance is itself reinforced through the diffusion of the technologies of the information society. In this sense, it is possible (though not a foregone conclusion) that the continuing expansion of the global information society may fatally compromise intellectual property as we currently know it.

Given the entrenched interests that are already mobilised in this area, intellectual property is unlikely to completely wither or fade away in the near future, whatever its contradictions. But, whatever the future may hold, effective political action now might bring reasonably immediate benefits to the 'info-poor' throughout the global system. If, as I have argued, change can be brought about through reconcep-tualisation allied to new technological possibilities, then it is incumbent on a critical theory to suggest some areas where political action can plausibly promote changes to the current state of affairs. If there is a contradiction between the information society presented as a property-based socio-economic organisation, and the 'logic' of the flow of information, such contradictions need to be firmly outlined. I will now make this explicit through discussions of the question of defining social utility, and the legal balance between the real individual and his or her legal counterpart (the legally constituted individual).

Re-enlarging social utility

The public realm in a sense is the corner-stone of intellectual property; justifications of intellectual property always include an expression of social utility. However, when examined closely this utility is only residual. The public realm represents only whatever is not claimed by the rights accorded to private intellectual property. There are therefore no effective safeguards to halt its erosion; indeed, in itself the expansion of private rights in knowledge has brought about the public realm's decline. The limits to the public realm flow from the particular social utility that *is* recognised.

> Business frequently advances the position that intellectual property rights spur innovation, the production of greater wealth and improved well-being. Frequently, however, the utilitarian argument of business is based upon a narrow set of stakeholders – those within national boundaries and with direct ties to the company in question.
>
> (Steidlmeier 1993: 162)

This narrow view of social utility, based as it is on a narrow group, needs to be reformed if any other concept of welfare is to be put forward. Many developing states' governments have argued in the past, and continue to argue post-TRIPs that social utility must be related to the global population not some small group of developed states' owners of IPRs. In these demands they have been joined by user groups who also see the limitation of the public realm as problematic.

During the December 1996 WIPO conference to adopt a new Copyright Treaty under the Berne Convention the recognition that the public interest needed to be stressed and (re)enlarged in the wake of the TRIPs agreement played a major part in the parties' deliberations. The original negotiating draft was 'heavily weighted against public and user interests' but during the negotiations the greatly enlarged reproduction right which 'would have deemed all digital or electronic copies, no matter how temporary or transient to be reproductions was deleted' (Mason 1997: 637, 639). Furthermore, a co-ordinated effort by a number of user groups highlighted elements in the original draft that would have seriously eroded public availability of knowledge under copyright. In much the same way the Intellectual Property Committee managed to make much of the running through their support of the US delegation in the TRIPs negotiations, user groups are starting to be aware of the need to mobilise their political resources during such negotiations, providing technical advice and preparing draft clauses. Though governments may still favour commercial interests, an effective and strong stand in these fora by direct users and others who value the public realm, may be able to start re-balancing legislation through political pressure at the national level to recognise wider social utility. There is a general feeling among these groups that they are likely to achieve more success at the national level, as the international negotiating forums seem excessively influenced by well-resourced multinational business groups (Mason 1997: 641). This leaves a major lacuna in the political project to enhance the recognition of social utility. Global social utility is not merely the sum of national social utilities, it reflects the identification of a global social sphere which states and their populations inhabit.

Multilateral actions are therefore still required to enhance the identification of a global social utility in information and knowledge flows. Perhaps the easiest action, though contradicting the current political dynamic, would be to reintroduce differential patent and copyright protection. Prior to the TRIPs agreement there was a *de facto* acceptance of some form of piracy and a lack of IPR protection in developing states. Thus, while some states did not even have intellectual property laws that related to developed states' companies conceptions of what was necessary, even those that did hardly enforced them. In a sense this was an intellectual property development strategy by stealth. The current system of patent

> protection has the effect of transferring income from consumers in the protected market to the monopoly inventor/producers. Since technological innovation is itself part of the development process and seems to occur more rapidly the more developed a country is, these monopolists reside permanently in the richest countries in the world. Therefore, extending patent protection to poor countries involves a transfer of welfare from the poor to the rich. Assuming that greater world-wide income equality is a desirable goal, for any number of reasons, this surely suggests that it should be the poorest of countries that are exempted [from the provisions of TRIPs].
>
> (Deardorff 1990: 505)

This sort of solution to the development issue comes up against three problems: first, it is not self-evident that in the short to medium term neo-Liberal models of economic organisation favour moves towards income equality. Indeed, given the emphasis in neo-Liberalism on the 'need' to reward effort so as to encourage economic activity, a tendency towards income equality might not reward actors sufficiently to ensure continued innovation. Thus a narrowly defined social utility serves to support the favoured social utility of innovative activity. To assume this is not the most important and prioritised social utility is to go against the prescriptions of neo-Liberalism itself. However, second, even if differential protection of IPRs were reintroduced, this strategy can hardly have been said to have been a development success in the past.

The problem with allowing some form of unlicensed diffusion of patented technologies, or other intellectual property, is that the aspects which it is possible to copy may not represent all the knowledge components of the item. As I have already suggested, technology transfer has stalled not only because of the lack of protection afforded to new technologies but because of an inability in many cases to take full advantage of technologies that are transferred. Even mature technologies and the know-how needed to maximise their use have been slow to appear in developing states. And when the technology does arrive, the tacit knowledge required to make the most (or even actually operate it at all) may not be fully developed or widely distributed. Thus, while weaker or absent patent protection in developing states may be a necessary condition for the resurgence of technology transfer (and with it a posited decline in global inequalities of wealth), it is not a sufficient condition. There is a connected need to establish the basic skills and technologies upon which newer developments can be deployed. It is seldom possible to leap-frog several stages of technological development effectively without major educational and infrastructural investment. Therefore, to actually enhance global social utility, where such utility is seen as the promotion of welfare and the promotion of more wealth equality, a more positive programme is called for.

Thus, John Frow has suggested the construction of a positive public domain which produces the rights to the raw materials of human life, in which he includes language and ideas. While currently language may in the main be free of intellectual property restrictions,[2] Frow's inclusion of ideas is interesting. He suggests rights to intellectual property in such a positive public domain

> are not 'natural' rights, located in an ordinary contract or a state of nature, but customary social rights, developed and recognised as a provisional end state of the struggle for civilised conditions of life . . . Like all rights, they represent a balance between conflicting demands, and they carry with them a corresponding set of obligations to the common good.
>
> (Frow 1996: 106)

If there was to be a right of public domain, what would the social obligations look like? These obligations, on which the enjoyment of rights would rest might plausibly include the transfer of patents and copyrights to a multilateral body which could then distribute them to developing states on a need basis rather than through the market. But, if there were obligations such as these, which states would benefit? The third issue raised by the proposal to re-establish differential protection would be the identification of those states not required to have intellectual property laws or to only provide some modified coverage. This group could not be fixed, rather, it would need to be constantly reviewed: as states developed there would become a need to introduce them into the global system, and therefore there would be an issue regarding the boundary moment. The review process would have to balance the interests of intellectual property owners in being rewarded for the exploitation of their IPRs, with the need for such property to be available socially to particular developing states' populations.

Alongside a reformulation of the notion of social utility (from a narrow innovation focus, to a wide global social welfare approach), some new multilateral body would be therefore required to govern the limits, but also subsequent re-extensions of the intellectual property regime. This body would then act as the clearing house for the flow of knowledge to those who needed it within the global system but lacked the immediate means to pay. This might plausibly be carried out by an agency of the United Nations, or some body affiliated to the WTO. However, without considerable political pressure this sort of shift in the global intellectual property settlement will not be possible. Indeed, for any change to be promoted, the issue of IPRs in the global system needs to attract more widespread political attention than it does currently. Any change is likely to be expensive: in political terms for those parties (in or out of government) prepared to take a position that goes against the dominant discourse of neo-Liberalism; for the current owners of IPRs who would see their income affected; and in the financial support required for some sort of global mechanism to positively manage any new system. The first step in any such political process would be for the public realm to be re-valued as a political priority, to justify such costs. James Boyle (1997) has suggested that this could be achieved in a similar manner to the Green movement's re-valorisation of the natural environment.

Boyle notes that the environmental movement was deeply influenced by two powerful perspectives: ecology and welfare economics. Drawing from ecology the recognition of complex and unpredictable connections between living things in the real world, and from welfare economics the failure of markets to fully internalise their costs, environmentalism sparked a movement which has had a major global political economic effect. Crucially, these ideas were not developed in the mainstream of political discourse but on the margins and then popularised. A similar position may currently obtain in the nascent global politics of intellectual property. Decisions are currently made on behalf of a small group of intellectual property owners whose perception of costs is linked to the narrow issue of innovation and reward. Though information flows can be economically modelled, there is little real public awareness of the interconnectivity of various types and flows of knowledge or of the way they work together to bring about effects both nationally and globally. While this brings together a number of disciplines in the social sciences (for instance, the sociology of knowledge, social psychology, information economics, philosophy), the overall complex knowledge environment is incompletely understood. A similar political effort that produced a change in the politics of natural resources and the environment could perhaps shift the conception of the knowledge environment to establish a significant role for a broad view of global social utility. The knowledge commons could be established as a global resource *not* one that should, or needs to be, carved up for individual gain.

Therefore, in much the same way that the environmental movement in one sense 'invented' the environment, a politics of intellectual property needs to (re)invent the public domain of knowledge – to re-embed individuals in the socialised body of knowledge. Intellectual property is not merely some arcane technical legal issue, the emergence of information society has made information and knowledge an important area of political conflict. As this becomes increasingly recognised, the effects of the mal-distribution of information and knowledge will become politically sensitive. It is likely that as information society affects more and more aspects of our lives, the shortcomings of intellectual property will become more apparent. However, this is not to suggest that the knowledge structure will let such perceptions emerge without trying to mould them to its own uses. Thus, the justificatory schemata I have explored will become more widely promulgated as the 'common sense' of the political economy of information and knowledge. A political effort will be required to organise against this narrowing of the agenda, and thus Boyle is correct to suggest environmentalism offers a good model from which to initially develop a grass-roots politics of intellectual property. But this is not the only way some sort of change could be affected. A complementary approach flows from the immanent critique I mobilised regarding the claims made within the justificatory schemata themselves.

Re-balancing individuals' rights

When the instrumental and self-developmental schemata are compared with outcomes in the real world of intellectual property relations, there is a significant disparity. Utilising an immanent critique, it is possible that intellectual property could be amended through a legal reformulation of private rights. This might be an attractive and immediate legal-political project as it essentially cuts with the grain of neo-Liberalism, unlike the previous proposal. It is possible that important political economic resources (information and knowledge) will become so diffused that intellectual property will not be able to govern them effectively. This is already evident in the general disregard of copyright at the level of the individual consumer. Indeed, the knowledge structure's attempt to uphold IPRs through the current settlement may turn out to be a rearguard action on behalf of capital to retain a particular form of property in important resources. Within the legal sphere this has led to attempts to re-configure various forms of intellectual property and the reiteration of the economic schema's assertion that some form of property is required for the continuity of economic life in a form that is socially beneficial. This suggests there is already some upheaval in the legal conception of intellectual property, which presents an opening for promoting an alternative agenda of legal change.

One avenue which would deal with a number of the justificatory issues revealed through the earlier immanent critique would be to reconsider the extension of individual rights to legally constituted individuals. Currently, though intellectual property is justified on the basis of the interests of an authorial functionary, in reality these rights are most often claimed and enjoyed by companies rather than individuals. Now markets have become oriented more towards intellectual creation and relatively less toward manufacturing, the greater emphasis put on the final audience for their products leads companies to find themselves approaching a position similar to that which was (and continues to be) occupied by the creators themselves. In the publishing, entertainments and software sectors companies increasingly stress their rights as (legally constituted) individuals to control their intellectual property. The political pressure from these important sectors has led states' policy-makers not to question this superimposition of one sort of individuality on another, but rather to attempt to strengthen the protection offered (Quaedvlieg 1998: 432–435). Thus, the knowledge structure's elision of these different individualities serves the purposes of the knowledge companies by expanding and reinforcing their rights in intellectual property whatever the effect might be on real individuals.

If technology continues to make the legal structure of copyright particularly difficult to sustain due to easy and high quality copying (the continuing 'piracy epidemic'), then there may be some recourse to mechanical means of limiting copying (Tang 1997). Rather than try to change the law to deal with technology, technology will be mobilised to deal with the problems it has raised. However, the conception of a mechanical or technical 'fix', even if temporarily successful will not last. Without the legal support allied to legitimised justificatory schema, the 'parasitic capitalists' described by Avernell and Thompson (1994) are likely to render such measures useless. Each new limiting device will spawn a new model from equipment makers intended to bypass its intervention. While the technology of reproduction was expensive relative to purchase of the 'original' the legal tensions underlying the private reproduction of knowledge objects were relatively unimportant. However, faced with cheap easy reproduction, and only partial acceptance of the 'copyright myth', digitalisation may have undermined intellectual property to a large extent in some sectors, even as it makes knowledge objects more valuable. But, while a technological fix may be chimerical, the possibility of remaking the law has been a fertile ground for discussion.

The swift emergence of new information technologies, and perhaps most significantly the rise of the Internet as a commercial arena, has led to attempts to fit new intellectual property relations into a previously existing legal framework. And while a number of legislatures have started to develop new glosses on intellectual property law to cover electronic commerce, the underlying distinctions between copyright and patent remain in place. However, some hybrid intellectual property rights, which rationalise the confusion between the spheres of protection delimited by copyright and patent at their margins have also started to be formulated. These include Plant Varieties laws as mandated under the TRIPs and UPOV agreements, the US Semiconductor Chip Protection Act for chip architectures and the UK Unregistered Design Right which accords copyright like protection to some industrial designs. Thus,

> because a product of today's most economically significant technologies *often bears its know-how on its face, like any artistic work, it may forfeit all lead time from the moment that the markets determines its value or even earlier should commercial success appear imminent.*
>
> (Reichman 1992: 356, emphasis in original)

Under the instrumentalist schema, the failure to protect innovative aspects of the new product will reduce or even nullify the reward and thus incentive to innovate: why risk investment if the rewards cannot be captured? And thus,

> intellectual property law has accordingly come under intense pressure *to alleviate this perceived risk aversion by providing innovators with artificial lead time through one device or another.* The response has varied with the technology in question, and the cumulative efforts are clearly mirrored in a patchwork quilt of protective legal hybrids, complemented by an increasingly supple law of trade secrets, that has strained the classical system of intellectual property law to the breaking point.
>
> (ibid., emphasis in original)

The pressure to extend copyright protection on the basis that it offers blanket protection to knowledge objects on the basis of authorship, but allows the ideas underlying such knowledge objects to remain in the public realm does not initially seem unreasonable. However, applied more broadly as currently conceived, copyright law would grant unacceptably wide protection to the tools and processes of the information age. Tools which might have been protected for twenty years by patent, under copyright might remain property for over 100. Additionally, trade secret law, especially as applied to employment contracts has started to produce problems for the very knowledge creators whom the justificatory schemata's arguments are supposed to benefit.

The innovations of the information society do not fit into the category of copyright or patent easily because 'the bulk of today's most valuable innovations flow from incremental advances in applied scientific know-how and because the line between theoretical and applied science has itself broken down' (ibid.: 356). The result has been a flow of hybrid laws and pragmatic *sui generis* legislation which have enhanced protection at the cost of social flows of information and knowledge. This has further shifted the balance of power in law between the individual and the legal individual. Companies, who have in the main pushed for widened protection, have the resources and the legal advice to ensure that where protection is available they can benefit from it. Real individuals, on the other hand, are confronted by a complicated legal structure that requires them often to transfer all their property rights to have some hope of profiting from them. And where those individuals are employed, such legal rights as they might enjoy for their products are automatically allocated to their employer as part of the contracted labour relation in most cases.

The developing states argued during and after the TRIPs negotiations that 'the priority of the right of a people to their livelihood and development takes precedence over the rights of private property' (Steidlmeier 1993: 163). Such an argument is not limited to the distinction between developing states' populations and multinationals, but in many cases (such as inevitable disclosure and employment law), may be an issue within developed states. Jessica Litman draws an interesting distinction between the myth of the author, someone who should benefit from their intellectual labours as generally accepted by consumers, and the limits on use which formal copyright law puts on the use of the copyrighted product. To the general user these limits seem draconian and fail to reflect *their* rights to use their own (purchased) property as they see fit. She suggests that intellectual property law fails to resolve the needs of the 'copyright myth' with the perception of the purchasing relation by consumers, and this lies at the root of copyright law's popular illegitimacy in this area (Litman 1991). A distinction between the individual as creator and the legal individual as rights holder remains in common usage. And as noted in the last chapter there have been cases (most especially in the music industry) where individuals have been able to assert these rights, however belatedly, in the face of legally constituted individuals.

A legal strategy for recognising this popular conception of different 'individuals' would be to entrench the rights of the real individual and remove (in intellectual property law) the recognition of companies as individuals under law. Intellectual property could then become inalienable. Margaret Radin has argued that 'although the right to hold property is considered inalienable in traditional liberalism, property rights themselves are presumed fully alienable and *inalienable property rights are exceptional and problematic*' (Radin 1987: 1851, emphasis added). This is exemplified under the TRIPs agreement by the move away from inalienable moral rights. This desire to re-establish inalienable property leads Radin to assert that

> the characteristic rhetoric is morally wrong when it is put forward as the sole discourse of human life . . . Instead of using the categories of economics or those of traditional liberalism, I think we should evaluate inalienabilities in connection with our best current understanding of the concept of human flourishing.
>
> (ibid.)

Radin's logic has an immediate resonance with the self-developmental schema. Inalienability recognises the 'flourishing' of the creative individual and their right to control their creations. Though often presented as a binary choice, market inalienability can also be partial. In a sense this is the situation that already exists for intellectual property, after passing through a period when ideas or knowledge can be traded, they pass into the public realm where they effectively cannot.

Given that there is already a recognition of a partial market inalienability this logic may be useful for rethinking intellectual property. Part of the problem with intellectual property has been the disjuncture between the personhood of the creator and the (lack of) personhood of the legally constituted individual enjoying much of the benefit of IPRs. Thus, if we do

> not assimilate our conception of personhood to the market, market inalien-abilities are justified. But market inalienabilities are unjust when they are too harmful to personhood . . . Incomplete commodification can help mediate this kind of injustice. To see the world of exchange as shot through with incomplete commodification can also show us that inalienability is not the anomaly that economics and more traditional liberalism conceive it to be.
>
> (ibid.: 1927)

The way forward may be to join final non-alienability in intellectual property with some sort of licence system; temporary and contingent alienability. Initially this may seem to be what already exists, but it is different in one important aspect. Rather than allow the final transfer of IPRs to companies, rights would be retained by real individuals: companies could contract for these rights but would not themselves *directly* enjoy the rights allocated to the creator, or innovator. Clearly some sort of leasing arrangement would be required, but in the same way that leasehold only transfers a discrete and well chosen set of rights, so might intellectual leasing transfer a discrete bundle of rights. Equally such licences need not necessarily be exclusive nor uniform. Tendencies towards monopoly could be tempered and made more explicit through the allowance of differential licensing. Where such licences were refused, political questions could be raised through public critique of the terms of a specific lease, for instance to a developing state organisation.

Making intellectual property formally inalienable would require a set of new legal parameters for the acceptable methods and durations of transferring rights to exploiters. In whatever manner the shape of rights were changed, large companies are still likely to have the resources and expertise to maximise returns for any knowledge object. But, by re-balancing IPRs to emphasise the real individual some of the problems which I have detailed in regard to the relationship between innovating individuals and companies might be avoided. Companies would act as service providers to the knowledge-producing individuals, rather than controllers of intellectual property themselves. They could offer (and compete) on the basis of the return they expected to be able to provide (much as publishers and record companies currently compete for their authors and artists). Similarly, for inventions or processes, the rights of reproduction (or use) could be auctioned on the basis of time limited enjoyment of the right to use. Though this would require careful drafting, and undoubtedly some problems would emerge once such a system was set up, the expanded rights of real individuals would allow the dominant justificatory schemata to fit better with the practice of intellectual property law. Like the widening of social utility this would be a major political undertaking. One of the key legal elements of modern capitalism is the recognition of the company as a legal entity enjoying rights like an individual in certain circumstances. But these rights are accorded in law and thus can be limited by law.

While such a development would retain the key element of dissemination to earn a reward, by recognising the inalienability of intellectual endeavours it would re-establish the continuing rights of the creator over their own ideas. Given the concentration of liberalism on individual rights, strengthening the real rights of real individuals could generate a powerful political block behind it. This would still leave the problem of how the incremental additions, which nowadays most often provide innovation, should be weighted against the publicly available elements. This re-balancing of individual rights needs therefore to be joined with the political re-valuing of social utility. Thus, not only should IPRs be limited to real individuals, there should also be a clear judgement of the newness and non-obviousness of any particular individual claim for intellectual property in a particular knowledge object. Essentially this would require in exchange for enhanced individual rights a limitation of the sorts (and extent) of knowledge objects to which these rights could be applied. And this would undoubtedly be a major area of political conflict among the various vested interests. Only by also (as part of the same process) re-valuing the social utility of knowledge could this issue start to be resolved.

Consequently it is likely that only a two-dimensional political project linking the re-balancing of individual rights with the re-enlargement of global social utility in knowledge would succeed in reformulating intellectual property's current settlement. This raises the possibility of some sort of hybrid law – part copyright, part patent: recognising the individual's expression while also acknowledging the novelty of some aspect of the underlying idea but with strict criteria for inclusion. Currently hybrid laws are changing the way that the legal structure of intellectual property operates, but are reproducing the unbalanced rights system and expanding the field of intellectual property. This two-dimensional political project could reverse this trend.

Not only does this response echo the Hegelian justification of property, it also takes up the project which Hirschman attributes to Proudhon: the construction of property as a response to absolutist power. Writing in the early 1860s (in *Philosophy of Property*), some twenty years after his resounding condemnation of property (in *What is Property?*), Proudhon's characterisation of property as a 'wild, boundless and revolutionary force' prompted him to rethink its significance, retreat from his 'property is theft' position and see property as the best counterweight against the increasingly powerful modern state (Hirschman 1977: 128). Rethinking intellectual property in a similar way is a method of resistance to absolutist authority in the social milieu of knowledge reproduction. It seeks to restrain the monopoly rights which have in the past accrued to knowledge owners; here it is no longer the state that is the object from which property might be a useful guard, but rather the powerful knowledge industrialists.

Thus, amending Proudhon analogously, we might conclude that intellectual property

> is born of Liberty, not as it may first appear, against right, but through the operation of a much better understanding of right. What indeed, is Justice other than an equal balance between forces? . . .
>
> There is a corollary to [the] principle that [intellectual] property is the only power that can act as a counterweight to [knowledge capital], because it shows no reverence to princes, rebels against society . . . The corollary is that [intellectual] property, an absolutism within an absolutism . . .
>
> [Knowledge capital's] power is the kind of power that absorbs everything else into it. If it is allowed to take its own way, all individuality will quickly disappear . . . [Intellectual] property, on the contrary, is a decentralising force. Being itself absolute, it is anti-despotic and anti-unitary.
>
> (Proudhon 1970: 140–141, from *Philosophy of Property*, with my additions)

Though Proudhon saw the state as the opposed element in an unbalanced relationship between individual and power, in the global information society (under neo-Liberalism) it is capital, or for intellectual property, knowledge capital. Property may be utilised to reorient the balance by making the individual's position more robust at the cost of the knowledge sector's companies.

Failing this sort of sea change in the law, one aspect of the changing nature of the information economy may favour individuals over companies in any case. If a technical fix to copying is unlikely, and legal fixes may continue to fail to fully protect intellectual property, one scarcity can be relied on: the physicality of the creating individual. The individual knowledge creator may themselves become the commodity that commands value. Thus the rise of the named consultant, the branded individual, the 'star' can be seen as a possible path for knowledge creators. While knowledge objects can be copied or 'stolen', individuals themselves are always scarce. Personal appearances will be the scarce commodity that commands value. For the entertainer the market for live shows always recognises this, as does the consultancy market, and increasingly the key to earning a return for knowledge work may become based on the appearances, on direct contact. As Handy (1994) and others have suggested, the worker of the future may hold a portfolio of jobs and careers. In the knowledge sector these may well be based on the fees that can be commanded to bring certain internalised knowledge assets to bear on particular problems. Intellectual property may become less vital with creators and innovators depending instead on their own material scarcity to generate the reward for their innovative and creative work.

A change is going to come

Like David Vaver, I will leave aside 'the paradox inherent in the fact that supporters of inventive activity often react so vehemently when any move is proposed to modify, inventively or otherwise, a system devised in the seventeenth century' (Vaver 1990: 117). This resistance to change in the intellectual property system is mobilised through the knowledge structure's support for the dominant justificatory schemata. Nevertheless, as Edith Penrose pointed out in the 1950s, if

> national patent laws did not exist it would be difficult to make a conclusive case for introducing them: but the fact that they do exist shifts the burden of proof and it is equally difficult to make a really conclusive case for abolishing them.
>
> (quoted in Vaver 1990: 115–116)

As I worked on this book I have moved towards a similar realisation. Having started from a position which regarded IPRs as largely indefensible, as I further explored the issues around intellectual property my position became less strident. I have concluded that the coverage of intellectual property needs to be tempered by a fully developed and robust public domain but not completely abolished. In any case, given that political action needs to start from the contemporary settlement, it may indeed be 'difficult to make a really conclusive case for abolishing' intellectual property which would gain widespread support from those it would effect. But as I have outlined above that does not mean that what we have is perfectly acceptable, nor that political action is pointless.

I make no claim to be the only political economist thinking about changes that might be made to the global system of intellectual property. For instance, Lester Thurow has suggested three principles that should be at the heart of any new system of intellectual property rights:

i.   A new system must strike the right balance between the production and the distribution of new ideas;
ii. Laws on intellectual property rights must be enforceable or they should not be laws;
iii. The system must be able to determine rights and resolve disputes quickly and efficiently.

(Thurow 1997: 101–102)

Unenforceable laws are useless, and while it may be the case that the information society will render some sorts of IPRs un-protectable, laws remain supple and commercial interests are likely to find one way or another of retaining some enforceability for intellectual property provisions. This is therefore primarily a technical issue, albeit an important one. The third principle is largely a procedural issue; as Thurow points out, many of the 'problems with the patent system flow from the lack of consistent, predictable, rapid, *low-cost* determinations . . . and a means of quick, *cheap* dispute resolution' (ibid.: 102, emphasis added). Certainly, the provision of cheap legal recourse for individuals would immediately go some way to achieving the re-balancing of individual rights. But without a limitation on who should enjoy the rights of the 'individual' to intellectual property, substantial imbalances would remain. Thus, it is the first issue where the serious political economic problems lie. Without some further limitation on what knowledge resources can be privately owned, problems of welfare mal-distribution will continue. Thus, my interest parallels Thurow's first principle as it seems to me to be the key issue. The two-dimensional political project I have briefly outlined seeks to address this balance from both directions – individual and social.

There are many ways such political action could bring pressure for change; for instance, some form of globalised anti-trust movement might be a plausible way to approach the problem (Barton 1995: 617/8). The monopoly rights enjoyed by multinationals over important intellectual property could be assessed and low-cost compulsory patenting reintroduced. Though this would require the wider notion of social utility to be institutionalised within the TRIPs agreement, the provisions for compulsory licensing remain in place and would respond to such a redefinition rather well. Political action could promote a programme to return intellectual property to the balance between production and distribution that obtained prior to the rise of the information society. This is to say it could also be presented as a programme to 'correct' distortions introduced by technological changes. As Quaedvlieg has pointed out, copyright was 'crafted to fulfil the role of a mediator between different interests and market forces. One *cannot* reduce copyright to the legal vehicle of a triumphalist information-economy without disturbing the underlying system of legal balances' (1998: 437). A similar assertion could also be made for patents. The increasing power of the knowledge capitalists *vis-à-vis* others in the global system has upset the balance of forces institutionalised by various forms of intellectual property law. The political programme above would aim to restore and enhance this system of legal balances. This would also need to be a positive move to transfer existing knowledge and information (as well as know-how or tacit knowledge) to reflect this new settlement; it would need to be retro-active.

Finally, as I have implied throughout this study, and as Drahos neatly summarises, property in knowledge is

> continually referred to by the aggregated term of rights. Through that process of reference they have become deeply entrenched in the discourse of private

property rights. Their relocation in the language of private property has obscured their origins in public privilege.

(Drahos 1996: 213)

By re-inscribing the monopoly privileges accorded to the holders of intellectual property as rights, the common interest of all individuals in upholding IPRs is asserted and the possibility of the possible obligations incumbent on the knowledge 'owner' is obscured. To a large extent the knowledge structure obscures this possibility, but if privilege is being awarded, then some form of connected duty should also be part of the logic of IPRs. This would require a revaluation of know-ledge benefits – both economic and extra-economic. The control of knowledge would no longer be based on the rights of individuals to hold property, constructing a false scarcity. Rather, it would require an assessment of the worth and usefulness of any information or knowledge that emerged socially, and the awarding of privilege on an instrumental basis, if it was to serve some socially valuable purpose. If this sounds familiar, this is because this is how the patent system should operate when its limitations on patentability are strictly adhered to. However, these new 'privileges' would come with duties and responsibilities that would make them entirely contingent. Again this would require a new politics of intellectual property and the public domain. It also requires a reassessment of the justificatory schemata which underlie intellectual property's current justification.

While I have argued for two complementary paths flowing from a critical theory of intellectual property, which though difficult and requiring political mobilisation, to my mind appear plausible, there is a more strident position which I was originally drawn to when preparing this study. Would it not be altogether better to abandon the notion of property in knowledge? This argument has the appeal of simplicity and logical consistency. If there are all these problems with intellectual property, surely it would be better just to abandon the attempt and deal with knowledge in some different way. However, as Brian Martin acknowledges, this desire to challenge the entire system of intellectual property 'is a daunting task'. This is partly because the current system is portrayed by the justificatory schemata as potentially rewarding all creators of knowledge objects so although

> the monetary returns to these [small intellectual producers] are seldom significant, they have been persuaded that they both need and deserve their small royalties. This is similar to the way that small owners of goods and land, such as homeowners, strongly defend the system of private property, whose main beneficiaries are the very wealthy who own vast enterprises based on other people's labour.
>
> (1998: 51)

And recognising that intellectual property is embedded within the structures of modern capitalism, Martin also accepts that to fruitfully challenge intellectual property in this way there would also be a need to challenge the whole economic system. As he feels this is far from practical, he suggests setting up an alternative structure for dealing with intellectual products. This would be based on shareware principles, and co-operation to ensure knowledge innovators' reputations were enhanced through a system of accreditation (ibid.: 54). However, intellectual property is only one of the techniques by which powerful groups control information and/or knowledge to protect their interests and consolidate their wealth. (Such a realisation led Proudhon away from his anti-property position to one which sought to reform property and make it fulfil its potential for the individual.)

The anti-intellectual property position is essentially a proposal for some form of 'sharing utopia'. Though as a strategy for intellectual creation it may have problems, as a transformational discourse it has its uses in pushing arguments forward (Halbert 1996). The possibility of different ways of thinking about the production of knowledge, most importantly outside a form of property regime, helps galvanise more instrumental criticism that might produce some valuable changes. Certainly, my path has been away from a 'sharing utopia', towards a critical theory of plausible reforms to the current global intellectual property settlement. There is a clear need for the promotion and recognition of a new politics of intellectual property which can utilise and engage with the technologies of the global information society. My understanding of the global political economy of intellectual property rights has emerged through the contradictions that have appeared between the TRIPs agreements provisions, the justificatory schemata and the real intellectual property relations in the global system. It is not self-evident that the TRIPs agreement will continue to pattern intellectual property relations, but neither is it self-evident that the two political paths I have suggested will necessarily be developed successfully. While the revelation of contradictions is one part of the dual-dialectic of change, the other side is material actions by agents within the global system. The knowledge structure will continue to attempt to obscure alternatives and lay out the usual justificatory schemata at every opportunity. Nevertheless, intellectual property politics have the potential to be varied, interesting and engaging; all we have to do is make them so.

Notes

1 On institutions and property

1 I do not intend to consider the origin of selfhood here, I have assumed that something called the self can be identified in the adult individual even if there may be a problem in suggesting when the onset of selfhood should be located in any particular individual's life.
2 While I have not explicitly used Margaret Archer's work (1988) in developing the arguments in this section, I first developed my understanding of the importance of contradiction and commonalty in the analysis of change through an engagement with and exploration of Archer's important and powerful analysis.
3 Derek Sayer reads Marx in such a way that Marx's dialectic is what I have called here the dual-dialectic (Sayer 1990). Though his is an attractive position, I make the bi-directional dynamic explicit within widespread (even popular) understanding of the positions of Marx *and* Hegel.
4 Again I acknowledge a debt to Margaret Archer (1988) in this approach.

2 Developing intellectual property

1 The question of what sorts of collections of otherwise publicly available data are subject to copyright protection is an area which has been the subject of two well-known cases that have actually reduced the coverage of intellectual property – the *Feist* case in the United States and the *Magill* case in Europe. Though they involve different legal arguments and problems, both cases moved away from the protection of publicly available information once it was collected in specific forms. In both cases directories of publicly available information were excluded from protection. Though neither *Feist* (Grosheide 1992: 300–301) or *Magill* (Miller 1994) changed the overall character of copyright law in their relevant jurisdictions, both are interesting precedents which dilute one area of the coverage of intellectual property law.

3 TRIPs as a watershed

1 Blakeney (1996) provides a useful, reasonably clear and well-laid out discussion of the agreement and readers requiring a clause-by-clause treatment of the TRIPs agreement will find his account illuminating. A shorter account is provided by Davies (1996) which while providing the text of the agreement and a gloss, does not go into the detail provided by Blakeney. The treatment in Hoekman and Kostecki (1995), while less detailed, sets the agreement in the context of the history and political economy of trade agreements, and is usefully read in conjunction with one of the previous studies.
2 An excellent discussion of the various meetings and diplomatic efforts before, during and after this series of conferences can be found in Sell (1998).

4 Sites of resistance: patenting nature, technology and skills?

1 Though this is not the case in broad patents which allow the holder to receive licence fees from second generation innovations using the original idea, such patents are the subject of continued contestation and are not particularly common – though they are important when issued. I have assumed here that broad patents can be subsumed within the general discussions of IPRs merely as a special case of general trends and problems.
2 This is similar to Amartya Sen's argument regarding the incidence of famine and the ability of the starving to operationalise their entitlements to food. Thus, in many cases famines are not caused by a shortage of food but rather by the inability of the starving to gain access to what food there is (Sen 1981).
3 The original 'aphorism that Newton made his own in that famous letter to Hooke [is]: "If I have seen further, it is by standing on ye shoulders of Giants".' (Merton 1988: 621).

5 Sites of consolidation: legitimate authorship?

1 Parallel imports are especially a problem for brand reliant manufacturers. If redundant styles or production over-runs have been sold in peripheral markets, it can dilute the brand if these products are imported into the developed or mature market to compete on price for brand rather than stylistic currency. Manufacturers have tried to utilise copyright and trademark laws to keep branded parallel imposts to a minimum but have seldom been completely successful. They have run up against problems of rights exhaustion or more significantly in Europe the legally enforced single market (*The Economist* 1998b; Koenig 1998).
2 The royalties which an artist receives from copyright does not come directly to them but is mediated by the record company's and publisher's offices. Until they have the major influence of a multimillion selling act many performers are still stuck with industry standard contracts. In these contracts all sorts of expenses that one might presume would be paid by the record company are actually charged to the artist. Thus it is not unusual for artists whose publishing is controlled by their record company not to earn significant money from a release even though the record company is turning a good profit (Dannen 1990). Though nowadays many artists assign their publishing separately, this is only a recent development and even then may not always ensure the record company is auditing their sales accurately. Most accounts of the industry contain horror stories of swindling and payment problems, for instance see Chapple and Garofalo (1977) and Eliot (1989). I have left this contract issue to one side here but this is not to deny its importance within the labour relations of the industry.
3 Further examples and discussion of the legal history of sampling can be found in Sanjek (1994) and Schumacher (1995).
4 Gaines (1992) discusses further cases including Oscar Wilde, Bela Lugosi (as Dracula) and Superman as a branded image.
5 While I do not address these important issues in this book I recognise them as vital subjects for investigation. Initial statements of their importance can be found in Foucault (1991), the discussion of Anthony Giddens in Webster (1995: 52–73), and on a more global scale Hewson (1994).

6 Between commons and individuals

1 This also requires a particular view of efficiency which is itself an ideological construct. However, space does not allow a detailed treatment of the arguments on the construction of 'efficiency' and its possible alternatives (see for instance, Sen 1987).
2 Some brand names in common generic usage (Jeep, filofax, Hoover) are trademarks which in extreme cases have led to their owners taking legal action against writers using these terms. Though this issue is not central to my current concerns, as the importance

of branding continues to grow with the homogenisation of commodities and the further commodification of knowledge, this may expand as an area of intellectual property disputes. For an interesting discussion of this and other linked issues see Friedman (1991).

References

Adelman, I. (1991) 'Prometheus Unbound and Developing Countries', in P. Higonnet, D.S. Landes and H. Rosovsky (eds) *Favourites of Fortune. Technology, Growth and Economic Development since the Industrial Revolution*, Cambridge, MA: Harvard University Press.

Almeida de, P.R. (1995) 'The Political Economy of Intellectual Property Protection', *International Journal of Technology Management* 10, 2–3: 214–229.

Altbach, P.G. (1995) *Copyright and Development: Inequality in the Information Age*, (Bellagio Studies in Publishing No.4) Chestnut Hill, MA: Bellagio Publishing Network.

Amsden, A.H. and Mourshed, M. (1997) 'Scientific Publications, Patents and Technological Capabilities in Late-industrialising Countries', *Technology Analysis and Strategic Management*, 9, 3 (September): 343–359.

Aoki, K. (1996) '(Intellectual) Property and Sovereignty: Notes Toward a Cultural Geography of Authorship', *Stanford Law Review* (Symposium: Surveying Law and Borders) 48, 5 (May): 1293–1355.

Archer, M. (1988) *Culture and Agency: The Place of Culture in Social Theory*, Cambridge: Cambridge University Press.

Avenell, S. and Thompson, H. (1994) 'Commodity Relations and the Forces of Production: The Theft and Defence of Intellectual Property', *Journal of Interdisciplinary Economics* 5, 1 :23–35.

Avineri, S. (1972) *Hegel's Theory of the Modern State*, Cambridge: Cambridge University Press.

Bae, J.P. (1997) 'Drug Patent Expirations and the Speed of Generic Entry', *Health Services Research* 32, 1 (April): 87–101.

Bale, H.E. (1988) 'A Computer and Electronics Industry Perspective', in C.E. Walker and M.A. Bloomfield (eds) *Intellectual Property Rights and Capital Formation in the Next Decade*, Langham, MD: University of America Press.

Barlow, J.P. (1993) 'Selling Wine Without Bottles: The Economy of Mind on the Global Net' available at http://www.eff.org/pub/publications.barlow (accessed 8 May 1998).

Barthes, R. (1977) 'The Death of the Author' in S. Heath (ed.) *Roland Barthes: Image-Music-Text*, Glasgow: Collins.

Barton, J.H. (1993) 'Adapting the Intellectual Property System to New Technologies', in M.B. Wallerstein, M.E. Mogee and R.A. Schoen (eds) *Global Dimensions of Intellectual Property Rights in Science and Technology*, Washington, DC: National Academy Press.

Barton, J.H. (1995) 'Patent Scope in Biotechnology', *International Review of Industrial Property and Copyright Law*, 25, 5: 605–618.

Becker, L. (1977) *Property Rights: Philosophic Foundations*, London: Routledge & Kegan Paul.

Bell, D. (1974) *The Coming of Post-Industrial Society*, London: Heinemann Educational.

Beniger, J.R. (1986) *The Control Revolution: Technological and Economic Origins of the Information Society*, Cambridge, MA: Harvard University Press.

Bettig, R.V. (1992) 'Critical Perspectives on the History and Philosophy of Copyright', *Critical Studies in Mass Communication*, 9, 2 (June): 131–155.

Bettig, R.V. (1997) 'The Enclosure of Cyberspace', *Critical Studies in Mass Communication*, 14 (June): 138–157.

Bhaskar, R. (1991) 'Dialectics' in T. Bottomore (ed.) *A Dictionary of Marxist Thought*, second edition, Oxford: Blackwell.

Biersteker, T.J. (1992) 'The "Triumph" of Neo-classical Economics in the Developing World: Policy Convergence and Bases of Governance in the International Economic Order', in J.N. Rosenau and E.-O. Czempiel (eds) *Governance Without Government: Order and Change in World Politics*, Cambridge: Cambridge University Press.

Bimber, B. (1995) 'Three Faces of Technological Determinism', in M.R. Smith and L. Marx (eds) *Does Technology Drive History? The Dilemma of Technological Determinism*, Cambridge, MA: MIT Press.

BIO (1997) *1997–98 BIO's Citizens' Guide to Biotechnology* available at http://www.bio.org/whatis/citizen1.dgw (accessed 8 July 1998).

Blakeney, M. (1996) *Trade Related Aspects of Intellectual Property Rights: A Concise Guide to the TRIPS Agreement*, London: Sweet and Maxwell.

Bourdieu, P. (1977) *Outline of a Theory of Practice*, translated by Richard Nice, Cambridge: Cambridge University Press.

Boyle, J. (1996) *Shamans, Software and Spleens: Law and the Construction of the Information Society*, Cambridge, MA: Harvard University Press.

Boyle, J. (1997) 'A Politics of Intellectual Property: Environmentalism for the Net?', *Duke Law Journal* 47, 1: 87–116.

Braverman, H. (1974) *Labour and Monopoly Capital: The Degradation of Work in the Twentieth Century*, New York: Monthly Review Press.

Burch, K. (1995) 'Intellectual Property Rights and the Culture of Global Liberalism', *Science Communication* 17, 2 (December): 214–232.

Burch, K. (1998) *'Property' and the Making of the International System*, Boulder: Lynne Rienner.

Castells, M. (1996) *The Rise of Network Society*, (The Information Age: Economy, Society and Culture: 1) Oxford: Blackwell.

Castells, M. (1997a) *The Power of Identity*, (The Information Age: Economy, Society and Culture: 2) Oxford: Blackwells.

Castells, M. (1997b) 'An Introduction to the Information Age', *City*, 7: 6–16.

Castells, M. (1998) *End of Millennium*, (The Information Age: Economy, Society and Culture: 3) Oxford: Blackwell.

Chapple, S. and Garofalo, R. (1977) *Rock 'n' Roll is Here to pay: The History and Politics of the Music Industry*, Chicago: Nelson Hall.

Chaudhry, P.E. and Walsh, M.G. (1995) 'Intellectual Property Rights. Changing Levels of Protection Under GATT, NAFTA and the EU', *Columbia Journal of World Business*, 30, 2 (Summer): 80–92.

Commons, J.R. (1959 [1924]) *Legal Foundation of Capitalism*, Madison: University of Wisconsin Press.

Cook, P.J. (1997) 'Science in a Market Economy', *Resources Policy* 22, 3: 141–159.

Corrigan, P. and Sayer, D. (1981) 'How The Law Rules: Variations on Some Themes in Karl Marx', in B. Fryer, A. Hunt, D. McBarnet and B. Moorhouse (eds) *Law, State and Society*, London: Croom Helm.

Cox, R.W. (1996) (with T.J. Sinclair) *Approaches to World Order*, Cambridge: Cambridge University Press.

Cribbet, J.E. (1986) 'Concepts in Transition: The search for a new definition of property', *University of Illinois Law Review*, 1: 1–42.

Curtis, T. (1988) 'The Information Society: A Computer-Generated Caste System?', in V. Mosco and J. Wasko (eds) *The Political Economy of Information*, Madison: University of Wisconsin Press.

Dannen, F. (1990) *Hit Men: Power Brokers and Fast Money Inside the Music Business*, London: Muller.

Davies, D. (1996) *The World Trade Organisation and GATT '94: A Guide to the New International Economic Law*, Pinner, Middlesex: Carlton Publishing.

Deardorff, A.V. (1990) 'Should Patent Protection be Extended to All Developing Countries?', *The World Economy* 13, 4: 497–507.

Demsetz, H. (1967) 'Toward a Theory of Property Rights', *American Economic Review*, 57, 2, May, 347–59.

Dhar, B. and Rao, C.N. (1996) 'Trade Relatedness of Intellectual Property Rights', *Science Communication*, 17, 3 (March): 304–325.

Drahos, P. (1995) 'Global Property Rights in Information: The Story of TRIPS at the GATT', *Prometheus* 13, 1 (June): 6–19.

Drahos, P. (1996) *A Philosophy of Intellectual Property*, Aldershot: Dartmouth.

Drahos, P. (1997) 'Thinking Strategically About Intellectual Property Rights', *Telecommunications Policy*, 21, 3: 201–211.

Drucker, P. (1993) *Post-Capitalist Society*, New York: HarperBusiness.

Ducatel, K. and Millard, J. (1996) 'Employment and Innovation in Advanced Communication Technologies: Strategies for Growth and the Growth of Employment', *Futures*, 28, 2: 121–138.

Duff, A.S. (1995) 'The "information society" as paradigm: a bibliometric inquiry', *Journal of Information Science*, 21, 5: 390–395.

Eaton, J. and Kortum, S. (1996) 'Trade in Ideas: Patenting and Productivity in the OECD', *Journal of International Economics*, 40, 3–4: 251–278.

Eisenstein, E.L. (1980) *The Printing Press as an Agent of Change*, Cambridge: Cambridge University Press.

Elger, T. (1979) 'Valorisation and Deskilling: A Critique of Braverman', *Capital and Class*, 7 (Spring): 58–99.

Eliot, M. (1989) *Rockonomics: The Money Behind the Music*, London: Omnibus Press.

Ely, R.T. (1914) *Property and Contract in their Relations to the Distribution of Wealth*, London: Macmillan.

Etzkowitz, H. and Webster, A. (1995) 'Science as Intellectual Property' in S. Jasanoff, G.S. Markle, J.E. Petersen and T. Pinch, (eds) *Handbook of Science and Technology Studies*, London: Sage Publications.

Farrands, C. (1996) 'The Globalisation of Knowledge and the Politics of Global Intellectual Property: Power, Governance and Technology', in E. Kofman and G. Youngs (eds) *Globalisation: Theory and Practice*, London: Pinter.

Feather, J. (1994) 'From Rights in Copies to Copyright: The Recognition of Author's Rights in English Law and Practice in the Sixteenth and Seventeenth Centuries', in M. Woodmansee and P. Jaszi (eds) *The Construction of Authorship Textural Appropriation in Law and Literature*, Durham, NC: Duke University Press.

Foucault, M. (1991 [1979]) *Discipline and Punish: The Birth of the Prison*, London: Penguin Books.

Fransman, M. (1994) 'Biotechnology: Generation, Diffusion and Policy', in C. Cooper (ed.) *Technology and Innovation in the International Economy*, Aldershot: Edward Elgar.

Friedman, D.D., Landes, W.M. and Posner, R.A. (1991) 'Some Economics of Trade Secret Law', *Journal of Economic Perspectives* 5, 1 (Winter): 61–72.

Friedman, M. (1991) *A 'Brand' New Language: Commercial Influences in Literature and Culture*, New York: Greenwood Press.

Frow, J (1994) 'Timeshift: Technologies of Reproduction and Intellectual Property', *Economy and Society*, 23, 3 (August): 291–304.

Frow, J. (1996) 'Information as Gift and Commodity', *New Left Review*, 219: 89–108

GATT (1988a) *News of the Uruguay Round of Multilateral Trade Negotiations*, 18 (2 August) Geneva: Information and Media Relations Division of the GATT.

GATT (1988b) *News of the Uruguay Round of Multilateral Trade Negotiations*, 20 (4 November) (Geneva: Information and Media Relations Division of the GATT.

GATT (1989) *News of the Uruguay Round of Multilateral Trade Negotiations*, 31 (16 October) Geneva: Information and Media Relations Division of the GATT.

GATT (1990a) *News of the Uruguay Round of Multilateral Trade Negotiations*, 35 (19 April) Geneva: Information and Media Relations Division of the GATT.

GATT (1990b) *News of the Uruguay Round of Multilateral Trade Negotiations*, 36 (1 June) Geneva: Information and Media Relations Division of the GATT.

GATT (1990c) *News of the Uruguay Round of Multilateral Trade Negotiations*, 41 (9 October) Geneva: Information and Media Relations Division of the GATT.

GATT (1992) *The Uruguay Round. A Giant Step for Trade and Development and a Response to the Challenges of the Modern World*, Geneva: GATT Publication Services.

GATT (1994) *Final Act Embodying the Results of the Uruguay Round of Multilateral Trade Negotiations*, Geneva: GATT Publication Services.

Geller, P.E. (1994) 'Must Copyright Be For Ever Caught Between Marketplace and Authorship Norms?', in B. Sherman and A. Strowel (eds) *Of Authors and Origins*, Oxford: Clarendon Press.

Giddens, A. (1990) *The Consequences of Modernity*, Cambridge: Polity Press.

Gould, D.M. and Gruben, W.C. (1996) 'The Role of Intellectual Property Rights in Economic Growth', *Journal of Development Economics*, 48, 2: 323–350

Grosheide, F.W. (1992) 'Copyright and Publishers' Rights: Exploitation of Information by a Propriety Right' in W.F. Korthales Altes *et al.* (eds) *Information Law Towards the 21st Century*, Derventer: Kluwer.

Grosheide, F.W. (1994) 'When Ideas Take the Stage' (Opinion), *European Intellectual Property Review*, 6: 219–222.

Halbert, D. (1996) 'Intellectual Property Law, Technology and Our Probable Future', *Technological Forecasting and Social Change*, 52, 2–3: 147–160.

Hamel, G and Prahalad, C.K. (1994) *Competing for the Future*, Boston: Harvard Business School Press.

Handy, C (1994) *The Empty Raincoat*, London: Hutchinson.

Harvey, D (1989) *The Condition of Postmodernity*, Oxford: Basil Blackwell.

Harvey, D.P. (1993) 'Efforts under GATT, WIPO and Other Multinational Organisations against Trade Mark Counterfeiting', *European Intellectual Property Review*, 12: 446–451.

Hegel, G. (1956 [1899]) *The Philosophy of History*, New York: Dover Publications.

Hegel, G. (1967 [1821]) *Philosophy of Right*, Oxford: Oxford University Press.

Heilbronner, R.L. (1985) *The Nature and Logic of Capitalism*, New York: W.W. Norton.

Helleiner, G.K. (1977) 'International Technology Issues: Southern Needs and Northern Responses', in J.N. Bhagwati (ed.) *The New International Economic Order: The North–South Debate*, Cambridge, MA: MIT Press.

Henderson, E (1997) 'TRIPs and the Third World: The Example of Pharmaceutical Patents in India', *European Intellectual Property Review*, 11 (November): 651–663.

Hepwoth, M.E. (1989) *Geography of the Information Economy*, London: Belhaven Press.

Hettinger, E.C. (1989) 'Justifying Intellectual Property', *Philosophy and Public Affairs*, 18, 1: 31–52.

Hewson, M (1994) 'Surveillance and the Global Political Economy', in E.A. Comor (ed.) *The Global Political Economy of Communication*, Houndmills: Macmillan Press.

Higham, N (1993) 'The New Challenges of Digitisation', *European Intellectual Property Review*, 10 (October): 355–359.

Hill, C (1972) *The World Turned Upside Down: Radical Ideas During the English Revolution*, London: Temple Smith.

Hirschman, A.O. (1977) *The Passions and the Interests: Political Arguments for Capitalism before its Triumph*, Princeton, NJ: Princeton University Press.

Hoekman, B.M. and Kostecki, M.M. (1995) *The Political Economy of the World Trading System: From GATT to WTO*, Oxford: Oxford University Press.

Hoffman, J (1975) *Marxism and the Theory of Praxis*, London: Lawrence & Wishart.

Horne, T.A. (1990) *Property Rights and Poverty. Political Argument in Britain 1605–1834*, Chapel Hill: University of North Carolina Press.

Kay, J. (1993) *Foundation of Corporate Success: How Business Strategies Add Value*, Oxford: Oxford University Press.

Khan, K-ur-R (1990) 'Transfer of Technology, Emerging International Responsibility of Transnational Corporations; Possible Impact of the Uruguay Round at the GATT', *Science, Technology and Development*, 8, 3: 209–221.

Khor, M (1990) 'Intellectual Property: Tightening TNC Monopoly on Technology', *Third World Network Features*, (Syndicated article 667/90).

Knights, D. and Willmott, H (eds) (1990) *Labour Process Theory*, Basingstoke: Macmillan.

Krugman, P. (1995) 'Technological Change and International Trade', in P. Stoneman (ed.) *Handbook of the Economics of Innovation and Technical Change*, Oxford: Blackwell.

Kumar, K. (1995) *From Post-Industrial to Post-Modern Society: New Theories of the Contemporary World*, Oxford: Blackwell.

Kumar, N. (1996) 'Intellectual Property Protection, Market Orientation and Location of Overseas R&D Activities by Multinational Enterprises', *World Development*, 24, 4: 673–688.

Lash, S. and Urry, J. (1994) *Economies of Signs and Space*, London: Sage.

Lehman, B. (1996) 'Intellectual Property: America's Competitive Advantage in the 21st Century', *Columbia Journal of World Business*, 31, 1: 6–16.

Litman, J. (1991) 'Copyright as Myth', *University of Pittsburgh Law Review*, 53: 235–249.

Little, B.H. and Trepanier, C.W. (1997) 'Untangling the Intellectual Property Rights of Employers, Employees, Inventors and Independent Contractors', *Employee Relations Law Journal*, 22, 4 (Spring): 49–77.

Locke, J. ([1690] 1988) *Two Treatises on Government*, Cambridge: Cambridge University Press.

Lukes, S. (1974) *Power: A Radical View*, Basingstoke: Macmillan Education Ltd.

Macdonald-Brown, C. and Ferera, L. (1998) 'First WTO Decision on TRIPs', *European Intellectual Property Review*, 2 (February): 69–73.

Maclean, J (1981) 'Marxist Epistemology, Explanations of "Change" and the Study of International Relations', in B. Buzan and R.B.J. Jones (eds) *Change and the Study of International Relations: The Evaded Dimension*, London: Francis Pinter.

McLellan, D. (1973) *Marx's Grundrisse*, St. Albans, Paladin.

Macpherson, C.B. (1962) *The Political Theory of Possessive Individualism*, Oxford: Clarendon Press.

Macpherson, C.B. (ed.) (1978) *Property. Mainstream and Critical Positions*, Oxford: Basil Blackwell.

Mansfield, E. (1988) 'Intellectual Property Rights: Technological Change and Economic Growth', in C.E. Walker and M.A. Bloomfield (eds) *Intellectual Property Rights and Capital Formation in the Next Decade*, Langham, MD: University Press of America.

Marlin-Bennet, R. (1995) 'International Intellectual Property Rights in a Web of Social Relations', *Science Communication*, 17, 2 (December): 119–136.

Martin, B. (1998) 'Against Intellectual Property', in *Information Liberation*, London: Freedom Press.

Martin, W.J. (1995) *The Global Information Society*, Aldershot: Aslib Gower.

Marx, K. ([1887] 1974a) *Capital: A Critical Analysis of Capitalist Production*, (Volume 1) London: Lawrence & Wishart.

Marx, K. (1974b) *Economic and Philosophic Manuscripts of 1844*, Moscow: Progress Publishers.

Marx, K. and Engels, F. (1965) *The German Ideology*, London: Lawrence & Wishart.

Maskus, K. (1990) 'Normative Concerns in the International Protection of Intellectual Property Rights', *The World Economy*, 13: 387–409.

Maskus, K. (1997) 'Implications of Regional and Multilateral Agreements for Intellectual Property Rights', *The World Economy*, 20, 5: 681–694.

Maskus, K and Penubarti, M. (1995) 'How Trade-related are Intellectual Property Rights?', *Journal of International Economics*, 39: 227–248.

Mason, A. (1997) 'Developments in the Law of Copyright and Public Access to Information', *European Intellectual Property Review*, 11 (November): 636–643.

Masuda, Y. (1980) *The Information Society as Post-Industrial Society*, Tokyo: Institute for Information Society, reprinted as: Masuda Y (1990) *Managing in the Information Society: Releasing Synergy Japanese Style*, (with a foreword by Ronnie Lessem) Oxford: Basil Blackwell.

Matsui, S. (1977) 'The Transfer of Technology to Developing Countries: Some Proposals to Solve Current Problems', *Journal of the Patent Office Society*, 59, 10 (October): 612–628.

May, C. (1996) 'Strange Fruit: Susan Strange's Theory of Structural Power in the International Political Economy', *Global Society*, 10, 2 (Spring): 167–189.

May, C. (1998) 'Capital, Knowledge and Ownership: The Information Society and Intellectual Property', *Information, Communication and Society*, 1, 3 (Autumn): 245–268.

Merton, R.K. (1988) 'The Matthew Effect in Science, II. Cumulative Advantage and the Symbolism of Intellectual Property', *Isis*, 79, (December): 606–623.

Micklethwait, J. and Wooldridge, A. (1996) *The Witch Doctors*, London: Heinemann.

Miller, C.G. (1994) 'Magill: Time to Abandon the "Specific Subject-matter" Concept', *European Intellectual Property Review*, 10: 415–421.

Minogue, K.R. (1980) 'The Concept of Property and its Contemporary Significance', in: J.R. Pennock and J.W. Chapman (eds) *Property (NOMOS XXII)*, New York: New York University Press.

Morris-Suzuki, T. (1988) *Beyond Computopia: Information, Automation and Democracy in Japan*, London: Kegan Paul International.

Mossinghoff, G.J. and Bombelles, T. (1996) 'The Importance of Intellectual Property Protection to the American Research-Incentive Pharmaceutical Industry', *Columbia Journal of World Business*, 31, 1 (Spring): 39–48.

Moufang, R. (1994) 'Patenting of Human Genes, Cells and Parts of the Body? – The Ethical Dimensions of Patent Law', *International Review of Industrial Property and Copyright Law*, 25, 4: 487–515.

Mumford, L. (1967) *The Myth of the Machine: Technics and Human Development*, London: Secker & Warburg.

Munzer, S.R. (1990) *A Theory of Property*, Cambridge: Cambridge University Press.

Murphy, R.F. (1972) *The Dialectics of Social Life: Alarms and Excursions in Anthropological Theory*, London: George Allen & Unwin.

Nance, D.A. (1990) 'Owning Ideas', *Harvard Journal of Law and Public Policy*, 13, 3: 757–773.

Negroponte, N. (1995) *Being Digital*, London: Hodder and Stoughton.

Noble, D.F. (1998) 'Digital Diploma Mills: The Automation of Higher Education', *Monthly Review*, 49, 9 (February): 38–52.

Nonaka, I. and Takeuchi, H. (1995) *The Knowledge-Creating Company*, Oxford: Oxford University Press.

North, D.C. (1977) 'Markets and Other Allocation Systems in History: The Challenge of Karl Polanyi', *Journal of European Economic History*, 6, 3 (Winter): 703–716.

North, D.C. (1981) *Structure and Change in Economic History*, New York: W.W. Norton.

North, D.C. (1990) *Institutions: Institutional Change and Economic Performance*, Cambridge: Cambridge University Press.

Nozick, R. (1974) *Anarchy, State and Utopia*, Oxford: Blackwell.

Oberschall, A. and Leifer, E.M. (1986) 'Efficiency and Social Institutions: Uses and Misuses of Economic Reasoning in Sociology', *Annual Review of Sociology*, 12: 233–53.

OECD (1997) *Towards a Global Information Society. Global Information Infrastructure, Global Information Society: Policy Requirements*, Paris: Organisation for Economic Co-Operation and Development.

O'Neill, J. (1990) 'Property in Science and the Market', *The Monist*, 73, (October): 601–620.

Paine, L.S. (1991) 'Trade Secrets and the Justification of Intellectual Property: A Comment on Hettinger', *Philosophy and Public Affairs*, 20, 3: 247–263.

Palmer, T.G. (1990) 'Are Patents and Copyrights Morally Justified? The Philosophy of Property Rights and Ideal Objects', *Harvard Journal of Law and Public Policy*, 13, 3: 817–865.

Park, W.G. and Ginarte, J.C. (1997) 'Intellectual Property Rights and Economic Growth', *Contemporary Economic Policy*, 15, 3 (July): 51–61.

Penner, J.E. (1997) *The Idea of Property in Law*, Oxford: Clarendon Press.

Poggi, G. (1978) *The Development of the Modern State*, London: Hutchinson.

Polanyi, K. (1957) *The Great Transformation: The Political and Economic Origins of our Time*, Boston: Beacon Press.

Polanyi, M. (1969) [1962] 'The Republic of Science: Its Political and Economic Theory', in *Knowing and Being: Essays*, (edited by M. Grene), London: Routledge & Kegan Paul.

Poster, M. (1990) *The Mode of Information. Poststructuralism and Social Context*, Cambridge: Polity Press.

Primo Braga, C.A. (1989) 'The Economics of Intellectual Property Rights and the GATT: A View From the South', *Vanderbilt Journal of Transnational Law*, 22: 243–264.

Proudhon, P.-J. (1970) *Selected Writings*, (edited by Stewart Edwards), London: Macmillan.

Proudhon, P.-J. ([1840] 1994) *What is Property?*, (edited and translated by Donald R. Kelley and Bonnie G. Smith), Cambridge: Cambridge University Press.

Purdue, D. (1995) 'Hegemonic Trips: World Trade, Intellectual Property and Biodiversity', *Environmental Politics*, 4, 1 (Spring): 88–107.

Quaedvlieg, A.A. (1992) 'The Economic Analysis of Intellectual Property Law', in W.F. Korthales Altes *et al.* (eds) *Information Law Towards the 21st Century*, Deventer: Kluwer.

Quaedvlieg, A.A. (1998) 'Copyright's Orbit Round Private, Commercial and Economic Law – The Copyright System and the Place of the User', *International Review of Industrial Property and Copyright Law*, 29, 4: 420–438.

Quah, D.T. (1997) 'Increasingly Weightless Economies', *Bank of England Quarterly Bulletin*, (February): 49–56.

Radin, M.J. (1987) 'Market-Inalienability', *Harvard Law Review*, 100, 8 (June): 1849–1937.

Reeve, A. (1986) *Property*, Basingstoke: Macmillan Education.

Reeve, A. (1991) 'The Theory of Property. Beyond Private versus Common Property', in D. Held (ed.) *Political Theory Today*, Cambridge: Polity Press.

Reich, R.B. (1991) *The Work of Nations: Preparing Ourselves for 21st Century Capitalism*, London: Simon & Schuster.

Reichman, J.N. (1992) 'Legal Hybrids between the Patent and Copyright Paradigms', in W.F. Korthales Altes *et al.* (eds) *Information Law Towards the 21st Century*, Deventer: Kluwer.

Reichman, J.N. (1993) *Implications of the Draft TRIPs Agreement for Developing Countries as Competitors in an Integrated World Market*, (Discussion Paper 73) Geneva: UNCTAD.

Rose, C.M. (1994) *Property and Persuasion: Essays on the History, Theory and Rhetoric of Ownership*, Boulder, COL: Westview Press.

Ryan, A. (1984) *Property and Political Theory*, Oxford: Basil Blackwell.

Sadler, D. (1997) 'The Global Music Business as an Information Industry: Reinterpreting Economies of Culture', *Environment and Planning A*, 29, 11: 1919–1936.

Samuelson, P. (1991) 'Is Information Property? (Legally Speaking)', *Communications of the Association for Computing Machinery*, 34, 3: 14–19.

Samuelson, P. (1992) 'Copyright Law and Electronic Compilations of Data', *Communications of the Association for Computing Machinery*, 35, 2: 27–33.

Sanjek, D. (1994) '"Don't have to DJ no more": Sampling and the "autonomous" creator', in M. Woodmansee and P. Jaszi (eds) *The Construction of Authorship Textural Appropriation in Law and Literature*, Durham, NC: Duke University Press.

Sayer, D. (1990) 'Reinventing the Wheel: Anthony Giddens, Karl Marx and Social Change', in J. Clark, C. Modgil, and S. Modgil (eds) *Anthony Giddens: Consensus and Controversy*, London: Falmer Press.

Schumacher, T.G. (1995) '"This is a sampling sport": Digital Sampling, Rap Music and the Law in Cultural Production', *Media, Culture and Society*, 17, 2 (April): 253–273.

Sell, S.K. (1995) 'The Origins of a Trade-Based Approach to Intellectual Property Protection', *Science Communication*, 17, 2 (December): 163–185.

Sell, S.K. (1998) *Power and Ideas: North–South Politics of Intellectual Property and Antitrust*, Albany: State University of New York Press.

Sen, A. (1981) *Poverty and Famines: An Essay on Entitlement and Deprivation*, Oxford: Clarendon Press.

Sen, A. (1987) *On Ethics and Economics*, (Oxford: Basil Blackwell.

Shiva, V. (1996) 'Agricultural Biodiversity, Intellectual Property Rights and Farmers' Rights', *Economic and Political Weekly*, (22 June); 1621–1631.

Shiva, V. and Holla-Bhar, R. (1993) 'Intellectual Piracy and the Neem Tree', *The Ecologist*, 23, 6 (November/December): 223–227.

Silverstein, D. (1991) 'Patents, Science and Innovation: Historical Linkages and Implications for Global Technological Competitiveness', *Rutgers Computer and Technology Law Journal*, 17, 2: 261–319.

Simon, E. (1996) 'Innovation and Intellectual Property Protection: The Software Industry Perspective', *Columbia Journal of World Business*, 31, 1 (Spring): 31–37.

Smith, A. (1996) *Software for the Self: Technology and Culture*, London: Faber and Faber.

Stalk, G. (1988) 'Time – The Next Source of Competitive Advantage', *Harvard Business Review*, 66, 4 (July–August): 41–51.

Stearns, L. (1992) 'Copy Wrong: Plagiarism, Process, Property and the Law', *California Law Review*, 80, 2: 513–553.

Stehr, N. (1994) *Knowledge Societies*, London: Sage.

Steidlmeier, P. (1993) 'The Moral Legitimacy of Intellectual Property Claims: American Business and Developing Country Perspectives', *Journal of Business Ethics*, 12, 3 (February): 157–164.

Steidlmeier, P. and Falbe, C. (1994) 'International Disputes over Intellectual Property', *Review of Social Economy*, 52, 3: 339–360.

Sterk, S.E. (1996) 'Rhetoric and Reality in Copyright Law', *Michigan Law Review*, 94, 5: 1197–1249.

Strange, S. (1988) *States and Markets*, London: Pinter Publishers.

Strange, S. (1996) *The Retreat of the State: The Diffusion of Power in the World Economy*, Cambridge: Cambridge University Press.

Subramanian, A. (1990) 'TRIPs and the paradigm of the GATT', *World Economy*, 13, 4: 509–521.

Tang, P. (1997) 'Multimedia information products and services. A need for "cybercops"?', in B. Loader (ed.) *The Governance of Cyberspace: Politics Technology and Global Restructuring*, London: Routledge.

Thurow, L.C. (1997) 'Needed: A New System of Intellectual Property Rights', *Harvard Business Review*, 75, 5 (September–October): 95–103.

Toffler, A. (1980) *The Third Wave*, London: Collins.

Vaver, D. (1990) 'Intellectual Property Today: Of Myths and Paradoxes', *Canadian Bar Review*, 69, 1: 98–128.

Verma, S.K (1996) 'TRIPs – Development and Technological Transfer', *International Review of Industrial Property and Copyright Law*, 27, 3: 331–364.

Vernon, R. (1971) *Sovereignty at Bay: The Multinational Spread of U.S. Enterprises*, New York: Basic Books.

Wade, R. (1996) 'Globalisation and its Limits: Reports of the Death of the National Economy are Greatly Exaggerated', in S. Berger and R. Dore (eds) *National Diversity and Global Capitalism*, Ithaca, NY: Cornell University Press.

Waldron, J (1988) *The Right to Private Property*, Oxford: Clarendon Press.

Wall, D. (1996) 'Reconstructing the Soul of Elvis: The Social Development and Legal Maintenance of Elvis Presley as Intellectual Property', *International Journal of the Sociology of the Law*, 24, 2 (June): 117–143.

Webster, F. (1995) *Theories of Information Society*, London: Routledge.

Webster, F. (1996) 'The Information Society: Conceptions and Critique', *Encyclopaedia of Library and Information Science*, 58, 21 (supplement): 74–112.

Wilkins, M. (1992) 'The Neglected Intangible Asset: The Influence of the Trade Mark on the Rise of the Modern Corporation', *Business History*, 34, 1 (January): 66–95.

Williamson, O.E. (1985) *The Economic Institutions of Capitalism*, New York: Free Press.

WIPO (1993) *World Intellectual Property Organisation – General Information*, Geneva: WIPO.

Woodmansee, M. (1984) 'The Genius and the Copyright: Economic and Legal Conditions of the Emergence of the "Author"', *Eighteenth Century Studies*, 17: 425–448.

Worthy, J. (1994) 'Intellectual Property Protection After GATT', *European Intellectual Property Review*, 5: 195–198.

News media sources

Bates, S. and Rafferty, K. (1996) 'West tries to silence Japan's "bootleg" tunes', *The Guardian*, 10 February: 3.

Bell, E. (1998) 'Rock is on the Block – But Will Anybody Buy', *Observer*, (Business section), 17 May 1998: 7.

Berger, D. J., DiBoise, J. A. and Mucchetti, M. (1997) 'Inevitable Disclosure Law Remains Unsettled', *The National Law Journal*, 12 May, Section C. p. 38, available at http://www.ljextra.com/practice/intellectualproperty/0512tsecr.html (accessed 21 July).

Dickson, D. and Jayaraman, K.S. (1995) 'Aid Groups Back Challenge To Neem Patents', *Nature*, 377, 14 September: 95.

Di Fronzo, P.W. (1996) 'A Little Knowledge is a Dangerous Thing', *Intellectual Property Magazine*, available at http://www.ipmag.com/difronzo.html (accessed 15 March 1998).

Durham, T. (1998) 'Rights Deal on Digitised Data', *Times Higher Education Supplement*, (Multimedia section), 13 March 1998: 1.

Elkin, A. (1998) 'Deconstructing Beck', *Index on Censorship*, 27, 4: 15.

Finch, J. (1997) 'Task Force Attacks Scandal of Fake Drugs', *The Guardian*, 17 January: 26.

Garrett, A (1997a) 'Professors Profit as Oxford Bags Biotech Millions', *Observer*, (Business section), 27 April: 7.

Garrett, A. (1997b) 'Technological Hot Properties: The Value Is All In The Minds', *Observer*, (Business section) 20 July: 9.

Gilbert, P. (1997) 'The Drummer from Lush Killed Himself Last Year . . .', *The Guardian*, (section 2), 7 April: 10–11.

Goodwin, C. (1997) 'Spielberg "Kidnaps" Tale Of Slave Revolt', *The Sunday Times*, 2 November: 25.

Halstead, R. (1997) 'Inventor Takes DTI to European Court', *Independent on Sunday*, (Business section) 12 January: 1.

Harding, L. (1998) 'BA Image Built on the Price Of Seven Cows', *The Guardian*, 11 July: 1.

Hayes, D. (1997) 'A Smash Hit for Song Thieves', *Independent on Sunday*, (Business section), 27 April 1997: 6.

Hinde, J. (1998) 'Fillip for State-Funded Scientists', *Times Higher Education Supplement*, 12 June: 64.

Jayaraman, K.S. (1995) 'Neem Unsheaths Contraceptive Potential', *Nature*, 377, 14 September: 95.

Julius, A. (1996) 'Whose Line is It Anyway?', *The Guardian*, (The Week section) 30 November: 5.

Kingston, P. (1996) 'No Copying, Now, Please', *The Guardian*, (Higher Education section) 12 November: v.

Koenig, P. (1998) 'Tommy v Tesco', *Independent on Sunday*, 14 June: 24.

Macilwain, C. (1996) 'Researchers Resist Copyright Laws That Could Endanger Data Access', *Nature*, 383, 24 October: 653.

Millar, S. (1997) 'Alarm as Music Piracy Reaches Record Level', *The Guardian* 8 March: 3.

Patel, K. (1998) 'Millions Lost on Patent', *Times Higher Education Supplement*, 17 July: 1.

Penman, D (1997) 'Swampy™: Been There, Dug That . . . Now Buy the T-shirt', *Observer*, 10 August: 4.

Rawlinson, R. (1995) 'Clampdown of Copyists', *Fashion Weekly*, 11 May: 7.

Reid, C. and McKie, R. (1996) 'Boots Suppressed its Own Survey on Cheaper Drugs', *The Observer*, 28 April: 1.

Roper, M. (1996) 'Parts of Distinction', *Sunday Business*, 20 July: 16.

Rowe, M. (1997) 'Hot on the Scent of the Calvin Klein Fakers', *Independent on Sunday*, 6 April: 5.

Spanner, R.A. (1996) 'Beyond Secrets', *Intellectual Property Magazine*, available at http://www.ipmag.com/span.html (accessed 15 March 1998).

Sweeting, A. (1998) 'You're Singing My Song. No, *you're* Singing *My* Song', *The Guardian*, (Review section) 17 January: 5.

Thayer, A. (1995) 'Scope of Agricultural Biotechnology Patents Sparks Dispute', *Chemical and Engineering News*, 21 August, available at:
  http://pubs.acs.org/hotartc/cenear/95082/art02.html (accessed 8 July 1998).

Tuck, A. (1994) 'Copy Cats', *The Guardian*, (Weekend section) 26 February: 22–26.

Tyler, C. (1997) 'The Enemy Within', *Financial Times*, (Weekend section): 12 April: 1.

Wilkie, T. (1995) 'Whose Gene is it Anyway?', *Independent on Sunday*, (Magazine Section), 19 November: 75–76.

Wroe, M. (1998) 'You Gotta Scroll with it', *Observer* 14 June: 23.

Wylie, I. (1996) 'Curbing the Copyright Copy-cats', *The Guardian*, (Upfront section) 23 November: 2–3.

The Ecologist (1992) *Whose Common Future?* (special issue), 22, 4 (July/August).

The Economist (1993a) 'Mr Lopez's Many Parts', 29 May: 73.

The Economist (1993b) 'Why Jose's Dream Car Matters', 24 July: 65/6.

The Economist (1993c) 'Pistols at Dawn', 31 July: 60.

The Economist (1994a) 'Intellectual Property . . . is Theft', 22 January: 72/3.

The Economist (1994b) 'Trade Tripwires', 27 August: 63.

The Economist (1996a) 'Intellectual Property. The Property of the Mind', 27 July: 69.

The Economist (1996b) 'Copyrights and Copywrongs', 27 July: 16.

The Economist (1997a) 'Glaxo: Coping with the Unwelcome News' 26 April: 87.

The Economist (1997b) 'Playing Godmother to Invention', 24 May: 124.

The Economist (1997c) 'Only the Bangs are Genuine', 28 June: 104.

The Economist (1997d) 'Stranded on the Farm?', 4 October: 128.

The Economist (1998a) 'In the Picture', 10 January: 89/90.

The Economist (1998b) 'A Grey Area', 13 June: 85–89.

The Economist (1998c) 'Software Piracy', 27 June: 140.

Observer (1996) 'Drugs Giant Fights off Patent Threat' (Business section) 5 May: 3

Pacific News Bulletin (1995) 'Bioprospecting: Another Wave Of Colonialism', May: 7–13.

Sunday Business (1996) 'Users the Losers in the Copyright Laws', (Computer Age supplement), 14 July: 16.

Index

Act of Anne, 1710 129
agenda setting 31, 32, 40, 41, 47, 52, 60, 64, 85, 89, 125
alienation 27, 96
Allen, Debbie 131
Antoni & Alison 154–155
appropriation *see* commodification
Archer, Margaret 182
Armani, Giorgio 154–155
Ashby, Roger 124
authorial function 14, 47, 50, 52, 54, 59, 135, 136, 160, 163, 172
Avenell, Simon and Tompson, Herb 138
Avineri, Shlomo 26

bargains (between authority and markets) 32–33
Barlow, John Perry 62, 140
Barthes, Roland 130
Beatles 140, 142; Harrison, George 141
Beck 142
Bell, Daniel 5
Beniger, James 2
Berne Convention for the Protection of Literary and Artistic Works 67, 68, 70, 73, 75, 131, 168
Bettig, Ronald 145
biotechnology 28, 74, 89, 91, 101–107, 147
Black Box 142
Boots 111
Bourdieu, Pierre 31
Boyle, James 171
branding 5, 100, 152–153, 155, 158, 183–184
Braverman, Harry 57
Brazillian government 86
British Airways 156
broadcasting industry 69, 72, 138–139

Brown, James 142
Burch, Kurt 72, 74

capitalism 2, 3, 4, 6, 12, 21, 27, 28, 29, 43, 53, 162
Capitol/EMI 142, 152
Castells, Manuel 2, 3, 4
Chase-Riboud, Barbara 131
change, theory of 30–42
China 99
Clarke, Angus 107
class 37
clothing industry 152, 154–155
Coca Cola 10, 11
Cohen, Stanley and Boyer, Herbert (recombinant DNA patent) 106, 110
collations of data 28, 50, 51, 75, 136
commodification 6, 12, 13, 25, 27–30, 32, 43, 48, 49, 51, 60, 61, 64, 65, 73, 95, 123, 162, 165, 175
common property 23
'common-sense' 22, 47, 63, 107, 130, 151, 171
complimentarity 34, 39, 41
compulsory licensing 73, 74, 79, 179
computer industry 144–150, 154; *see also* software
Condé Naste 135
conflict 40, 42
contradiction 34, 38, 39, 41, 161, 181
control revolution 2
Convention on Biodiversity Conservation 103
copyright 8–9, 25, 46, 49, 50, 52, 54, 55, 65, 68, 75, 86, 97, 109, 111, 122, 127, 128, 130–137, 139–142, 144, 145, 147, 148, 151, 155, 156, 157, 163, 168, 170, 172, 173, 174, 176, 179; moral rights 9, 73, 96, 128

Copyright Licensing Agency 133
Cox, Robert 1, 12, 34, 43, 93
critical theory 1, 32, 43, 164, 167, 180

Dhar, Biswajit and Rao, C. Niranjan
    78–79
Diana, Princess of Wales 157
Dior, Christian 158
division of labour 27, 129
DNA 102, 106, 107, 110
Doisneau, Robert 159
Drahos, Peter 88–89, 179
Drucker, Peter 4
dual-dialectic 14, 35–42, 54, 78, 181
Dyson, James 124

education sector 123, 132, 133, 134
efficiency 18, 19, 21, 49, 51, 52, 53, 85,
    92, 183
Ely, Robert 16
employment 5, 27 144, 149
employment law 58, 121–123
enclosure 13, 43, 48, 49, 60, 61, 64, 78,
    86, 89, 95
environmentalism of the net 15, 171

Faulkner, William 130
Feist Publications vs. *Rural Telephone Service*
    136, 182
first occupancy 24
Food For Our Future 105
foreign direct investment 113
Friends of the Earth 105
Frow, John 170

General Agreement on Tariffs and Trade
    (GATT) 67, 68, 69, 74, 81, 82, 87,
    165; Tokyo Round 81; Uruguay
    Round 67, 68, 71, 80, 81, 86, 162
General Motors 59, 120
geographical indicators 68
globalisation 2
Gould, David and Gruben, William 116
W.R. Grace and Co. 103
Grateful Dead, The 140
Greenpeace 105
Group of 77 83

Hamilton, Walter 16
Handy, Charles 178
Hegel, Georg 2, 7, 26–28, 29, 35–36, 177
Herodutus 127
Hettinger, Edwin 62
Hill, Damon 158–159

Hirschman, Albert O. 177
Holloway, Loretta 142

IBM 122
identity politics 4
ideology 13, 93, 151
Indian government 87, 99, 100, 103
industrial designs 10, 68
inequality 2, 27, 78, 83, 99, 114, 137,
    151, 167, 171
inevitable disclosure 58, 120–122
information 6, 30, 31, 51, 85, 133–134,
    136, 137, 162, 167, 171
information services 5, 128–129, 176
information society 1–6, 30, 43, 81, 82,
    94, 128, 162, 164–167, 171, 174
information and communication
    technology 3, 75, 81, 133, 162, 165,
    173
innovation 4, 6, 50, 53, 65, 73, 78, 81, 86,
    97, 102, 109, 110, 112, 115, 116, 125,
    127–130, 150, 154, 163, 165, 166,
    173, 174
institutions 29, 31–34, 37, 39, 45, 47, 51;
    see also property, as an institution
integrated circuits 68
intellectual property 1, 6–14, 22, 27, 30,
    38, 43, 45–67, 72, 75, 81, 89, 91, 93,
    95, 96, 98, 101, 102, 104, 105, 108,
    109, 110, 112, 119, 127, 128, 129,
    131, 135, 138, 139, 140, 144, 147,
    148, 149, 153, 160, 162–167,
    170–173, 175, 178, 180 181; *see also*
    law
Intellectual Property Committee 82, 84,
    168
intellectual property rights 7, 22, 28,
    42–44, 49, 50, 51, 53, 57 60, 61, 63,
    68, 70, 71, 72, 74, 75, 77, 81, 83, 84,
    86–89, 91, 93, 96, 97, 98, 100, 103,
    112, 113, 115, 116, 140, 144, 148,
    150, 151, 154, 156, 160–163, 165–170,
    172, 175, 176, 179, 180
International Convention for the
    Protection of New Varieties of Plants
    (UPOV) 74, 103, 173
International Federation of the
    Phonographic Industry 152
internet 2, 4, 53, 61, 79, 81, 89, 133,
    134, 137, 140, 143–146, 148, 161,
    173

Jackson, Michael 158
Jefferson, Thomas 62

justificatory schemata 7, 12–15, 22–29, 43, 45, 46, 49–52, 60, 61, 66, 77, 85, 89, 91, 92, 93, 113, 127, 128, 129, 160–164, 171, 180; instrumental schema 7, 24–27, 29, 47, 49, 50, 62, 92–96, 99, 104–107, 111, 113, 118, 125, 127, 134, 136, 144, 150, 159, 163, 166, 172, 173; self-developmental schema 7, 26–29, 49, 61, 92, 93, 96, 97, 107, 112, 127, 128, 134, 136, 145, 155, 157, 159, 163, 172, 175; economic schema 7, 48, 51, 61, 63, 92, 93–94, 97, 109, 112, 135, 159, 163, 166, 172

Kay, John 123–124
Khor, Martin 64
knowledge 6, 12, 29, 30, 31, 43, 46, 47, 51–54, 59, 62, 85, 94, 109, 128, 133, 134, 137, 139, 151, 153, 162, 164, 165, 167, 170, 171, 175, 179, 180; *see also* tacit knowledge, theoretical knowledge
knowledge and information (distinction between) 6, 51
knowledge entrepreneurs *see* knowledge industries
knowledge industries 4–6, 49, 50, 54, 59, 60, 72, 81, 82, 122, 124, 128, 139, 144, 154, 155, 156, 161, 176
'knowledge objects' 42–43, 46–51, 53, 55, 61, 64, 96, 127, 128, 135, 156, 159, 160, 173
knowledge structure 13, 15, 29–32, 39–42, 60, 61, 64, 88, 89, 107, 109, 119, 124, 125, 128, 151, 156, 160, 163, 164, 166, 167, 171, 172, 181
knowledge workers 5, 62, 89, 96, 97, 122, 125, 130, 137, 144, 156–157, 163, 177–178

labour process 57
law 12, 13, 17, 18, 21, 26, 43, 53, 58, 61, 66, 68, 70, 82, 88, 89, 100, 104, 107, 113, 120, 124, 128, 131, 134, 136, 139, 140, 145, 150, 157, 158, 160, 169, 170, 173, 176– 179
Led Zeppelin 141
legal individuals 15, 119, 125, 151, 159, 160, 163–164, 167, 172–178
Lehman, Bruce 119
Litman, Jessica 174
Little, Bruce and Trepanier, C. 123
Locke, John 7, 24–26, 27, 29, 47, 62, 63

Lopez, Jose Ignacio 120–121

McGee, Alan 143
Macpherson, C.B. 22, 25
Madonna 158
Magill (decision of European Court of Justice) 182
management literature 59, 123–124
Mansfield, Edward 118
Mark, R.T. 142
market inalienability 174–175
markets 7, 19, 20, 21, 23, 26, 29, 31, 42, 47, 51, 52, 61, 63, 65, 72, 93, 110, 111, 139, 165, 166, 172
Martin, Brian 180
Martin, William 133
Marx, Karl 27, 35–37, 92, 96, 182
Matsui, Shoji 114
Merton, Robert 108, 130, 148
Microsoft 146, 153
monopoly 52, 53, 65, 78, 93, 119, 126, 134, 151, 163, 169, 175, 179, 180
Monsanto 105
Morris-Suzuki, Tessa 94–95
Most-Favoured-Nation treatment 69
MP3 143
Multi-Fibre Arrangement 88
multinational corporations 115, 116, 117
Mumford, Lewis 38
Munzer, Stephen 46
music industry 69, 72, 75, 81, 128, 138–144, 152, 154, 174, 183; rap 141–142; sampling 141–142, 183

national treatment 69, 71
Natural Law 24, 25
Neem tree 99, 103
neo-liberalism 164, 167, 169, 170, 172, 177
New International Economic Order 112
Newton, Sir Isaac 183
Nike 142
Nonaka, Ikujiro and Takeuchi, Hirotaka 124
North, Douglas 19
Nozick, Robert 95–96
Ntcox'o, Cg'oso 156

OECD 3, 117, 119
Okri, Ben 131
Olson, Douglas 105
Onassis, Jackie 158
O'Neill, John 111

parasitic capitalists 138, 173
Paris Convention for the Protection of Industrial Property 67, 68, 70, 83
Park, Walter and Ginarte, Carlos 116
passing off 10, 155, 157
patents 8, 11, 25, 46, 49, 50, 53, 54, 57, 65, 68, 72, 74, 75, 76, 78, 79, 80, 83, 86, 96, 97, 99, 100, 102, 103, 105–112, 114–118, 123, 124, 125, 127, 128, 134, 135, 147, 163, 169, 170, 173, 174, 176, 178, 180, 183; process patents 76, 112, 149
Penrose, Edith 178
Perry, Rupert 152
PepsiCo 121
pharmaceutical industry 72, 74, 91, 98–102, 105, 118, 153
'Piller, Anton' law 71
piracy 51, 60, 72, 75, 80, 81, 84, 86, 98–101, 128, 131, 132, 137–140, 145, 149, 150–157, 161, 172
plagiarism 129–131, 154–155
Porat, Marc 128
power 19, 20, 30–34, 39–42, 47, 85, 125, 162, 177, 181
Presley, Elvis 157–158
privacy 157, 158, 159
product cycle 113
property 16–21, 28–29, 72, 165; active and passive property 28, 48, 77, 95 159, 160; analogous with intellectual property 11, 42, 43, 45, 46, 47, 52, 56, 64, 93, 97, 98, 126, 151, 162, 163, 166, 167; history of property 17, 19, 21, 22, 29; institution, property as an 16, 18–21, 29; *see also* institutions; intangible property 46; leasehold property 54–57, 175; state, property and the 16; *see also* intellectual property
Proudhon, Pierre-Joseph 23, 177, 181
public and private (balance between) 7, 11, 12, 24, 54, 60, 64, 65, 68, 77, 85, 87, 91, 94, 98, 100, 101, 106, 110, 111, 112, 118, 125, 157, 163, 164, 165, 167–171, 176, 178
publishing industry 51, 72, 128–138, 140, 144, 172

Quaedvlieg, Antoon 166, 179
Quah, Danny 2

Radin, Margaret 174–175
reciprocity 69
Redmond, William 121

Reeve, Andrew 23
Reich, Robert 4–5
Reichman, Jerome 86, 149
reverse engineering 10,76
rights of owners 11, 12, 23, 24, 48, 50, 54, 58, 64, 72, 73, 74, 76, 77, 79, 83, 88, 91, 98, 118, 125, 139, 147, 168, 172, 174, 176, 180
Robinson, Joan 49, 78
Rolling Stones 140–141
Rousseau, Jean-Jacques 24
'rules of the game' 33, 40
Ryan, Alan 24, 27

Saunders, John 101
scarcity 18, 21, 42, 45, 49, 52, 57, 60, 61, 63, 65, 93, 102, 105, 144, 152, 166, 167, 177
science 96, 98, 106–112, 136–137, 174
scientific management 57, 58
Seagate Technology 122
Sell, Susan 82
Sen, Amartya 183
Shiva, Vandana 104
Silverstein, David 109
Simon, Emery 146–147
Sinatra, Frank 140
Smith, Anthony 2
Smiths, The 143
Snapple 121
software 75, 84, 115, 123, 128, 133, 146, 149, 153, 163, 172; shareware 147–148, 181; *see also* computer industry
Spielberg, Stephen 131
states 6, 8, 16, 17, 20, 21, 26, 65, 68, 72, 73, 74, 78, 79, 83, 88, 91, 92, 96, 99, 105, 109, 111, 113, 116, 117, 151, 164, 169, 170, 174
Stearns, Laurie 130
Strange, Susan 14, 29–31, 38, 39; four structures 30–32, 38, 39, 40–42; *see also* knowledge structure
structural interactions 31–32
Subramanian, Arvind 78
Swampy 159
Swift, Graham 130

tacit knowledge 6, 59, 79, 114–115, 169; *see also* knowledge
technology 13, 28, 53, 65, 66, 81, 89, 96, 112,113, 114, 131, 134, 138, 139, 141, 143, 147, 148, 160, 165, 169, 172

technology transfer 73, 78–81, 83, 86, 91, 112–119, 125, 137, 163, 169; theft *see* piracy
theoretical knowledge 5, 6; *see also* knowledge
Thurow, Lester 178–179
Toyota 59, 120
trademarks 9–10, 68, 72, 76, 155, 159
Trade Related Aspects of Intellectual Property Rights agreement (TRIPs) 12, 14, 40, 43, 44, 65, 67–91, 96, 97, 99, 100, 101, 103, 105, 112, 114–119, 125, 128, 131, 135, 136, 139, 140, 151, 152, 160, 161, 162, 164, 166, 168, 169, 173, 174, 175, 179, 181, 182; TRIPs negotiations 80–90, 119, 137
trade-related-ness 77–78, 89, 156, 160, 161, 165
trade secrets 10, 57–59, 62, 65, 68, 109, 114, 122, 173, 174
transaction costs 19

United Nations 68, 170; Conference on Technology and Development (UNCTAD) 83; Food and Agricultural Organisation (FAO) 104; World Health Organisation (WHO) 153
United States of America 82, 83, 85, 87, 89, 119, 136, 168; Office of Technology Assessment (OTA) 94; Patents and Trademarks Office 103; Semiconductor Chip Protection Act 173; Uniform Trade Secrets Act (UTSA) 121
Unregistered Design Right (UK) 173

Verma, S.K. 80
Verve, The 141
Volkswagen 59, 120–121
Voltaire 131

Waldron, Jeremy 27, 46
Waters, Muddy 141
Webster, Frank 6
Workbench 124
World Intellectual Property Organisation (WIPO) 67–71, 84, 87, 131, 132, 136, 168
World Trade Organisation (WTO) 12, 28, 67–72, 74, 76, 81, 82, 87, 88, 99, 100, 103, 104, 116, 162, 170